Topics in Energy
Edited by L. Bauer, W. K. Foell, M. Grenon, G. Woite

B. Chateau
B. Lapillonne
Energy Demand: Facts and Trends

A Comparative Analysis of Industrialized Countries

Springer-Verlag Wien NewYork

Dr. Bertrand Chateau
Dr. Bruno Lapillonne
Institut Economique et Juridique de l'Energie, Grenoble, France

With 26 Figures

Library of Congress Cataloging in Publication Data. Chateau, Bertrand. Energy demand. (Topics in energy.) Includes bibliographical references and index. 1. Energy consumption. 2. Energy policy. 3. Power resources. 4. Renewable energy sources. I. Lapillonne, Bruno. II. Title. III. Series: Topics in energy (Springer-Verlag). HD9502.A2C46. 333.79'12. 82-704

ISBN 3-211-81675-5 Springer-Verlag Wien-New York
ISBN 0-387-81675-5 Springer-Verlag New York-Wien

Foreword

The first oil crisis of 1973–74 and the questions it raised in the economic and social fields drew attention to energy issues. Industrial societies, accustomed for two decades or more to energy sufficiently easy to produce and cheap to consume that it was thought to be inexhaustible, began to question their energy future. The studies undertaken at that time, and since, on a national, regional, or world level were over-optimistic. The problem seemed simple enough to solve.

On the one hand, a certain number of resources:

coal, the abundance of which was discovered, or rather rediscovered

oil, source of all the problems . . . In fact, the problems seemed to come, if not from oil itself (an easy explanation), then from those who produced it without really owning it, and from those who owned it without really controlling it

natural gas, second only to oil and less compromised

uranium, all of whose promises had not been kept, but whose resources were not in question

solar energy, multiform and really inexhaustible

thermonuclear fusion, and geothermal energy, etc.

On the other hand, energy consumption, though excessive perhaps, was symbolic of progress, development, and increased well being.

The originality of the energy policies set up since 1974 lies in the fact they no longer aimed to produce (or import) more, but to consume less. They sought, and still seek, what might be emphatically called the control of energy consumption, or rather the control of energy demand.

Firstly, it should not be forgotten that the energy sector is one with highly rigid structures: it takes time to change installations, structures and habits.

Furthermore, to control it is necessary to understand. The decision-makers and researchers, quickly realized their poor understanding, both on a practical and theoretical level, of consumption problems (inadequacy of statistics for example).

How can we forecast for ten, twenty or fifty years — as is necessary in energy policy making — how much energy our children and grandchildren will want? The questions, mentioned above, have disrupted the regular growth curves to which we were accustomed: how can we extrapolate fluctuations? Development models — the American model for Europe and the Japanese model for other countries — no longer seem possible or desirable. The "good old recipes", such as the elasticity energy/GDP are no longer feasible. On the one hand, forecasting has become increasingly necessary as mistakes become more expensive, on the other hand energy studies have not so much brought solutions as shown by the inadequacy of methods. The same disillusionment was rapidly felt beyond the energy field in other consumption sectors, and about other questions concerning the future.

It is therefore with pleasure that we present this book by Dr. B. Chateau and Dr. B. Lapillonne on energy demand and consumption published in an entirely new collection. These two authors have spent many years studying this problem both at a national level, and at the European Community and world level – with the International Institute of Applied System Analysis (IIASA) amongst others. Furthermore, they have developed a method, the MEDEE approach, which has aroused much interest. As opposed to purely econometric approaches, MEDEE includes reflections on development in life styles necessary to the understanding and control of future energy demand.

In view of the wealth of information and originality of thought it contains, this volume should rapidly become a work of reference. I wish every success to the authors with whom I have had the pleasure to discuss – notably B. Lapillonne during our years of collaboration at the IIASA – this currently difficult but potentially rich subject; I consider their study to be one of the most useful and pertinent amongst an abundance of literature of lesser interest.

M. Grenon*

* Michel Grenon has been closely associated with the Energy Program of IIASA from 1974 to 1981. He is the author of several books on energy policy.

This book is dedicated to the memory of Marc Alinhac with whom we had so many interesting and fruitful discussions on energy demand analysis and forecasting

Acknowledgements

This book synthesizes eight years of work on energy demand analysis, modelling and forecasting. It could not have been written without the scientific support and emulation of the "Institut Economique et Juridique de l'Energie (IEJE)", which is a research team of the "Centre National de la Recherche Scientifique (CNRS)": many thanks to all members of the Institute and especially J. M. Martin, IEJE's director, who initiated this study in 1973, P. Godoy and I. Renzetti for their participation in data collection and analysis, and F. Blamoutier and her team who provided us with most of our bibliographical support.

We wish also to acknowledge with many thanks the organizations which sponsored our work on energy demand during all these years:

the French energy organisations "Commissariat à l'Energie Atomique (CEA)", "Electricité de France (EDF)" and "Société Nationale Elf Aquitaine (SNEA)", and especially MM. M. Alinhac (EDF), P. Bernard (EDF), B. Laponche (CEA), Moury (SNEA) and B. Ploton (SNEA) who provided us with precious advice and information,

the Commission of the European Communities which sponsored the development of the MEDEE 3 model and its extension to all countries of the EEC, and thus gave us the opportunity to improve our knowledge and information on these countries; especially MM. Strub and Romberg who were responsible for the development of the EEC energy modelling system, and Mr. P. Valette who has continually organized the work on MEDEE 3.

Many people helped us to get hitherto unpublished information. We wish to thank in particular: M. Adawchowsky (SNEA, France), M. Brascamp (TNO, Netherlands), MM. van Baarsels et Beerens (Ministerie van Volksherisveling en Ruimtelijke Ordening, Netherlands), M. Norgard (Technical University, Denmark), M. Elbek (Niels Bohr Institute, Denmark), M. Josephsen (Danish Energy Agency), M. Merzagora (CNEN, Italy), MM. Schmidt and Suding (Energiewirtschaftliches Institut, Köln, Federal Republic of Germany), MM. Klaiss and Hocker (IKE, Stuttgart, Federal Republic of Germany), M. Leach (IIED, U.K.), MM. Schipper (Lawrence Berkeley Laboratory, U.S.A.) and M. Romig (ECE, Geneva).

Many thanks also to Mrs. Ingman and Mr. Dixon who helped us to write this book in good English.

Last, but not least, we wish to acknowledge with many thanks Professor Grenon who agreed to review and comment on a preliminary version of this book, and, above all, gave us the opportunity of writing it.

Grenoble, March 1982   **B. Chateau** and **B. Lapillonne**

Contents

Table of Conversion

1 MJ = 10^6 J = 239 kcal = 0.278 kWh
1 GJ = 10^9 J = 278 kWh
1 TJ = 10^{12} J = 0.278 Gwh = 23.9 toe
1 PJ = 10^{15} J = 0.278 TWh = 0.0239 Mtoe
1 EXJ = 10^{18} J = 23.9 Mtoe = 278 TWh

1 kWh = 3600 kJ
1 kcal = 4186 J
1 Gcal = 10^6 kcal = 4.18 GJ
1 toe = 41.8 GJ
1 BTU = 1055 J = 0.252 kcal

1 Mtce = 29.3 PJ
1 Mtoe = 41.8 PJ
1 Mboe = 38.7 Mtoe = 1620 PJ
1 TWh = 3.6 PJ
1 QUAD = 1.055 EXJ = 25.2 Mtoe (= 10^{15} BTU)

Introduction

Towards the close of 1973, the four-fold increase of oil prices heralded the end of an era of plentiful and relatively cheap energy. For some countries (Europe, Japan) this era had begun in the late fifties with the commercialization of Middle East oil; for others — i.e. the U.S.A. and Canada — it started as far back as the beginning of the century. First of all in North America, then in Europe and Japan, the energy abundance, both real and expected, encouraged or even generated rapid economic growth and energy intensive development patterns, characterized by the important and rapid spread of road transport and of the car, by the growing consumption of materials with a high energy content, by the urban sprawl, by the generalization of energy intensive habits and behaviours (heating, travels, . . .) and especially, by the development of a whole energy intensive technological infrastructure (badly insulated dwellings, low-efficiency industrial kilns, . . .). This generally resulted in an explosive growth of commercial energy consumption, the world-wide level of which underwent a threefold increase between 1950 and 1973 (previously such an increase had required fifty years).

Paradoxically, in spite of its spread to all levels of industrial societies and although it has become essential to their functioning, energy aroused little interest — especially with respect to consumption — in the last two decades, due to the widespread ill-founded notion that cheap energy sources would be available for a long time — with oil until the turn of the century and nuclear energy thereafter. In addition, the small share of energy expenditure in household budgets or in industrial production costs, with a few exceptions (low income families, basic industries such as steel processing or the cement industry), by no means highlighted the importance of the energy factor. In such a context, the 1973/74 oil crisis came as a real shock, economic indeed, but especially psychological, by revealing how the life styles and more generally the development patterns of industrialized countries were dependent upon energy and how far the countries were vulnerable to restrictions in the amount of available energy or to sudden price increases (inflation, commercial balance, . . .). Today it is undeniable, and the recent 1979/80 "oil shocks" well illustrate this, that the world is facing a long-term crisis. Thus industrial societies should henceforth be prepared for much higher fuel prices than in the past. This brings into focus two great issues concerning the development of the energy market, which underlie this study: how will industrial societies react to this reversal of trend in energy prices, and more especially what will be its consequences upon the

evolution of the energy demand? Which energy sources will be able to be mobilized to replace hydrocarbons in order to satisfy this demand, and how soon?

In view of the time-constants of the energy sector, these issues are only
meaningful if considered over a long time span. Indeed, the delays between the
decision to invest (opening of a coal mine, or construction of a nuclear power
station, for instance) and the beginning of production (approximately 7 to 10
years), as well as those necessary to amortize the energy investments (approximately 15 to 20 years) oblige energy firms and governments to consider, within
their investment decisions, the development of the energy market over a 20–25
year period – what we refer to as long term. In addition, for similar reasons and
in view of the delays necessary for the success of research development programmes, the definition and the implementation of energy policies (supply and
demand) can only take place in a long-term context.

One of the paradoxes of the present situation is precisely that one must
look at the long-term development of the energy market, at a time when the
major uncertainties facing the world (economic crisis, oil supply, . . .) render
bold any forecasting attempt. This leads some experts to consider long-term
forecasting as a purely academic exercise, or even, in some cases, to refuse the
very idea of forecasting. Such an attitude seems to us as dangerous because it
ignores the time constraints; it delays the investment decisions or favours
random measures, taken in answer to immediate problems, to the detriment of
long-term solutions. As emphasized by C. Wilson in the WAES [1] synthesis
report, "Time is our most precious resource. It must be used as wisely as energy":
the energy decisions upon which rests the future of society, must be made now,
but these decisions must rest on a far-reaching perception of the energy market.

Indeed, long-term prospects can no longer simply extend past trends or rely
upon the inertia of economic systems, as was currently done for the short and
medium term. Too many changes or upheavals in the economic development
and structures, in the consumption modes and in the conditions of the energy
supply may occur over the next twenty or thirty years, which we can neither
ignore nor cast aside. In order to fully comprehend the long-term evolution of
the energy market, it is essential to understand how industrial societies use
energy and how this consumption changes in time: thus may be identified the
major fundamental trends which determine this evolution and upon which one
may accurately base the exploration of the distant future. This pre-supposes a
deep and detailed analysis of the energy demand, undertaken within an historical and comparative context; this is what we have set out to do in this study.

Such an analysis must be disaggregated and must look at energy at the end-
use level (domestic uses such as heating and cooking, industrial uses such as
steam production, high-temperature production etc.) for at least two reasons.
The evolution dynamics of energy needs are specific to each end-use and thus
any attempt to understand the evolution of the energy demand can only be done
at the end-use level. In addition, each end-use corresponds to specific energy
needs determined by the quantities and the thermodynamic characteristic required: between low temperature thermal energy needs (less than 100 °C,
heating, hot water) and average or high temperature, mechanical or electric

energy needs, there is little reason to resort to the same energy vector, and the knowledge of the quality of energy required, only possible at the end-use level, is necessary for a satisfactory understanding of future substitutions for hydro-carbons.

The historical and comparative dimension of the analysis is essential to fully identify the dynamic processes and to define possible future developments. An historical analysis limited to a single country is indeed necessary to understand the evolution dynamic of that country's energy consumption but does not allow one to set this development pattern within a more general context; be-cause of this, it only provides partial elements for the evaluation of possible future changes.

The comparative analysis alone, though it does allow one to understand from the differences among countries the links between the technological and economic characteristics of a society and its energy needs, does not help in the understanding of the dynamic processes. The excellent comparative study of Europe, the U. S. A. and Japan, carried out by J. Darmstatter et al. [2] is ex-tremely convincing in its explanation of the different levels of per capita energy consumption, at a given time (1972); it does not, however, explain the dynamics which led to these situations and is of little help in prospective studies. Thus the historical and comparative analyses are obviously complementary for the ex-haustive understanding of the phenomena and for any forecasting attempt. A few examples will suffice to illustrate this complementarity.

First of all, the experience acquired in certain energy utilization techniques by some countries may be used as reference by other less advanced countries: for instance, Japan for steel processing, Italy or France for the private car, Denmark and Sweden for the development of heat networks and the insulation of dwellings, and the U. S. A. for solar energy and heat pumps. In addition, the development of public transport networks, both urban and interurban, has been quite different from one country to another, and the experience of certain countries, where transport modes are highly developed, such as Germany or Japan, can prove quite enlightening. Finally, with respect to housing, the differ-ences observed between countries in the spread of household equipment (central heating, electrical household appliances, . . .) allow for a better definition of the range of possible developments.

The countries around which this comparison will centre are OECD countries: for simplification purposes, and in view of the available information, we have restricted this study to countries with a well-established industrialization, providing sufficiently broad field of investigation on the geographic as well as the economic and social levels. Thus we shall frequently include the U.S.A., Sweden, Japan and the main European Community Countries (France, the Federal Republic of Germany, the United Kingdom, Italy, the Netherlands, Belgium and Denmark). In certain cases, other countries, such as Switzerland, Austria or Canada may also be mentioned.

We shall only deal with comparisons which are likely to add to our knowl-edge of the development dynamics of energy needs and of the links between these needs and the technological, social and economic features of industrial societies; thus, whenever the comparisons prove to be of little interest in this particular field, we shall merely study one country as being representative of all the others.

Similarly, we shall attempt, in this analysis to go as far back as 1950, whenever the information available allows us to do so, and whenever the expected teachings justify this: in the opposite case, we shall use shorter historical reference periods, sometimes as short as one year.

As an introduction to the energy demand analysis the chapter 1 will be devoted to the definition of the main concepts used in this analysis and to some theoretical considerations upon the interaction between energy prices and the quantities of energy demanded (in others words upon the energy demand function).

Once the conceptual and theoretical framework set up, the energy demand analysis will be developed in the next three chapters, each one being devoted to a major energy consuming sector: residential and tertiary, transport and industry.

Given the specific nature of each of these sectors and of the information available, the sectoral analysis will be carried out differently stressing sometimes the socio-economic aspects, elsewhere the technical aspects, insisting either on the historical dimension or on prospective considerations.

Thus, chapter 2, devoted to the residential and tertiary sector, mainly emphasizes the role of technology — at the level of housing, heating techniques . . . — and gives a high priority to prospective considerations.

Chapter 3, about the transport sector, is, as opposed to the previous chapter, much more centered around socio-economic aspects, both because they play a fundamental role in transport energy demand, and because they are by far the most uncertain and the least known.

Chapter 4, on industry, will be more balanced both on the technical and economic aspects, and on the historical and prospective dimensions. However, the large heterogeneity of this sector, both on the economic or energy level, will lead us to limit the general considerations and to focus particularly on two energy intensive industries, the steel and cement industries.

After these sectoral analysis, we will come back in chapter 5 to methodological considerations, showing how the conclusions of the analysis can be used in energy demand forecasting. We will then review the main methods and models developed and used so far in industrialized countries. Particular attention will be devoted to phenomenological (or technico-economic) models — and especially to the MEDEE models since they represent a direct extension of the analysis carried out before.

This book will end up with an outline of the major prospective trends in industralized countries for the next three decades in the energy demand field. We will take this opportunity to present the main view points on the long term energy demand as well as the main scenarios developed so far.

Although restricted to the industrialized countries of the OECD, this study is sufficiently broad in certain of its aspects, to be of interest to less industralized countries or to countries with different economic systems.

I. The Analysis of Energy Demand: An Overview

For a good understanding of energy demand issues, it is necessary to recall the content of the most common concepts used by the energy economist (demand,consumption, primary, secondary and final energy), and to propose a definition for the more recent and less well-defined concepts such as "useful energy" and "energy needs". After these introductory definitions, we shall give the main outlines of our method of analysis. Then will follow a series of more general considerations concerning the role of prices in the energy field, which will serve as a background to the analysis of the energy demand in the various energy-consuming sectors of the economy.

1. Concepts and Methods

1.1. Usual Concepts

For the economist, consumption is indicated by the market transaction: namely the quantity that is purchased. It may be measured either in physical terms (e.g. number of kWh purchased) or in monetary terms (e.g. electricity bill); one form of measurement may be replaced by the other by using the price at which the transaction was carried out. On the other hand, demand represents the quantity which the buyer would obtain depending on the various price levels; in general it cannot be observed on the basis of current statistics. Consumption will be equal to demand for a given transaction price if there is no constraint on the quantities offered.

The concept of demand is often misused for that of consumption, and vice versa: under the condition of allowing demand and quantities demanded to be assimilated, which is frequently the case, this is of little consequence if the price is known. In this book, we shall use "consumption" for everything concerned with statistical observations in the past, and we shall use "demand" in all other cases.

Let us now consider "energy" concepts. The distinction which is made in scientific literature between primary, secondary and final energy is due to the desire — and necessity — to pin point energy products at the different stages of their manufacture:

primary energy represents both energy sources which have been taken from nature and which may eventually be used as such (petroleum and natural gas for example) and those which have no economic value before being processed (hydropower, geothermal energy, fissile materials);

secondary energy represents any form of primary energy of the first type which has been processed once or several times: this could also be called "derived energy";

final energy represents any form of primary or secondary energy which is available to the final consumer (for example, petrol, electricity, district heat, etc.); if the latter produces goods or services, then the final energy is considered as an intermediate good; if the consumer is a household, then it is considered as a final consumer good. Final energy is measured by directly observing the quantities supplied on the market by the producers to the consumers, taking also into account the quantities of energy which are directly available to the consumer (solar energy, wood and waste products, for example).

All the consumption of primary, secondary and final energy are grasped simultaneously, for a given year, by means of an energy balance; this balance is a synthetic translation of energy flows, from primary energy to final energy. In order to allow aggregation operations, these flows are materialized by means of a common physical unit of account used to measure all production, processing and consumption. This presupposes the use of a set of energy conversion coefficients between the various sources of energy.

Two accounting systems, differing both in their object and their spirit are traditionally used to define the unit of account and the energy conversion coefficients. The so-called *"substitution"* accounting system aims at measuring the energy flows and consumption which would have resulted from one single energy source, which would thus have been "substituted" for all the other energy sources on a primary level. Thus the common unit of account is the unit quantity of the reference primary energy (ton of oil equivalent (toe), ton of coal equivalent (tce)). The measurement of the energy conversion coefficients (mistakenly called equivalence coefficients) is based on the relative heat value of the other sources of energy in relation to that of the reference energy. In order to limit the distorsions introduced by such an accounting system, the dominant source of primary energy is usually chosen as a reference: until the mid-sixties this was coal, and everything was measured in terms of tce; since then coal has been ousted by petroleum and the unit of measurement is now the toe (or the barrel of oil equivalent: boe).

The other accounting system is based on the notion of the *"heat content"* of the various forms of energy. The unit is, in this case, a conventional unit of energy measurement — calory, joule or kWh — and the conversion coefficients express the quantities of thermal energy which can be obtained from the various sources when consumed (1 kWh of electricity is equal to 3600 kJ).

Finally, a word should be said about the accounting of consumption of electricity, and of energies such as solar energy, district heat, and geothermal energy.

Electricity is a special case, in that it is both a primary energy (hydropower or wind) and a secondary energy. The application of the substitution method, in the strictest sense of the term, would mean measuring electricity production from hydropower or wind energy on the basis of the heat value of electricity, and electricity production from thermal power plants on the basis of the quantity of the reference primary energy (coal or oil) necessary to produce it. Although certain countries have chosen to measure electricity in this way (Norway, for example), others have decided to simplify the calculation and measure everything in the second way (France, for example). Even at the present time the situation is far from clear, and it is necessary to remain very attentive when reading statistical yearbooks, all the more to since the conversion coefficients may vary from one country to another, and for a single country, from one period in time to another[1]. The use of the other accounting system is less ambiguous since the electricity is measured on the basis of its heat value.

As far as new energies (solar, geothermal, waste heat, etc.) are concerned, it has become common practice (mistakenly) to account for them on the basis of their heat content alone, even in those energy balances which have been set up by means of the substitution accounting system. Although the correction which is then necessary raises no real problems with solar and geothermal energy, this is far from being the case for combined heat and power generation. In this case the substitution rule raises fundamental problems, as it results in accounting for the same quantity of primary energy twice; firstly in the form of electricity, and secondly in the form of heat[2].

1.2. New Concepts

Two new concepts have appeared in energy literature: *useful energy* and *energy needs*. To be more precise, these concepts are "new" only in relation to what has been written and said over the last twenty years: it would be more correct to talk of a "renewal" of their use, inasmuch as certain authors made use of them in the nineteen fifties. Despite the fact that they are used more and more frequently, there is as yet no precise and generally accepted definition of these concepts. As they will appear often throughout this book, it is of interest to propose a definition and explain exactly its meaning.

Theoretically, and in the physical sense, useful energy represents energy in the form that it is actually wanted by the consumer: heat for heating, light for lighting, mechanical power for movement, etc. However, this useful energy is seldom directly available and most often has to be obtained by processing final energy (petrol, electricity, . . .) in equipment designed for that purpose (boiler, oven, engine, . . .). This processing involves different losses — and thus different efficiencies — according to the final energy and equipment used (for example an efficiency of 95% for electric heating, and 50% for coal heating). It is of interest to adopt the concept of useful energy because statistical observation of the energy consumption is based on final energy, and is therefore distorted by the disparity between end-use efficiencies: two households heated at the same temperature in identical dwellings will consume different quantities of final

---

[1] See OECD and EUROSTAT statistics for instance.

[2] The reader will find a more thorough discussion of these questions in Reference [1].

energy, depending on whether they use electricity, gas or coal, simply because the end-use efficiencies of these energy products are different. The measurement of useful energy, which is carried out downstream of the end-use equipment, avoids this inconvenience, and gives the only true indication of the energy which is actually required to obtain a given service.

Up to this point the concept of useful energy raises no problems: the difficulties begin when it becomes necessary to measure it. Let us take an example: how can one measure the useful energy in an industrial smelting furnace? Should one use the thermal energy necessary for maintaining the furnace at a certain temperature, or the thermal energy necessary for smelting? The diversity of possible answers to this type of question gives some idea of the disparate nature of the definitions and concrete measurements of useful energy. Given our objective — to rid the measurement of energy demand of the distorsions introduced by substitutions between energy forms — and the fact that the consumption of final energy alone is statistically known, we prefer to argue in terms of "relative useful energy": in a given end-use of energy (heating, kiln, engine, . . .) the relative useful energy is measured by the consumption of the most efficient energy in the most efficient currently-used technique. From this definition it becomes clear that relative useful energy can be measured each time that one has knowledge of the consumption of final energy and of the *relative efficiencies* of the couple final energy/equipment in relation to the reference couple. If the absolute efficiency of the reference couple is approximately 1, then our measurement of the relative useful energy will be close to the theoretical measurement of useful energy (this is the case for electric heating for example).

The concept of *energy needs*, although it has long been in use, has taken on a new meaning. This concept is ambiguous in that energy does not correspond to any need in itself: one does not consume energy because one needs energy, but rather in order to meet a need for comfort, or mobility, or to produce a good or a service. Let us take accomodation as an example: one heats one's house or appartment during the winter because of a need to maintain a certain indoor temperature, a certain comfort; depending on whether the house is large or small, well or badly insulated, the amount of thermal energy necessary to maintain this level of inside comfort may vary substantially. Similarly, in the steel industry the quantity of energy required to produce a ton of steel, for example, varies considerably according to whether the steel is produced from scrap or from iron ore. Thus it can be seen from these examples that it is meaningless to discuss energy needs unless this notion is intrinsically linked to that of the satisfaction of a social need (comfort, for example), or the realization of a production activity, *in a given physical and technological context* (a house of a certain type in a certain climate, a given production process, etc.). In this sense, it may be relevant to talk of a need for thermal energy to heat a given housing unit, in a given climate, to a given temperature; on the other hand it is quite meaningless in this case to talk of a need for final energy or primary energy, since according to the energy products used, the efficiencies — and therefore the quantities of energy required — may vary. If we generalize this example, then it can be seen that there is a close relation between the concept of useful energy and that of energy needs as we have just described it. When we use the term energy needs we will implicitly be referring to *useful energy needs*, i.e. to *the quantity of relative useful energy necessary to satisfy a social need or to carry out a production activity, in a given physical and technological context.* Social needs should be understood in this case in the narrow sense of the term, i.e. in the sense of a consumer need (mobility, comfort, etc.) which results, directly, in energy consumption. The physical and technological context is defined as the geographical, climatic and technological environment in which the social need is expressed or the production activity carried out; it is appre-hended in a concrete manner by means of physical parameters which establish the link between the original social need or production activity and the resultant useful energy need. It is characterized by time constants which may be either infinite (climate), or very long (geography, technology), as opposed to end use equipment whose time constants are most often short. We will return to this aspect of the problem later when analysing consumer reactions to price rises.

1.3. Method of Analysis

The analysis which we are referring to should be understood as that of the mechanisms by which final energy demand is generated and evolves; it makes direct use of the concepts which we have just described and does not include any consideration on the conversion primary energy/final energy.

The first phase consists in identifying the groups of social needs and pro-duction activities which are homogeneous in relation to the useful energy needs which they give rise to; in specifying the characteristics of the physical and technological contexts in which these useful energy needs arise; in identifying and characterizing the equipment used to transform final energy into the re-quired useful energy.

The second phase consists in analysing the phenomena and mechanisms which explain the evolution in time firstly of social needs and production activities, secondly of the physical and technological context, and lastly of the end use equipment (Fig. 1.1).

More generally, this analysis makes it possible to identify a certain number of factors — or determinants of energy demand — which explain to a greater or lesser extent the generation of energy demand at a given time, as well as its evolution. We shall attempt to show how, in the past, these various determinants have influenced the evolution of energy demand, quantitatively whenever this is possible, but most often qualitatively. In particular we will show, when the case arises, the changes provoked by the oil crisis in 1973–74.

Statistical measurement of these determinants is highly uneven. Certain, mainly technical and economic, determinants have been the object of statistical observation over more or less long periods of time (for example the car owner-ship ratio, or specific energy consumptions in the iron and steel industry); others, however, have only given rise to short-term studies or surveys, to the extent that their historical evolution is difficult to apprehend (for example, indoor temperature). Unfortunately, the fact that a determinant has been the object of a thorough statistical observation in no way guarantees that it is of importance in determining energy demand; in fact, some key factors have never been analysed statistically (for example the average consumption of cars, or the indoor temperature already mentioned above). By considering the data resulting from long-term statistical observation alone, and thus discarding the less well known factors, the effect on our analysis would of course have been detrimental.

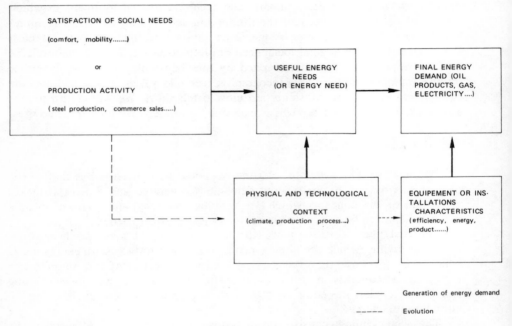

Fig. 1.1. Analysis of energy demand: main determinants of energy demand and relationships

Thus, we will attempt to deal with the main determinants of energy demand whether they have been well covered statistically or not. The reader should keep in mind the differences in the quality of the data used (e.g. statistical observation — as opposed to surveys). We will add another dimension to this analysis by using, whenever possible, comparisons between various countries: the choice of the country which of course depends on the availability of the necessary information, may vary according to the determinants and energy uses under consideration. We have generally included in these comparisons the main OECD countries.

The historical analysis will be followed by an appraisal of future prospects, in which we shall attempt to distinguish the main trends which can be envisaged for the next twenty years: the year 2000 will be the time horizon of most observations. Given the upheavals in the energy field since 1973, we shall particularly emphasize, on the one hand the role of public authorities (energy saving policies) and factors or constraints of an institutional type, and on the other hand, the influence of high and possibly continually rising energy prices. In our conclusion we will attempt to bring out the dominant tendencies, which are unlikely to be fundamentally altered, and to distinguish in the agitation which followed the 1973—74 crisis between short-term phenomena and more fundamental changes which will inevitably profoundly alter medium- and long-term trends in the energy field.

Although these analyses deal mainly with energy problems, we will be led to explore more or less related fields of activity, such as transport, construction, industries, etc. As we are not specialists in these particular areas, we hope that those who are more familiar with them will be indulgent. It should not be forgotten that the aim of these explorations is to improve our knowledge of energy demand, and certain simplifications, short-cuts or ommissions will only have minor consequences on the analysis.

2. The Role of Prices

Demand, as we have already seen, is a concept in which prices and quantities cannot be dissociated, and thus the interaction price-quantity must be situated at the core of any analysis of demand. Our method of analysing energy demand may be characterized, among other considerations, by its highly disaggregated nature, and throughout this analysis we will deal on many occasions with price-quantity interactions. In order to maintain a certain homogeneity and to proceed in a coherent manner, and also to avoid useless repetition, we consider it of more interest to carry out a general analysis of these interactions before going on the detailed study of energy demand.

Before entering into the heart of the problem, it is nonetheless necessary to be more precise about what is meant by "energy prices". Energy is a heterogeneous economic good, which appears in the form of products which barely resemble one another (electricity and fuel oil, for example): thus to discuss the "price of energy" may lead to some confusion. In general, and unless we indicate otherwise, when discussing the "price of energy", we are referring to the price of the dominant energy, be it the dominant final energy at the level of the household or of producers for a given use, or the dominant primary energy at the overall level of the economy as a whole.

Throughout the nineteen-sixties and up until the oil crisis in 1973—74, little attention was paid to the role played by prices in the generation and evolution of energy demand[1]: the extremely low levels and the non-evolution — or even the decline — in prices during the period were the justification for such indifference. Thus the crisis found most Western economies with a methodological and statistical apparatus which was totally inadequate to take into account and measure the immediate and long-term impact of the substantial increases in the price of oil. Although most of the experts were in agreement in recognizing the

---

[1] Unless we indicate otherwise, we will from now on use the expression "energy demand" in place of "quantity of energy demanded".

reality of this impact, none of them were able to evaluate correctly and quantitatively the extent and depth of the problem. Various attempts have been made since the crisis to make up for this weakness, but in general they have been unsuccessful due to the extreme shortage of statistical data and the complexity of the problem. It is not our intention to provide a solution to this vast problem, nor even to analyse price-quantity interactions in all their complexity. Rather, we shall attempt to identify the main effects of an increase in the price of energy on demand. Several cases will be envisaged, depending on whether the energy corresponds to a final consumption (satisfaction of a social need) or an intermediate consumption (production activity), and whether we are discussing the short term (less than one year), the medium term (1 to 10 years) or the long term (more than 10 years).

2.1. Micro-Economic Aspects

Final Consumers and Energy Prices

The theoretical developments in micro-economics enable us to give a satisfactory explanation of household behaviour in the case of an increase of the price of energy, at least in the short term[1]. As we have already explained, every energy need may be assimilated instantaneously with the need which the energy helps to satisfy; thus the cost of the energy may be assimilated to the cost of the service thus rendered. For instance, the cost of space heating is assimilated to the cost of the energy consumed for that purpose, or the cost of running a car is assimilated to the cost of petrol. Within their budget, households choose between their various needs according to their particular preferences. Some of their energy needs correspond to relatively incompressible needs (e.g. heating and hot water). If the price of energy increases faster than their incomes, then households will tend not only to reduce their energy demand corresponding to the most compressible needs, but also all their demand for goods and services which are not directly energy-related but which they consider relatively less important. Perhaps we should point out that by the evolution of prices and incomes, we are talking in real terms, i.e. once inflation has been deduced. The concepts of price elasticity of demand and cross elasticities enable us, in theory, to account for and to measure household reactions to such price increases. Elasticity is defined as the measurement, in percentage terms, of the variation in quantities demanded determined by a variation of 1% in prices. In practice, the stability — and even the decrease — in energy prices before 1973 made it impossible to measure in a meaningful way the elasticities over this period[2]. This helps to explain the inability of the experts to apprehend correctly the short-term phenomena which followed the 1973—74 crisis. A retrospective of the consequences of the increases in petroleum prices in 1973/74 and 1979/80 should probably make it possible to measure short-term elasticities more ac-

---

[1] See for instance Mainguy [2].

[2] For an exhaustive discussion of the various types of elasticity and ways of measuring them, see Girod [3] and Nera [4].

curately. However, given the close relations between these elasticities and individuals ways of life, it is clear that they are meaningful only for a given moment in time, in a given social and technological context, and that they can hardly be transposed in time and in space. For instance, the elasticities measured in a given country after the 1973—74 oil price increases are probably not valid for assessing the effect of new increases in 1980; similarly elasticities measured in the U.S. cannot be transposed to European countries and vice versa since the possbilities of switching to public transport as well as the initial price levels of petrol are radically different.

If we leave aside short term problems, for the time being, then we are immediately confronted with a more complex situation. Energy is not a simple economic good; it is in fact a complementary good, i.e. energy must be used with capital (complementarity energy/capital). Although in the short term, households can only react on the basis of a "given equipment" (e.g. the heating or cooking appliances), in the long run they have the possibility of changing their equipment in order to increase or maintain the degree of satisfaction of either their energy-related needs (e.g. space heating) without a correlative increase in their energy expenditure, or their other needs (by decreasing their energy expenditure[3]). Thus the cost of the service rendered can no longer be assimilated to the energy cost, but rather to the total cost of the equipment and the energy. If we go back to the previous examples of space heating and car running, the cost of the service rendered must be considered, in the medium term, as the sum total of the cost of the energy consumed plus that of the investment in the space heating installation or in the car itself. The application of economic theory in order to explain the behaviour of the consumer in this case comes up against two obstacles which are difficult to overcome:

The notion of medium term elasticity of energy demand becoming meaningless, one must recourse to the notion of elasticity linked to that of a "service rendered", which is problematic to measure inasmuch as the technological, social and economic context changes, as do the preferences and the way of life of individuals; it is obvious, for example, that the medium-term elasticity of car mobility to petrol price will be very different if technology moves towards very light cars as against heavy cars or if the car is more and more devoted to professional uses as against leisure uses.

The extent to which the consumer controls the choice of equipment varies considerably according to circumstances, either for purely technical reasons (collective or district heating installations, for example), for economic reasons (amortization rate of the existing equipment, access conditions for loans, etc.) or for social reasons (tenants versus landlords, for example).

From a practical point of view, the medium-term mechanisms are translated in the energy field, essentially by substitutions of one form of energy for another (these substitutions being conditioned by the relative efficiencies and prices of these energy forms) and, should the occasion arise, by a slowdown of overall

---

[3] Provided, of course, that the price of equipment does not rise faster than that of energy!

demand resulting from both these substitutions and a general improvement of the equipment.

In a longer run, households will have greater freedom in that they cannot only choose between various equipments, but also between various alternatives (choice of accomodation which is insulated or not, choice of modes of transport). What we have just discussed is even more pertinent in this case, in that not only the relation between useful energy need and final energy demand may change (which is the case in the medium term), but also the relation between the underlying social need and the useful energy need: for an unchanged indoor temperature, a well insulated house needs up to two times less heat than a badly insulated one.

The most important long-term effect will be a change — perhaps even a reduction — both of useful energy needs and final energy demand. This will be the result of a transformation of the physical and technological context, along with a substantial modification of the household expenditure structure (a decrease in the "energy" share, and an increase in "equipment goods" and "housing investment"). The further one advances in time, the more the short-term effects (reduction of needs) give way to the medium- and long-term adaptations, and the more hazardous it becomes to attempt to transpose the short-term phenomena observed at the beginning of the price increase and the price elasticities measured over a short period. Thus any study dealing with forecasts or prospects of energy-demand — in particular if the time horizon is a long-term one — must necessarily abandon the concept of price elasticity of demand, since its theoretical significance becomes increasingly problematic as one moves away from the short term and since short term elasticity is less and less transposable as one advances towards the future. The concepts of medium- and long-term elasticity would seem to us to be more or less meaningless, except in order to give an ex post synthesis of the combined effects of prices on the many determinants of energy demand. The variations in the results obtained in the numerous studies which have attempted to measure this type of elasticity reinforces our scepticism[4].

Nevertheless, household reaction to a price increase will not only depend on its rythm compared to the evolution of incomes and the cost of equipment, but also on the way it is spread out over time. Roughly, we may oppose a sudden increase which takes place over a short period of time, of the type observed for oil in 1973—74 and 1979—80, and a gradual increase. A sudden increase obviously has a more marked immediate impact: a psychological impact on the one hand, and an economic impact on the other (on the household budget). Generally — i.e. inasmuch as this sudden increase has no lasting effects on the nature of consumer needs (for example, on the temperature at which he heats his house) — the impact tends to decline with the increase in income, in such a manner that in the long run the effect will be similar to that resulting from a gradual increase. A sudden increase could have different medium- and

---

[4]   See References [5, 6, 7].

long-term consequences, by making overall changes in equipment and more generally in technology more rapidly economically viable. In the absence of financial or budget constraints limiting investment, the consequences will be an acceleration in the modification of equipment, and the installation of new equipment (this is also reinforced by the "psychological effect"). However, after a certain period of time, the impacts of these two types of price increase should tend to become identical, provided however that the increase of the energy price in relation to the evolution of incomes and of the cost of equipment has been the same. In reality, unless the anticipation of relative price increases has been correct or too high for energy (regular increase) it is probable that there will be a phenomenon of over-investment in the case of a sudden increase in the price of energy which will result in a more substantial decrease in energy demand. In other words, theoretically and apart from the case which we have just mentioned, the long-term effects of a sudden or gradual price increase should be identical, and only the intermediate stages will differ. However in reality, the situation may be somewhat different since a sudden increase can reduce, for an indefinite period of time, household investment capacities and therefore hinder both equipment substitution and more long-term technological adaptations. It would not be so much the overall level of household energy demand which would be affected but rather the structure of that demand, and more fundamentally, the degree of satisfaction of the underlying social needs. A contrario, a sudden price increase, if substantial, may modify long-term energy patterns in a totally different manner. It may on the one hand, bring about radical changes in the behaviour of the consumer and the nature of his needs, and on the other hand, result in decisions on investment, research, development and regulations which would otherwise not have been made in the case of a regular price increase and a progressive adaptation of techniques to the economic system. The French nuclear programme and its implications on the uses of electricity, the setting up of new standards concerning insulation and specific consumptions of equipment, are good examples of such a development.

Intermediate Consumers[5] and Energy Prices

Certain of these observations concerning households may of course be applied to producer of goods and services. In this section we will deal only with the specific aspects of these latter.

A producer faced with a price increase may, in the short term adopt three possible attitudes: carry over the price increase on to his selling price, recover the price increase by lowering his profit margin – thus maintaining his selling price at a constant level – or make up for the price increase by reducing other costs (wages, overheads, etc.). In reality, his attitude depends on his ability to increase the selling price (legal possibilities given the regulations in force, and commercial possibilities given national and international competition). It also depends on his desire (tactical, strategical) to maintain full production capacity,

---

[5] An intermediate consumer is an economic agent using energy in order to produce a material good or a service.

and his freedom of action concerning profit margin and certain budget categories.

In the longer term, the producer has a greater freedom of action in that he can modify his energy equipment and his production techniques. However, if he can carry over the price increase in a lasting manner onto his selling price, or simply for strategic reasons, it may be that he will be prompted to direct his investments towards the extension of his production capacities and the conquest of new markets rather than towards modifying existing equipment (this is what has been observed in numerous industries since 1974). Of course, when the producer decides to extend his production capacities, or in the case of technical obsolescence, the new equipment which he will install will be adapted to the evolution of energy price and will have better energy performances. The technical substitutions will in this case also result in substituting one form of energy for another and reducing energy demand per unit produced. However these effects will be felt more or less rapidly depending on the producer's attitude towards investment.

A sudden increase in the price of energy may have unforeseen effects which are generally ignored by economic theory: whereas the "normal" reaction to such a price increase should be an intensified investment effort over a short period of time, as a matter of fact the opposite phenomena is often observed. In this case, both the inflationary-type response (increase of selling-price) and the recessionist-type response (lowering of production level or of profit margin) undermine investment capacities and imprison the producer in a vicious circle from which he will find it difficult to extricate himself: the sudden price increase leads to a drop in investments and a slowdown (or even a standstill) in the mechanisms of technical substitution, which leads to a loss of competivity, which leads to a drop in investments etc. Thus, depending on whether the increase is sudden or gradual, and whether it gives the producers the time for technical adaptation or not, the increase in the price of energy may have in this case very different effects in the medium- and long-term: a reduction in energy consumption resulting from a reduction in production activity in the first case; a reduction in consumption without any effect on production activity in the second.

In the long term, the producer will finally be confronted with two major alternatives: either he may readapt on a technical level to the evolution of prices, while remaining competitive, and in this case the readaptation involves not only substitution of energy equipment but also changes in the production processes; or he may not remain competitive vis-à-vis other producers who are subject do different constraints (in particular abroad, in the countries which have their own energy resources), and gradually his production will drop or he will attempt to maintain his competivity in other geographical areas (by spreading production activities around). Thus the two marked long-term effects of the increase in the price of energy are the modification of the production structure, and of the technological context in which production takes place. In the first case, there is a decrease in energy demand linked to energy-intensive production activities, and in the second, a significant decrease in energy demand per unit produced through technical adaptation.

2.2. *Macro-Economic Aspects*

Throughout the analysis which we have just developed, concerning both industrial producers and consumers, we have left aside the interactions which may exist between the increase in the price of energy on the one hand, and the evolution of incomes, production levels, and the general price level on the other. Similarly, it has been implicit in our analysis that the level of this price increase is irrespective of the reactions of the various economic agents. Indeed, it is not possible to proceed otherwise on the micro-economic level on which we have argued until now. However, one cannot deny that there do exist real interdependences that any accurate analysis of price mechanisms must attempt to integrate. At this stage, the analysis must deal with the economy as a whole, and thus becomes considerably more complex. As we do not intend to undertake a thorough investigation of the macro-economic aspect, we will simply provide here a schematic description of the main macro-economic phenomena related to an increase in energy prices.

Firstly, it is necessary to distinguish between energy produced within the country and imported energy. In the first case, a price increase translates a change in the income structure of the economic agents (an increase in mining revenues, for example) which should not necessarily have any considerable effect on the overall level of economic activity: at the most, in the medium- and long-term it may affect the structure of the economic sectors and of the final consumption. In the second case, any increase in the price of imported energy corresponds to a transfer of income outside the economic system. Depending on whether this transfer is recycled or not within the system (either by purchases of goods or services, or by investment) such a transfer has different consequences. If it is recycled, then this will not have any considerable effect on the overall level of activity but will reduce the internal consequences of such activity (domestic consumption and investment), and in this way will modify the structure of this activity (relative weight of industrial sectors, of consumption and investment, etc.); if not, it will result in a slowdown of economic activity and will thus have a recessionist effect (the logical consequence of lower overall consumption and or lower overall investment), accompanied by structural changes. In addition, an increase in the price of energy may lead to medium and long term technical and structural adaptations, as shown at the micro-economic level, which tend to offset those impacts. Once again it should be stressed that the nature of the increase is of importance. In order to bring about structural and technical adaptations a large investment is necessary; in the case of a substantial and sudden increase in the price of imported energy, the sudden loss of domestic income may considerably hamper this investment effort, even over a long period of time, and thus prevent the offsetting mechanisms of the economy from operating and favour the recessionist tendencies mentioned above. In turn, the development of such tendencies may hamper the necessary effort of investment, and thus reinforce the initial effect and increasingly restrain the readaptation mechanisms. In this case, there will be a fall in energy demand, not resulting this time from structural and technical adaptation, but rather from a lowering both of the level of economic activity and of the degree of satisfaction of a certain number of social needs.

When discussing an increase in the price of energy, we are in fact discussing a real increase in relation to the average rate of inflation. This conventional manner of posing the problem is particularly attractive and effective, since in this way it is possible to put aside all inflation-related problems. However, it is also extremely simplistic and thus a source of error in our present discussion. Inflation (measured by the change in the average consumer price index) may be roughly explained by a disequilibrium between the evolution of the money supply and that of the real activity of economy. One can make the hypothesis that this disequilibrium is itself related to a disequilibrium between the evolution of the renumeration of one factor of production (wages, revenue, profit, . . .) and that of the real contribution of this factor to production (productivity increase)[1]. From this point of view, energy, which as a raw material may be considered as a factor of production, may generate or encourage an inflationary trend, if its price, *in current terms*, increases more rapidly than its productivity[2], and if this difference is not offset by differences in the opposite direction on the other factors of production. Without entering into the polemical debate on whether inflation can be "explained" by the increase in the price of energy, we would simply like to stress that to talk of an increase in the price of energy in real terms — whatever the increase may be — is equivalent to admitting implicitly a certain increase in the productivity of energy, which can only be obtained by technical and structural adaptations. This means that it is legitimate to talk of an increase in the price of energy in real terms only if these adaptations have been carried out either at the same time as the increase if it is spread out over time, or after the increase if the latter is sudden. A contrario — and this may be applied in particular to the case of a sudden increase — one may wonder what could possibly be the significance of an increase in real terms (in the medium- or long-term) of the price of energy if the technical and structural readaptation of the economy is extremely slow, or even non-existent. In this case, should it not be admitted that the inflationary mechanisms tend increasingly to "inhibit" this increase, and that any attempt to maintain it can only reinforce these mechanisms, and help to put the economic systems in an even greater state of disequilibrium.

Thus, depending on the circumstances and the country under consideration (energy produced in the country or imported, imports payed in domestic or foreign currency, more or less adapted industrial structure, etc.), and whether the increase is sudden or spread out over time, a substantial increase in the price

---

[1] We do not deny the very schematic and incomplete nature of these explanations of the mechanisms of inflation, and we agree that the complexity of this problem is such that it is impossible to find at the present time a single theory which can provide a complete and convincing explanation of this phenomenon.

[2] Productivity has two meanings here: the quantity of goods or services produced by one unit of energy in one case, the degree of satisfaction of a social need provided by one unit of energy in the other.

of energy may give rise to two extreme situations. The first may be characterized by a considerable slow-down (perhaps even a reduction) in economic
activity, a low, or even negative growth of income of economic agents, and
soaring inflation; all this being related to poor or non-existent technical and
structural adaptation. The second, however, corresponds to a sustained growth
of economic activity and moderate inflation rate, because of a rapid technical
and structural adaptation.

Before drawing this macro-economic analysis to an end, two additional
remarks are necessary:
— in general, the unforeseen effects of sudden price increase would seem to
indicate that such increases, in real terms, can only be lower, over a long time
span, than those resulting from continuous and regular processes, because they
generate more accentuated inflationary mechanisms;
— the fact that countries differ in their sensitivity to the evolution of the price
of energy does not necessarily mean that substantial increases will bring out
lasting divergences in the evolution of the various economies: the latter are in
fact largely interdependent, and any disruption in one economy ends up by
affecting, to a varying extent it is true, all the others.

We hope to have shown in this discussion in what way price mechanisms
applied to energy demand are complex, generally poorly apprehended by economic theory, and what is more, extremely difficult to describe historically
from a statistical point of view. This reinforces the necessity, previously outlined, to go beyond the conventional economic (econometric) analysis, and
to use both a more global approach, integrating the social, technical and political
components of demand which are so often absent from economic analysis stricto
sensu, and a more detailed approach in order to pin-point all the cases in which
price mechanisms operate differently.

II. Energy Demand in the Residential and Tertiary Sector

What is really meant by the "residential and tertiary sector" is often ambiguous in energy studies. Although the "residential" part would seem a priori easy to define — it covers everything to do with the energy demand of households for their dwellings — it is in general poorly apprehended from a statistical point of view. The tertiary sector is far more vague both in its definition and its statistical coverage: it includes of course all so-called tertiary activities (administration, shops, offices, education), but also other sectors which have nothing in common with these latter, such as farming, handicrafts, and sometimes even the building and construction industry. Since we are dependent on energy statistics, we have had to abandon any attempt at a rigourous definition of the tertiary sector, which would be identical for all countries, and to accept the particular meaning given to this term in each of the countries we have studied.

Our study on the residential and tertiary sector is in two parts: firstly, we will provide a historical analysis of the evolution of its energy consumption and of the main factors determining that consumption; secondly, we will examine long-term prospects.

From a statistical point of view, we have (with the qualifications mentioned above) fairly long series (1950—78) on the evolution of energy consumption for the residential and tertiary sector as a whole — excluding wood[1]. These latter will enable us initially to bring out the main trends for the sector as a whole over the last thirty years. We will then attempt to identify specific trends in the residential sector on the one hand, and the tertiary sector on the other. We will then proceed on to a more detailed level by attempting to pinpoint the main determinants of energy demand in these two sectors, by examining their historical evolution and appreciating qualitatively and if possible quantitatively their role in the evolution of energy consumption. In this case it will not be possible to use the same historical perspective nor to deal systematically with all the countries under study: we will be obliged to adapt our observations to the available information, which is to be found mainly in estimates and surveys

---

[1] Some may think it more oppurtune in this historical study to go further back in time. Such an exercise would seem to us to be of little interest, perhaps even somewhat dangerous, since wood cannot be taken into account. By beginning in 1950, at which date wood had become relatively insignificant, we believe that we avoid distorting the analysis.

rather than actual statistics. We will end this historical study, by stressing the main lessons of the 1973–74 oil crisis.

After this historical survey, we will then turn towards the future and discuss the main changes which are likely to take place in this sector by the year 2000. At this stage, the analysis will be sufficiently general in nature to be applied both to the housing and to the tertiary sector.

1. Historical Survey

1.1. Overall Energy Consumption 1950–1978

Trends in energy consumption in the residential and tertiary sector in the industrialized countries between 1950 and 1973 have two main characteristics: on the one hand, highly differentiated growth according to the country, and on the other, fairly regular growth, slower in the first decade and accelerating afterwards.

The disparity of population growth certainly helps to explain these differences. By setting these consumptions in relation to population[1], one can better appreciate the specific aspects of each country, both concerning absolute consumption levels but also growth rates. Thus Table 2.1 shows the substantial differences in per capita consumption in 1950 – very low consumption levels in France, Italy and Japan compared to the other European countries as a whole; very high levels in the U.S.A. and the U.K. – and extremely divergent trends from 1950 to 1970. We can observe a high growth rate in Japan and Italy (11–12% a year), fairly high in France (compared to the other European countries – about 10% a year); a growth rate of about 5 to 6% in Denmark, Sweden, the Netherlands and W. Germany; a slower evolution in the U.S.A. and Belgium and stagnation in the United Kingdom. Thus, towards the end of the period there is a narrowing of the differences in per capita consumption levels in Europe, with the exception of Italy (in particular the other European countries catch up with the U.K.). Another characteristic feature, which can be observed from Table 2.1, is the slow evolution of per capita consumption from 1950 to 1960 in Japan, Belgium, the Netherlands and the U.S.A.

Since a major part of the consumption of this sector covers heating needs, it may be that part of the differences between countries can be explained by different weather conditions – in particular for Japan and Italy. Thus we have corrected the consumption figures in order to base them on the same reference climate. The results of this readjustment show a marked slowdown in the seventies of consumption levels in most European countries around 40 GJ (i.e. about the equivalent of 1 ton of petroleum). The U.S.A. have a consumption level which is about twice as high as that in the European countries, however the gap between the U.S.A. and Europe tends to be reduced. As a matter of fact, we believe that the weather conditions have a far more marked effect than the

---

[1] See Table 2.1, and statistical tables in Appendix 1.

Table 2.1. *Per capita final energy consumption in the residential and tertiary sector* * (GJ/cap)

	1950	1960	1970	1975	1978
U.S.A.	55	63	83	79	83
	(16)	(16)	(16)	(15)	
Japan	2	5	17	22	22
		(8)	(14)	(11)	
France	5	19	33	36	43
	(4)	(11)	(12)	(11)	
F.R. Germany	14	25	46	47	
	(10)	(10)	(12)	(11)	
Italy	2	8	19	23	24
	(4)	(10)	(14)	(17)	
U.K.	40	41	42	41	43
	(28)	(23)	(19)	(17)	
Netherlands	21	24	51	63	65
	(15)	(13)	(18)	(20)	
Belgium	29	29	49	56	60
Denmark	26	35	73	63	71
Sweden	21	36	69	68	64
	(6)	(8)	(11)	(−)	

* Figures between brackets: per capita consumption with climatic correction per unit of GDP (in GJ/capita/1000 US $ 1970).

Source: Appendix 1, Tables R.3, R.4, and R.5.

figures tend to show — and this is particularly so in the nineteen-fifties — because the countries with temperate climates like Italy, Japan and even France were probably all less well equipped in heating appliances than the other countries: this may well explain the very low levels of per capita consumption in 1950 in France, Japan and Italy.

One question which may be raised now is in what way income growth affected trends in energy consumption. To simplify matters, and also because there is a lack of adequate statistical series, we will take the gross domestic product (G.D.P.) per inhabitant as an indicator of per capita income. An examination of the series of values obtained (Table 2.1) indicates the following phenomena: a parallel progression of income and consumption in France, Federal Republic of Germany, the U. S. A. (constant ratio); consumption progressing more rapidly than income in Japan, Italy and Sweden; and lastly, in the U. K. consumption progressing very much less rapidly than income. This shows that there is no simple relation between income and energy consumption, and that the influence of income on energy demand varies according to the country. How about the relative levels, between the various countries, of energy consumption per capita and per unit of G.D.P.? Although in 1950 there are significant differences, these tend to lessen with time to the extent that in 1970 consumption levels have become fairly close to one another. In order to draw pertinent conclusions concerning present differences between countries, it would be necessary to convert the G.D.P. not in terms of rates of exchange, but rather on the basis of "purchasing power parities", and this is beyond the scope of our study[2].

Let us now examine the energy substitutions which took place in this sector. The most striking feature is, of course, the decline of coal and the rise of hydrocarbons. In 1960, coal accounted for more than 40% of energy consumption for all the countries, except Sweden and the U. S. A. (where hydrocarbons had already penetrated the market in a considerable manner). From this date on, the rhythm of substitution of coal by hydrocarbons varies according to the country: extremely rapid in Japan, Italy, the Netherlands, and Denmark; slower in Federal Republic of Germany and France, and very slow in the U. K. and Belgium where coal continues to account for a substantial share of the market (about 20%).

These differentiated rates of substitution are obviously related to the rate of growth of energy demand: rapid growth (Italy, Japan) involves a more rapid renewal and development of heating equipment as a whole (and, a contrario, for countries with low consumption growth rates such as Belgium or the U.K.). They are also related to the energy resources availabilities, e.g. gas in the U.S.A. and the Netherlands. The share of electricity has generally increased little in most countries, apart from the U. K. and the U. S. A., where it has penetrated rapidly on to the market (more than 20% of consumption in 1974).

The differences in price levels between countries and energy forms on the one hand, and in the rythms of evolution of these prices (or in the consumer anticipation) on the other, probably explain some of the phenomena which we observed previously. Nonetheless as we have already mentioned[3] we consider that at the aggregated level on which we are arguing, it is difficult to analyse to what extent prices can explain these phenomena. Consequently, we will not return to this question.

Until now, we have mainly discussed the historical trends up until the oil crisis in 1973–74. This crisis marks a break with past trends since energy consumption of the residential-tertiary sector has ceased to grow in all the countries under study. In practically all these countries the absolute level of consumption in this sector was lower in 1977 than in 1971. For the member countries of the I.E.A. (International Energy Agency) as a whole, the progression rate of energy consumption in this sector fell from 5% a year over the period 1960–73, to 0.4% between 1973 and 1977. This slowdown in relation to past trends may be explained by various phenomena whose respective impact is difficult to isolate: slowdown in income growth (a G.D.P. growth rate of 1.6% a year between 1973 and 1977 compared with 4.5% a year between 1968 and 1973 for the countries of the I.E.A.), consumer reaction to the substantial price increases in 1974, or the consequences of energy-saving measures taken by governments (insulation

---

[2] The reader should consult the comparisons carried out by Darmstadter, Dunkerley and Alterman for 1972 [28].

[3] See our remarks in Chapter I, concerning the relation energy price/energy demand.

standards for new buildings, tax incentives, subsidies, . . .).

We will now try to understand in more detail past rates of growth of energy consumption and the slowdown which followed the crisis. We will do so by examining the evolution of the main determinants of energy demand in this sector; firstly in housing, then in the tertiary sector.

1.2. Energy Needs in Dwellings

Energy is used in dwellings for four main purposes:
— to maintain a certain inside temperature for comfort (heating or air conditioning)
— to heat water for domestic purposes (bathing and washing)
— to cook
— to use a certain number of household electrical appliances (washing machines, . . .) and for lighting.

As we have already pointed out, statistical sources generally give no indications concerning energy consumption in the residential sector, and even less concerning the breakdown of consumption according to end-uses. Nonetheless, a certain effort has been made in some countries in order to estimate such data since the oil crisis. The figures for estimated energy consumption per dwelling shown on Table 2.2 indicate a relative stabilization — even a decrease — in the 1970s, and this applies to almost all countries. The present distribution of these consumptions can be estimated roughly in the following manner: heating accounts for about 80% of consumption in France, Federal Republic of Germany, Denmark and Italy, but little less than 70% in the U.S.A. and the U.K. (Japan should be considered as a special case, in that heating is far less developed in this country and accounts for only 40% of consumption). In the U.S.A. and the U.K. water-heating accounts for a greater share (about 15%) of the overall figures than the 10% in the other countries (Japan once again is a special case, water-heating accounting for 30% of the total consumption figures). The share of household electrical appliances and lighting varies considerably from one country to another, from 6% in France (where household electrical appliances are relatively less developed) to 8% in the U.K. and Denmark and 14% in the U.S.A. Cooking activities account for between 4 and 5% of energy consumption in France, Federal Republic of Germany, and Denmark, and between 8 and 9% in the U.K. and the U.S.A. Lastly, air conditioning accounts for only 3% of energy consumption in American homes.

Space Heating

Energy demand for heating is induced by the need to maintain a certain inside climate in the home (temperature, humidity in the air, . . .). This need, which may be called a "need for inside temperature" generates firstly a *need for heat* which is a function of the insulation and ventilation characteristics of the home, the volume to be heated, the climate, and the "free" heat (generated by the occupants, the sun and the heat losses of the household electrical appliances). This need for heat is translated in turn into a demand for energy products (electricity, hot water, fuel oil and gas, for example), or a final demand, to use

Table 2.2. *Final energy consumption per dwelling (GJ/dwelling)*

	1955	1960	1970	1973	1974	1975	1976	1977
U.S.A.	153	166	192	179	174	163	–	–
U.K.	104	96	82	81	81	78	–	78
France	–	44*	–	86	83	79	81	84
F.R. Germany	–	57	87	88	78	77	83	81
Japan	14	14	30	30	29	32	32	–

* 1962.
Source: Appendix 1.

the usual terminology, determined by the efficiency of the heating equipment.

In order to understand the past evolution of energy demand for domestic heating, it is necessary to examine the evolution of each of these factors.

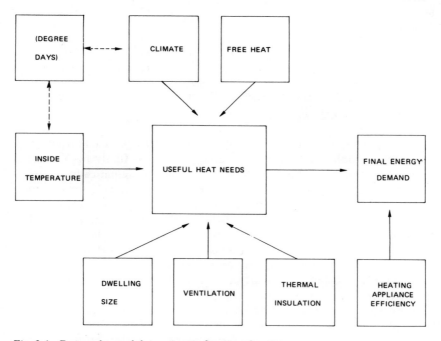

Fig. 2.1. Energy demand determinants for space heating

Temperature. Although we have no reliable information on the temperature at which people heated their homes in the past, it is quite certain it has constantly risen for two reasons: firstly, the development of central heating, which generalizes heating to all the rooms in the house, has contributed to increasing the average wholehouse temperature; secondly, quite distinct from this latter phenomenon, people have tended to seek ever-higher inside temperatures, considered by many as a condition for comfort and well-being. Related to living and working habits, this second phenomenon is far more difficult to analyse.

When comparing energy consumptions in homes with or without central heating, one may observe differences from 2.5 (84 GJ compared with 34 GJ) in France, to 1.7 in the Netherlands and about 1.3 in the U.K. (Table 2.3.).

Table 2.3. *Final energy consumption according to space heating modes. Unit: GJ/dwelling*

	F.R. Germany (1974)	France (1974)	Netherlands (1972)
Individual houses	88	–	96
with central heating	99	111	119
with room heating	76	–	72
Flats			
with collective central heating	} 65	72 } 66	} 100
with individual central heating		50	
with room heating	57	–	52
All dwellings types	74	59	91
with central heating	81	84	113
with room heating	67	34	66

Source: Data estimated for the MEDEE models using the following sources: F.R.G. [1], France [2], Netherlands [3, 4].

The development of central heating in most industrialized countries took place extremely rapidly, as is shown on Table 2.4. This is firstly because most new constructions built over the last 20 years have been systematically equipped with central heating, whatever the climatic conditions: in France, for example, 90% of new homes built since 1962 contain central heating, and there is practically no difference between the north and the south of the country. Secondly, the demolition of old dwellings has reduced the number of homes without central heating. Lastly, there has been a substitution in old dwellings of central heating systems for room heating (in France, this substitution has covered approximately 150,000 homes a year, i.e. 1% of the total number of homes, over the last 15 years).

Of course, this substitution process has been a consequence of the substantial progression in household income and of the existence of low interest rate loans, but it has also been accelerated, in many countries, by the penetration of petroleum products onto the heating market: the move from coal or wood to fuel oil has often been accompanied by the installation of central heating. Thus, in those countries which continue to make use of wood and coal on a large scale, Austria and Belgium for example, central heating has penetrated far more slowly. The move from independent heating to central heating is also determined by individual ways of life and by the internal organization within the home: thus, in farms, where a more traditional way of life subsists, characterized, in particular, by the existence of a large kitchen where the occupants live most of the time, central heating has hardly been developed at all (in France, for example, only 25% of all farms had central heating in 1975).

Table 2.4. *Development of central heating* ownership*

	1960	1970	1975	References
France	20% (1962)	35% (1968)	53%	[5]
F.R. Germany	12%	45%	55%	[6, 7]
U.K.	5% (1961)	27% (1972)	38%	[8, 9]
Netherlands	5%	24%	41%	[4, 10]
Belgium	11%	32%	34%	[11]
Italy	9%	28% (1971)	29%	[12, 13, 14, 15]
Denmark	47%	84%	88%	[16, 17]
Austria	–	–	38%	[18]

* Electric storage heating not considered as a central heating mode (11% of the dwellings in U.K. and 6% in F.R. Germany in 1975).

The inside temperature in homes which are centrally heated depends also on the type of heating used: temperatures are generally higher in the case of district or collective heating, firstly because the regulation of such systems is often poor, and secondly because heating costs are seldom individualized. A survey carried out in France by the Agence pour les Economies d'Energie found the following temperatures (winter 1979–80): flats with collective central-heating, 19.6 °C; flats with individual central heating 18.7 °C; individual houses with central heating 18 °C. The individualization of heating costs in the case of collective heating may either be on a meter basis, or in the form of a base supply of heat from the collective system and the use of back-up appliances in each individual home. A second survey, covering state subsidized housing alone, shows that the average inside temperature is 19.9 °C (floor heating) and 20.6 °C (radiators) in the case of a collective heating system, and 18.8 °C in the case of a collective base plus individual heating.

Size of the home. Heating needs are directly proportional to the size of the home, and thus to their surface area. Historically, in all countries, there has been a slow progression towards larger homes (the average size rising by 0.5 to 0.7 m²/year, see Table 2.5) despite a constant reduction of the number of persons per home. This trend, which has been facilitated by a progression in income greater than that of building costs, reflects a growing desire among individuals to have more living-space for themselves: it is far more marked in the case of new dwellings added each year to the stock, as is shown in Table 2.5. It may be observed that apart from the U.S.A. and Denmark there are no significant differences between countries as far as the size of dwellings is concerned, whether it be existing dwellings or new constructions. The average size of an existing flat is about 60 m² at the present time, and the size of newly-built dwellings varies between 100 to 115 m² for individual houses and 70 m² for flats. This slow increase in the average size of dwellings could indicate that size has been of little account in the increase of energy consumption per dwelling: in fact, the homes

Table 2.5. *Change in dwellings size* (average floor area in m²/dwelling)

	Average size for the dwelling stock				New dwellings built in				References
	1950	1960	1970	1975	1960	1965	1970	1975	
U.S.A.			110 {120 / 90}					113 {145 / 83}	[20]
F.R. Germany		62 {73 / 54}	66 {79 / 58}	70 {83 / 61}	77 {/ 62}	80 {93 / 67}	84 {105 / 68}	91 {115 / 71}	[6, 24]
France				72 {83 / 61} (1973)	64	73	77 {93 / 66}	83 {101 / 68}	[46, 47]
Belgium		71	77	78 (1974)					[11]
Denmark	67 {80 / 50}	71 {83 / 53}	77 {93 / 58}	84 {101 / 60}			114 {138 / 79} (1971)	123 {139 / 79}	[28, 29]
Sweden				77 {99 / 61}				94 {107 / 64}	[48]

All dwellings { individual houses / flats }

which were built in the sixties and seventies were much larger than average, as we have just seen, and far better heated since they were generally equipped with central heating.

Heat Losses. Heat losses in a dwelling are caused by the dissipation of heat through the boundary surfaces and by air infiltration, be it by voluntary air renewal (aeration) or uncontrolled renewal (leaks). The losses through the outside boundary surfaces (walls, windows, bottom floors, ceilings or verandahs) vary according to their heat transmission coefficients, which are related to the thermal characteristics of the construction material employed. Table 2.6 gives for Sweden and the U.K. the evolution of the average coefficients of the different types of boundary surface. It is not a matter in this case of comparing insulation practices in these countries, which differ too greatly as far as weather conditions are concerned, but rather of showing in what way, in the only two countries for which we have sufficient data, insulation in homes has developed in time. In contradiction with the commonly expressed idea that very old dwellings were better insulated than more recent constructions (for example, dwellings built after the second World War), it can be seen on Table 2.6 that the development of building techniques resulted in a constant improvement of the insulation of dwellings in both countries at a time when energy prices were falling in real terms.

Table 2.6. *Change in the insulation practices in Sweden and U.K.* (insulation coefficient U in $W/m^2 \cdot {}^\circ K$)

Year of construction		Before 1920	1920–1940	1940–1960	1960–1975
Outer walls					
Sweden	individual houses	0.6–0.9	0.6–0.85	0.55–0.6	0.35–0.4
	flats	0.84–1	0.9–1	0.65–0.7	0.45
U.K.		2.1–2.7	1.4–1.7	< 1.4–1.7 >	
Roofs					
Sweden	flats	0.4–0.65	0.46–0.6	0.43–0.5	0.3–0.37
	individual houses	0.42–0.6	0.35–0.5	0.35–0.45	0.28–0.30
U.K.		3	1.9	< 0.8–1.4 >	

Source: Sweden: [30]   higher figure: National Swedish Board of Physical Planning and Building
lower figure: National Swedish Institute for Building Research

U.K.: [25].

We have some less detailed information on other countries which nonetheless brings some light onto this problem. In France, two surveys were carried out in 1975 and 1976 concerning the thermal characteristics of existing dwellings. Although the average insulation figures given in these surveys should be considered with some caution there are nonetheless two clear trends: firstly, insulation characteristics differ little from one weather zone to another, and secondly, insulation in immediate post-second world war dwellings (1948–59) is far poorer than in other periods of construction[1]. In the U.S.A. it is possible to measure the development of insulation practices on the basis of the standards imposed by the administration (Federal Housing Administration) for state sub-sidized dwellings (20 to 30% of construction-work each year). These standards, which first appeared in 1953, were reinforced in 1959, and in 1971, so that dwellings built since 1953 have been increasingly well insulated (the maximum heat loss for individual houses was cut by 1.7 between 1953 and 1971) [32]. Although they are restricted to public construction, these standards have certainly had some effect on the insulation practice of private builders. According to the specialists it would seem that in the U.S.A. very old constructions were badly insulated. Lastly in Denmark, a systematic study has shown a clear progression in the thickness of the insulation material used in new constructions, which corresponds to the trends observed in the U.K. and Sweden [28].

Efficiency of Heating Appliances. The average conversion efficiency of energy products into useful heat is largely determined by the type of fuel used. This end-use efficiency has without doubt regularly increased over the last two decades because of the substitution of fuel oil and gas for coal, coal having a lower efficiency than fuel oil and gas. Quite apart from this phenomenon of sub-stitution, there has been, over the years, a continuous improvement in the end-use efficiency of each type of fuel, due to the development of central heating, which gives better performances than individual stoves, and also to intrinsic technical progress. A number of estimates have been made concerning the average efficiency of heating appliances in several countries, but these figures should be considered with caution. As a matter of fact, to our knowledge, there has not been any reliable survey carried out in this field, and most testing has been done in laboratories, i.e. in very different conditions from those in which this equipment is actually used. Nevertheless, we have attempted to give a synthesis in Table 2.7 of the main efficiency estimates which are currently used in certain industrialized countries. This table clearly shows the differences, mentioned above, between central heating and individual heating on the one hand, and between coal, fuel oil and gas on the other. The differences between countries are partly caused by the use of different heating techniques (for example the widespread use of low efficiency open coal stoves in the U.K., which explains the very low figure in this country for individual heating by coal), but mainly by the uncertain nature of such measurements as well as varying definitions of what is meant by "efficiency".

The improvement of average heating efficiencies due to substitutions be-tween modes of heating may be roughly estimated on the basis of a constant efficiency per mode of heating and fuel. Thus in the U.K. this average efficiency has risen from 41% in 1963 to 60% at the present time. The result has been that

---

[1] For example nearly 70% of collective dwellings built before 1949 had average heat losses (insulation + ventilation) of less than 1.6 $W/m^3 \cdot {}^\circ K$ as opposed to 20% in the 1949–59 period, and 50% for homes built after 1959: for reference, the insulation standards which have been in force in France since the oil crisis correspond to an average heat loss of 1.1 $W/m^3 \cdot {}^\circ K$.

Tabelle 2.7. *Space heating efficiencies**

	Room Heating				Central Heating				Average		
	Electricity	Petroleum products	Gas	Coal	District heating	Petroleum products	Gas	Coal	Petroleum products	Gas	Coal
F.R. Germany (IKE [1], 1974)	0.95	0.66	0.70	0.66	0.95	0.73	0.75	0.66	0.70	0.70	0.66
(JULICH [6], 1975)	0.90	0.45	0.60	0.41	0.71	0.51	0.53	0.45	0.49	0.55	0.42
U.K. (NEDO [34], 1970)	0.97	0.63	0.63	0.30	–	0.7	0.7	0.6	0.68	0.67	0.39
France (IEJE [35], 1978)	–	–	–	–	0.72	0.6	0.65–0.72**	0.50	–	–	–
U.S.A. (SRI [36], 1972)	0.94	–	–	–	–	0.63	0.63	0.30	–	–	–
Netherlands [10]	–	–	0.60	–	–	–	0.55	–	–	–	–

* Depending on the studies these efficiencies represent either the successive efficiencies from the boiler to the dwelling (boiler, distribution and regulation efficiencies) or the boiler (or stove) efficiency only.

** Lower figure: collective central heating; higher figure: individual central heating.

Table 2.8. *Occupied dwellings by type of heating and source of energy* (in %)

	France 1960	1968	1975	Denmark 1970	1976	Belgium 1961	1970	U.K. 1961	1972	1978	F.R. Germany 1960	1970	1975	U.S.A.** 1960	1976	Sweden 1976
Central heating																
District heating	–	0.5	1	27	33.5	–	–	–	1	1	1	4	8	–	–	22
Fuel oil	3	19	28.5	53	52	6	22.5	1	3.5	4	5	28	38	33	22	64
Gas	–	4	9.5	4	–	–	4	–	13.5	29	–	3	11	43	61	–
Coal	11.5	10.5	4.5	–	–	5	3	4	8.5	7	7	6	3	22	3	–
Electricity*	–	–	1	–	–	–	–	–	–	–	–	–	–	2	14	14
Room heating																
Fuel oil	3			10	9	2	10.5	95	73.5	59	10	17	14			
Gas					2.5	0.5	6				1	3	5			
Coal	82.5	66	55.5	6	–	86.5	54				76	37	15			
Electricity	–			–	3	–	–				–	2	6			
References	[58]	[44]	[44]	[16]	[17]	[11]	[11]	[9]	[9]	[9]	[6]	[6]	[6]	[45]	[56]	[80]

* Electric storage heating excluded.
** Central and room heating together.

the average consumption of energy per dwelling has decreased whereas the level of satisfaction of the useful energy needs has risen over the same period. Table 2.8 shows the trends in heating systems and fuels used, which enables us to have some idea of the evolution of efficiencies in other countries.

Space Heating: Conclusions

From, the previous analysis, it seems that the increase in the average size of dwellings had a secondary (although non-negligible) effect on the development, of the energy use for heating, whereas the spread of central heating and the substitution of one energy form for another have been the most determining factors.

In Table 2.9 we have set up comparisons between the various industralized countries of average energy consumption for heating purposes. In order to underline the role of the main determinants (type of dwelling, size of dwelling, climate, insulation characteristics and average efficiencies), we have evaluated for each country several indicators of energy needs for heating purposes:
— average consumption of final energy for heating purposes per dwelling (dwellings as a whole),
— average useful energy needs in individual houses and flats (dwellings as a whole);
— useful energy needs per unit of surface area for these two types of dwelling (per m²);
— useful energy needs per m² and degree-day, in order to take climate differences into account; this latter indicator gives some idea of the differences between countries concerning the average insulation of existing dwellings.

The figures which we give include the best estimates which we have available for each of the countries under consideration; they do not all correspond to the same year of reference, but this is of little significance since the variations from one year to another are probably of less importance than the uncertainty of these estimates. A certain number of remarks must be made on Table 2.9. Firstly it can be seen that the margins between average final energy consumptions are fairly wide, from 1 to 2.5 between the two countries on the extreme limits, Italy and the U.S.A. If we now look at the average useful energy needs both within flats and individual houses, then the differences between countries are considerably reduced: they range between 40 to 50 GJ in blocks of flats (we have not used the figures for the U.K. which would seem inaccurate). Individual houses consume on average 1.4 to 1.7 times more, depending on the country, than flats. In order to offset the effect of the size factor, we have evaluated specific heat needs per m² of dwelling: the result shows only a slight difference between individual houses and blocks of flats, which tends to prove that the effect of better average insulation in flats (smaller surface area in contact with the outside) is largely cancelled out by the increase in inside temperature induced by collective heating systems (see above). Lastly, heat needs have been corrected in order to take climate differences into account: the coefficient which is thus obtained (measured in MJ/m² degree-day) gives some idea of the differences in insulation (perhaps also combined with differing heating

Table 2.9. *Average energy consumption for space heating*

	Final energy GJ/dwelling (1975)[*]	Reference year	Useful energy GJ/dwelling		GJ/m²		MJ/m²·degree-day[**]		References
			Individual houses	Flats	Individual houses	Flats	Individual houses	Flats	
France	61	1976	61	41	0.73	0.67	0.30	0.28	[2, 35]
F.R. Germany	74	1974	62	45	0.75	0.75	0.25	0.25	[1, 51]
Denmark	88 (1976)	1976	70	40	0.7	0.67	0.26	0.23	[17, 52]
U.K.	51	1975	40	18	0.5	0.31	0.21	0.13	[25, 53]
Netherlands	91 (1972)	1972	67	56	0.57	0.62	0.31	0.34	[13, 54]
U.S.A.	125 (1977)	1972	90	52	0.75	0.58	0.30	0.23	[49, 56]
Sweden	104	1975	89	58	0.90	0.95	0.24	0.26	[48]
Italy	49	1974	–	–	–	–	–	–	[14]

* Average for the dwelling stock.
** Number of degree-days: France 2400; F.R. Germany 3000; Denmark 2900; U.K. 2400; Netherlands 2700; U.S.A. 2500; Sweden 3700.

practices) between countries. The comparison shows that the differences between countries are very small after all and hardly meaningful given the uncertain nature of such calculations. This tends to show that insulation practice is fairly similar from one country to another and to confirm the observation made earlier concerning the connexion between better insulation and increase in inside temperature.

Table 2.8 indicates the changes observed in the last 15–20 years in the heating systems. Until 1974 the trend was of course towards a rapid spread of oil and gas heating. In the section 1.4 we shall analyze the changes that have been brought about since 1974.

Water Heating

Domestic hot water needs cover hot water for cooking, bathing (baths and showers) and washing up. Very few surveys and statistical data are available on this question, and the few that do exist are difficult to compare with each other because of the development of dishwashers and washing-machines for which the water is heated directly in the appliances themselves, thus corresponding either to an electricity consumption, or sometimes a hot water consumption. In this section, when we use the term domestic hot water, we do not include, unless otherwise stated, hot water in dishwashers and washing-machines.

Trends in hot water needs are connected to the development of living standards; more exactly, they are related to the fact of having hot water on the one hand, and ownership of a bath or shower on the other. A symbol of comfort and luxury which concerned the well-off strata of the population only in the nineteen fifties, hot water for domestic uses became rapidly more widespread in the sixties and seventies, as is shown in Table 2.10. Apart from the U.K. where homes were equipped with hot water systems long before the other countries of the EEC, the percentage of homes equipped with hot water installations moved from about 30–40% in 1960 to 75–95% in 1975. Denmark and Federal Republic of Germany have now reached the U.K. at saturation level, and should be joined sometime in the next decade by the other countries of the EEC. The fact that dwellings tend increasingly to be equipped with baths and showers has played an important part in the increase in hot water needs in dwellings which already have hot water. In fact, it is generally estimated that, for a dwelling with all modern conveniences, about 60% of its annual hot water needs are accounted for by baths and showers [6, 28] (of course this is only an average figure which may vary according to the habits of the occupants).

Table 2.10. *Equipment of dwellings in hot water, and baths or showers* (in %)

Rate of equipment in		Denmark	France	U.K.	F.R. Germany	Belgium	Italy
Hot water	1960	47	–	85 (1964)	–	–	–
	1975	95	76	98 (1974)	84 (1972)	–	75
Baths/Showers	1960	44	29	77 (1961)	51	24 (1961)	29 (1961)
	1975	80	70	91 (1971)	82 (1972)	54	65 (1971)
References		[12, 28]	[12]	[12, 28]	[12, 6]	[12]	[12, 55]

As we have already mentioned above, there is little reliable information concerning hot water needs per dwelling; however in order to give a rough idea of the nature of the problem we will put forward some estimates which have been taken from studies on several countries (Federal Republic of Germany [6], France [37, 43], U.K. [25], Denmark [28]) and which support one another. Thus, it may be said that hot water needs vary between a minimum of 25 litres/day/person, in the case of a dwelling without bath or shower, and a maximum of 70 litres/day person; moreover, it would seem reasonable to use an average of 35 to 45 litres/person as being typical of the most advanced European countries (the U.K. and Denmark being in the upper part of this bracket and France in the lower part[2]). Average consumption in the U.S.A. is estimated at 50 litres/day/person; however, this figure cannot be compared directly with the European figures as in the U.S.A. there are a great many washing-machines and dish-washers which are connected up directly onto the hot water supply. If we take as a reference the consumptions observed in dwellings with the highest hot water consumption it can be considered that the saturation level is about 70 litres/person/day.

Table 2.11. *Efficiency of hot water systems* *

	France	F.R. Germany	U.K.**	U.S.A.	Netherlands
Fuel-oil (collective) (central)	0.5–0.65 (0.5) (0.65)	0.5–0.58	0.56–0.66	0.5	
Gas (collective) (geysers)	0.5–0.74 (0.5) (0.61–0.74)	0.63–0.7	0.48–0.58	0.64	0.56 (0.4) (0.58)
Electricity	0.81–0.85	0.9–0.94***	0.72	0.92***	0.72
Coal		0.3–0.45	0.34–0.44	0.15	
References	[36,37,38,39]	[6, 11]	[25]	[40]	[10]

  * This efficiency represents the ratio between the useful energy delivered at the tap and the final energy.
 ** The lowest value pertains to the summer period.
*** Tank and pipe losses probably excluded.

To move from hot water needs to final energy demand it is necessary to take into account the efficiency of the hot water-producing equipment. Of course the efficiency of such equipment depends on the energy form which is used, but also on the mode of production of the hot water. It is possible to distinguish three major hot water systems: systems combined with central heating (combined systems), electric storage-heaters, and lastly gas water-heaters (geysers) which produce on demand. The centralized systems are generally very inefficient on

---

[2]   The range in France is about 25 to 40 litres (water at 60–70 °C).

the one hand because of heat losses from the storage tanks and the distribution networks (all the greater if the number of flats covered by the circuit is high), and on the other hand, because in summer the boiler efficiency drops (to about 20%): in most cases the same boiler is used for heating purposes in winter and hot-water production in summer, and thus the boiler is too large in relation to the level of production necessary in the summer. The losses of storage tanks, as of electric immersion heaters, represent about 15% in Europe [6, 25, 38], and as much as 20% in the U.S.A. Distribution losses vary, of course, according to the size of the distribution network and the degree of heat insulation on the pipes (from 10 to 30%, the latter figure applying to major heating systems for flats). Gas geysers are generally more efficient: however an important source of energy loss is the pilot-light which may account for 15 to 25% [10, 41] of annual consumption when it operates continuously[3]. Table 2.11 gives the figures for what are considered to be typical efficiencies in the various industrialized countries. Although these figures must be considered with caution, they are probably the best available estimates for these countries. Because of the approximate nature of the figures (they are approximations rather than exact, accurate estimates) we will not attempt to make inter-country comparisons.

Table 2.12. *Final energy use per hot water producing appliance (GJ/appliance)**

	Electricity	Gas central	Gas independant	Fuel-oil central	References
U.S.A.	16.2	28–32	–	–	[41, 42, 49]
(1970)	(25%)	(60%)		10%	[41, 49]
U.K.**	6.1	21.1			[60, 73]
(1978)	(51%)	(19%)	(10%)	(3.5%)	[66]
France	6.1	11.9	5.4	17.3	[2]
(1975)	(24%)	(9%)	(42%)	(23%)	[2]
Netherlands**	6.3	19	8.2	–	[10, 4]
(1972)	(16%)	(7%)	(70%)	–	[10]
F.R. Germany**	3.5	12.6	–	–	[1, 64]
(1978)	(45%)	(17%)	–	–	[63]

  * Figures between brackets: share of each energy in the stock of hot water appliances.
** Estimated from the households ownership.

Although it is difficult to evaluate for a whole country the average hot water needs of dwellings as well as the average efficiency of the hot water supply, there are fairly solid criteria for estimating average final energy consumption according to type of appliance used (these estimates are most often made by the energy utilities on the basis of the equipment stock). In Table 2.12 we present a

---

[3] The consumption of pilot lights varies according to the type of installation from 800 to 1600 kWh/year; 1200 kWh may be considered as an average reference consumption [16, 57].

synthesis of available estimates for several industrialized countries. Two remarks should be made about this table if we are to make comparisons between countries: firstly, in the North American figures, the hot water consumption of washing-machines and dishwashers is included, and these are numerous in American homes; secondly, a certain number of dwellings have two distinct sets of hot water equipment (for example gas water heater + electric water heater) and the existence of several types of equipment, which varies from one country to another, may distort the apparent average consumptions.

Cooking

Energy needs for cooking purposes are directly related to individual eating habits. Throughout this paragraph we will not attempt to examine this interdependence which would lead us too far from our subject for an energy use which, after all, accounts for only a fairly small share of household energy needs in the industralized countries (between about 4 to 5%). Rather, we will try to indicate present final energy consumptions for this particular use, distinguishing between the two main energies used, i.e. gas (city gas or natural gas) and electricity. In a first group of industrialized countries, there has been, over the last twenty years, a rapid development of electricity most often to the detriment of gas (the U. S. A., Denmark, Federal Republic of Germany, the U. K.). Thus the share of households possessing electric cookers rose in the U. K. from 25% in 1955 to 45% in 1978 [8, 66] and in Federal Republic of Germany from 20% in 1953 to 68% in 1975 [63]; although we do not have sufficiently long statistical series for other countries, it is certain that, for example, Denmark and the U. S. A. underwent similar developments. In France, Italy and the Netherlands electric cookers have been far slower in penetrating the market. Table 2.13 gives the breakdown of the use of gas and electricity at the present time in a certain number of industrialized countries. This table also gives some estimates

Table 2.13. *Final energy use for cooking (GJ/dwelling)**

	Electricity	Gas	References
U.S.A.	3.6–4	14.4	[41, 42, 49]
(1972)	(43%)	(56%)	[49]
U.K.	3.6	8.4	[60, 71]
(1974)	(45%)	(55%)	[66]
France	3.1	4	[62, 65]
(1975)	(21%)	(79%)	[62]
Denmark	2.7	4.4	[61, 13]
(1970)	(47%)	(53%)	[16]
Netherlands	4.7	3.5	[14, 10]
(1972)	(6%)	(90%)	[10]
F.R. Germany	1.8–2.2		[1, 13, 64]
(1978)	(73%)	(22%)	[63]

* Figures between brackets: share in the stock of cookers.

concerning the specific energy consumptions of cookers (these estimates are most often obtained from energy utilities). As far as electricity is concerned these consumptions are approximately 1000 kWh/year or 3.6 GJ/year, except for Federal Republic of Germany where the estimates we have obtained are difficult to explain. The average consumption of gas cookers in Europe is about 4 GJ/dwelling; the very high consumption which is indicated for the U.S.A. is due to the existence of voracious pilot-lights.

Household Electrical Appliances and Lighting

Specific household electricity consumption includes the consumption of large household electrical appliances (refrigerators, washing-machines, freezers, dishwashers and television sets), miscellaneous electrical and electronic appliances (irons, vacuum cleaners, Hi-fi sets, etc.) and lighting. These consumptions depend on how well equipped the household is with such appliances and also on the conveniences existing in the home (electrical gadgets, intensity of lighting, etc.). They also depend on the technical characteristics of the equipment, and its size.

Table 2.14 shows trends concerning the equipment of households with refrigerators, freezers, washing-machines and dishwashers in some industrialized countries. Income differential explain to a great extent both differences in time between one country and another, and differences between categories of households. There is a very clear correlation between the amount of electrical equipment in a household and household income. The constant progression of incomes over the last twenty years in the industrialized countries has facilitated the spread of most large household electrical appliances: households are now equipped almost to saturation level with refrigerators, washing-machines and television sets; on the other hand, the least well-off strata of the population do not yet have any real access to dishwashers and freezers. Besides income level, other factors may play a determining role in the development of household electrical equipment: living or eating habits (freezer), number of persons per household (dishwashers), existence of community facilities (washing machine), distance from shops selling foodstuffs (freezer)[4], etc. Clothes dryers are now fairly widespread in the U.S.A. (20% of all households were equipped with this appliance in 1960, 56% in 1975, including both electric and gas clothers dryers), but they have had only a very limited impact in Europe.

In Table 2.15 we compare the estimated specific consumptions of household electrical appliances for several industrialized countries. The consumption figures represent the average quantities of electricity used each year in order to operate these appliances. These estimates have generally been obtained from energy utilities and are most often arrived at by cross-checking several methods: technical estimates made by the equipment manufacturers, surveys among consumers, econometric estimates made by the equipment manufacturers, surveys among consumers, econometric estimates made on the basis of the

---

[4] That freezers have largely penetrated the markets of certain countries, such as Federal Republic of Germany, is due to the fact that food stores have fixed opening hours in these countries.

Table 2.14. *Ownership level for household electrical appliances (in %)*

	Refrigerator			Freezer			Washing machine*			Dishwasher			References
	1960	1970	1978	1960	1970	1978	1960	1970	1978	1960	1970	1978	
U.S.A.	98	100	100	23	31	44 (1975)	55	62	75	7	27	38 (1975)	[69]
U.K.	18	59	88	–	3	24	36	63	75	–	1	3	[60]
F.R. Germany	41	85	93	–	22	47			89	–	–	16	[63, 68]
France	25	77	93	–	7 (1972)	21	24	54	76	–	2	21	[70]

* Electric washing machines only for the U.S.A.

Table 2.15. *Specific consumption of household electrical appliances (in kWh/year/dwelling)*

	U.K.		France	U.S.A.	Denmark	F.R. Germany
	1960	1978	1976	1970	1975	1975
Refrigerator	375	350	290	1300	485–550	380–430
Freezer		1000	800	1380	750–800	580–815
Washing-machine	80	200	450	360	575–700	330–410
Dishwasher		500	1000	360	650–665	565–725
Television	250	365	180	410	200	
Lighting	220	330	260	750	750	
Miscellaneous	235	450	160			
References	[60]	[60, 61]	[2, 62]	[67]	[61, 95]	[6, 68, 76]

increase of total electricity consumption and the growth of the stock of appliances. The energy consumption figures for refrigerators do not differ very greatly (300 to 400 kWh/year) from one European country to another, but they are three to four times higher in the U.S.A. than in Europe. This is due firstly to the greater size of American refrigerators (200 litres capacity on average in Europe compared to 500 litres in the U.S.A.) and probably also to their lower efficiency (insulation). The differences in the energy consumptions of freezers is less substantial between Europe (800 to 1000 kWh/year) and the U.S.A. (approximately 1400 kWh/year). However, there are considerable differences in the energy consumption figures for dishwashers between European countries, which are probably due to different eating and cooking habits (they range from 500 to 1000 kWh/year); the low consumption figures in the U.S.A. are probably due to the fact that many dishwashers are connected directly onto the hot water supply and thus the related hotwater consumption does not appear on the table. The same remarks could be made in order to explain the differences in the consumption figures for washing machines between Europe and the U.S.A. It can be seen that dishwashers and freezers are by far the appliances which consume the greatest amount of electricity.

Table 2.16. *Breakdown of the specific household electricity consumption according to major headings* (in %)

	F.R. Germany 1977	France 1976	U.S.A. 1972	U.K. 1978
Large electrical appliances	67.5	59	45.5	38
(refrigerators)	(22.5)	(19.5)	(28.5)	(17)
(freezers)	(18)	(11.5)	(9.5)	(13)
(washing-machines)	(19.5)	(22.5)	(5.5)	(8)
(dishwashers)	(7.5)	(5.5)	(2)	–
Lighting	13	18	16.5	18
Miscellaneous	19.5	23	38	44
(television)		(11.5)	(11)	(19)
Average consumption per dwelling (kWh)	1550	1400	4600	1700
References	[64]	[2]	[67]	[60]

Table 2.16 breaks down the specific household electricity consumption figures according to major headings. The main headings are, firstly, the most common large electrical appliances, i.e. refrigerators (17 to 30% of total consumption) and washing machines (about 20% in France and Federal Republic of Germany, but less in the U.K. and the U.S.A.), and secondly, lighting (13 to 18%). Despite the high specific consumption figures for freezers and dishwashing machines, their share of total energy consumption remains low because they have not yet really penetrated the market. Overall the average specific electricity consumption per household varies at the present time in Europe

between 1200 kWh/year and 2500 kWh/year, compared with 4600 kWh/year in the U.S.A.

The levels of electricity consumption per inhabitant have developed differently from one country to another, due, on the one hand, to the amount of equipment in each household — which is what we have just examined — and, on the other, to the spread of electric heating and, to a lesser extent, of electric water-heaters and cookers. The U.S.A. and the U.K. both have particularly high consumption levels compared to the average level for European countries, be it in the early sixties or at the present time[5]. In these two countries, and particularly in the U.K., the share of electrical household goods and lighting is much smaller, to a great extent because of the development of electric heating. In general, the consumption of electricity for household electrical appliances and lighting has tended to increase more slowly than for the other uses of electricity.

Air Conditioning

There has been little development of air conditioning in homes in Europe. In the U.S.A., on the other hand, there has been a very rapid development as Table 2.17 shows. However, the penetration of air conditioning would seem to have slowed down over the last few years, and it is hard to say whether this has been a reaction to the U.S.A. present energy situation or the fact that the market is nearing saturation level. In the about 50% of all homes have an air-conditioning system. In the same way as we have distinguished between central heating and individual heating, one may distinguish between central air conditioning and room air conditioning (window air conditioner). In the U.S.A. there is an estimated average annual electricity consumption of about 3600 kWh per dwelling in the case of a central air conditioning system, and 2000 kWh for a room by room system (this gives an average of 2500 kWh if we take account of the relative weight of each system). The efficiency of an air conditioner is expressed by a coefficient of performance (C.O.P.) which measures the relation between the useful energy which is supplied to homes and the electricity consumed by the air conditioner (at the present time most air conditioners work on electricity). The average value of this coefficient is at present estimated at 2 (heat pumps operating as air conditioners have a slightly lower C.O.P. than electric air conditioners — about 5%) [56].

Table 2.17. *Fraction of U.S. homes with air conditioners*

	1950	1960	1970	1974	1976
Window air conditioners	1	11	25	30	30
Central air conditioners	—	2	11	19	21
Total	1	13	36	49	51

Sources: References [49] and [56].

---

[5] See Appendix 1.

1.3. Energy in the Tertiary Sector

The tertiary sector resembles in many ways the residential sector both on the level of energy uses and that of techniques employed. In this section we will insist only on the specific aspects of this sector.

As we have already pointed out, the tertiary sector is variously defined on a statistical level, and hence the indicators of economic activity (value added, employement) and of energy consumption are difficult to compare from one country to another. Despite this we have nonetheless brought together in Table 2.18 the main available data concerning past trends of economic activity and energy consumption in this sector. From this table it can be seen that, apart from the U.K., energy consumption per person employed in the tertiary sector has risen steadily between 1950 and 1975, and that on this indicator major disparities between countries can be observed (the U.S.A. and Federal Republic of Germany are very close, as are France and the U.K.; however these figures for one group are double those of the other). It should be noted that, although certain disparities and similarities are very close to those observed in the residential sector (U.K., France, U.S.A.), others are quite radically different (Federal Republic of Germany in comparison with all the other countries). Differences in climate and insulation techniques are not sufficient to explain these differences; similarly, it is much less convincing, in this case, to explain the evolution in time, for a same country, of energy needs per employee as being a result of the installation of central heating systems.

Table 2.18. *Activity level and energy consumption in the tertiary sector*

	1950	1960	1970	1975	References
U.S.A.					
employment (10^6)	31.0	36.5	47.7	53.9	[69]
m^2/employee	26	34	44	45	[45]
GJ/employee	71	80	102		[45]
U.K.					
employment (10^6)	10.4	11.2	12.4	13.6	
m^2/employee		24.4	27.8	28.0	[25]
GJ/employee	53	54	60	54	[25]
France					
employment (10^6)	7.1*	7.2	8.6	9.8	
m^2/employee				37	[2]
GJ/employee		31**		51	[2]
F.R. Germany					
employment (10^6)	8.0	10.0	10.7	10.8	
m^2/employee					
GJ/employee				72***	

* 1954, ** 1961, *** includes small industries.

The more thorough studies which have been made in France [110] and the U.K. [25] show that in the tertiary sector there is a fairly great heterogeneity concerning both floor area in relation to employment and energy needs per unit of floor area, which may, to a certain extent, help to explain the differences between countries. Thus in France [110] in the education sector in 1973, the floor area per student varied from 7.5 to 11.2 m^2 (between secondary and university education); and when this is related to jobs in this sector this results in floor areas of between 110 and 270 m^2 per employee; in the retail trade, on the other hand, the floor area per employee varies between 19 and 36 m^2; similarly in offices it is between 13 and 16 m^2 depending on whether this is measured in the public or private sector[1].

If we now take a look at specific energy consumptions per unit of floor area, still according to the studies mentioned above, it can be seen — as is indicated on the table — that there are similarly great disparities from one sector to another. These differences, as far as specific electricity is concerned, are due both to the degree of illumination (much higher in offices and supermarkets than in teaching premises), and to the amount of electric or electronic equipment (lifts, refrigerating systems, computers, etc.); as far as space heating is concerned, it is probably the daily and seasonal occupation rate of premises which explains most of the differences, the remainder being a result of different heating temperatures and the free heat from occupants and electrical equipment.

1.4. Impacts of the 1973/1974 Oil Crisis

The oil crisis in 1973—74 has undoubtedly had two direct consequences that the new increases in oil prices in 1979—80 can only reinforce: on the one hand, most countries have implemented energy-saving measures, which are accompanied most often by the setting up of new administrative entities to deal with these tasks (in particular the creation of Energy Conservation Agencies); on the other hand, people have become aware of the existence of an energy crisis, or, more exactly, of the end of an era of cheap energy.

The authorities have generally made use for four types of intervention in order to promote energy-saving in the residential sector:
— regulations: the setting up of insulation standards or the reinforcement of existing standards for new dwellings, the setting of a maximum inside heating temperature (20 °C in France in 1974, then 19 °C in 1979), limiting of the space heating period (measure under study in Italy), individual metres for hot water and heating consumption in the case of a community distribution system, in order to individualize the heating bill and thus make the consumers more aware of their real consumption; Tables 2.9 and 2.22 give some idea of the changes in average consumptions which have been the result of the new insula-

---

[1]   By way of comparison, the surface areas per office employee in other countries are as follows: Rotterdam: 12—16 m^2/empl. in old office blocks, 20 m^2 in new office blocks; London: 18 m^2/empl. in 1966; 19 m^2/empl. in 1969; New York: 21 m^2 in Manhattan; Tokyo: 12 m^2/empl. in 1975 (source: reference [110]).

tion standards for new dwellings, and thus of the impact of these measures,
— incentives: the attribution of subsidies for investments which aim at reducing
energy consumption in homes or at using new techniques (improvement of
insulation or temperature regulation in existing dwellings, use of heat pumps
or solar techniques for example); these subsidies can either be in direct grant
form, or as tax-exoneration;
— demonstration measures: financial aid in order to promote or experiment
on projects using new techniques;
— general information and advertising in order to bring the problem of energy-
saving to the attention of general opinion (for example the "Save it" and "Chasse
au gaspi" campaigns in the U.K. and France respectively).

Households have become aware of the energy crisis mainly because of two
phenomena: firstly the often alarmist information provided abundantly by the
mass media since 1974; and secondly, the successive increases in energy prices
between 1973 and 1979. The latter phenomenon has been of particular importance in the lower income groups. It is however worth noting that on average the
share of the household budget devoted to energy-related spending has remained
fairly stable since 1973 in the major industrialized countries, as Table 2.19
shows. Since these price increases followed an up and down movement, it is
possible that their real economic effect has been how until now, although they
have had a certain psychological impact.

Table 2.19. *Household energy expenditures* (in % of their budget)

	Denmark	F.R. Germany	Italy	France	U.K.	U.S.A.
1970	4.6	3.4	3.1	3.1	4.8	2.5
1974	6.1	3.9	3.3	3.8	4.4	2.7
1977	5.5	4	3.2	3.8	5.1	3.1

Source: Appendix 1, energy used in the dwellings only.

Energy-saving measures and household reactions to price increases and to the
idea of an energy crisis brought about clear changes, in the 1974—78 period, in
historical trends, without it being possible to separate out the respective weight
of political factors and consumer behaviour. We will concentrate here on three
marked changes: a stop in the growth of energy consumption per dwelling, the
beginnings of improvements on the insulation in existing dwellings, and lastly
often radical changes in the choice of energy for space heating.

Thus, we observe a stabilization of average energy consumption per dwelling
since 1973 in the industrialized countries as a whole. To be more precise, this
consumption fell slightly between 1973 and 1975 (by about 10% in Federal
Republic of Germany, Denmark and France), which in fact represents a far
greater reduction compared with historical trends. It then rose again slowly
and was in 1978, around 1973 levels. In France, it is believed that this reduction is almost entirely due to a decrease in the consumption of energy for heating
in those homes which have central heating. As in the 1974—75 period only a

small number of dwellings underwent changes in order to improve their insulation, the reduction in consumption must mainly be explained in this country by the reduction of heating temperatures: this reduction was voluntary in the case of homes equipped with individual central heating and came as an immediate reaction to the substantial increases in the price of fuel-oil (an increase of 175% between 1973 and 1975, in real terms), and also to the information campaign carried out by the public authorities. The reduction of the heating temperature in flats with collective heating was a result of the new regulations which in 1974 set the maximum heating temperature at 20 °C. What is more, although this had only a negligible effect on overall energy consumption, the average specific energy consumption per hot water appliance has fallen slightly since 1973, in France, which has resulted in the increase in overall energy consumption for hot water being less than the increase in the number of appliances. It may be assumed that in the other countries similar phenomena have taken place, and that reduced energy consumption per dwelling may largely be explained by lower temperatures.

The increase in energy prices has made most people aware of the bad insulation of dwellings and of the possibilities of improvement. A certain number of households, mainly owner-occupiers, have thus undertaken insulation investments to reduce their heating costs. Various surveys carried out after the oil crisis in 1973–74 in several industralized countries give some idea of the impact of this movement; these figures of course should be handled with caution since they include both light household repairs and very heavy investments.

– In France, about 15% of households undertook energy-saving investment in 1974 and 1975 which was intended to reduce heating costs (heat insulation or regulation) [71]; this investment corresponded mainly to light repairs and had only a very small effect on overall consumption.

– In the U. S. A., an estimated 10% of households improved the insulation of their dwellings between 1973 and 1975 [72].

– In the U. K. [73, 76] in 1975 an estimated 38% of dwellings had insulated roofs which rose to 43% in 1978. Similarly the number of dwellings with double-glazing rose from 9% to 14%; the insulation of cavity walls however progressed very slowly (8% of walls in 1978).

– In Denmark, because of an extremely voluntarist policy adopted by the public authorities with the intention of improving the insulation of existing dwellings (a grant of 25%) a larger number of dwellings than in other countries underwent energy-saving repairs: thus from an analysis of the market in insulating material it can be seen that 19% of dwellings underwent repairs for roof insulation between 1973 and 1975, 10% for outside walls and 10% for windows [13]. The resultant energy saving has been estimated for 1978 at 5 PJ i.e. about 5% of the energy used for heating dwellings.

Until 1974, fuel-oil was the main source of energy used in heating homes, with the exception of certain gas-possessing countries such as the Netherlands and the U.S.A. The brutal rise in the price of fuel oil put into question its dominant position, and in most countries other forms of energy were developed in order to substitute them for fuel-oil, mainly electricity and gas: firstly as far as new dwellings were concerned fuel-oil's share of the market dropped substantially immediately after the crisis; then in existing dwellings gas and electricity came to be substituted for fuel-oil. The reaction in the various countries differed according to the pricing policies implemented by the authorities and market conditions. Thus in the U.S.A. and in France there has been a massive development of electric heating. In the U.S.A. [56] the share of new dwellings heated by electricity rose from about 30% in 1970 to 50% since 1974; some of these dwellings in fact use heat-pumps. However recent trends would seem to show that there has been a revival of gas-heating which could well slow down the development of electricity. In France [35], the rise of electric heating has been even more rapid and has resulted from a government strategy of developing nuclear electricity: over the 1975—78 period, 35% of new dwellings were equipped with electric heating and the penetration of electricity had reached 50% by 1978 (compared with a quite negligible percentage in 1972). The share of fuel-oil in new constructions fell from over 70% before the crisis to 15% in 1978 (an average of 20% over the 1975—78 period). On the other hand, apart from France and the U.S.A., electricity has little benefited from the decline of petroleum in other countries. In the Netherlands, as petroleum played a negligible role on the new construction market there has been no change since the petroleum crisis (99% of the new constructions are equipped with gas heating). In the U.K. [73] gas has substantially increased its share of the new construction market at the expense of fuel-oil and electricity; this trend may be largely explained by the differing evolution in prices of these forms of energy since 1974 (decrease in 15% in the price of gas because of the North Sea discoveries, increase of 30% in the price of electricity and about 50% for fuel-oil between 1973 and 1978 in real terms [78]). In Federal Republic of Germany, whereas fuel-oil accounted for 62% of new constructing in 1972—73, this figure dropped to 49% in 1976, which indicates a less rapid reduction than in other countries: gas and district heating have progressed in more or less the same manner to offset the decline of fuel-oil, and ther share in the new construction market rose respectively from 17 to 25% and from 14 to 20%. In Denmark, a large share of new flats and single family houses has been traditionally heated by district heating and the penetration of this mode of heating has only slightly increased since 1974: the share of district heating in new flats rose from 53% on the period 1960—69, to 68% on 1970—74 and 73% on 1975—77 (for single family dwellings the figures are respectively 30, 33 and 35%). Table 2.20 indicates the changes which have taken place concerning the equipment of new constructions on an energy form basis.

In existing dwellings the substitution of one energy form for another takes place in a far slower manner. This may happen when a room heating system is replaced by central heating, or when an obsolete boiler is replaced, or when a dwelling is connected onto a gas network or a district heating grid. In the first case, electricity may be developed, most often in electric storage heating form, but also sometimes in the form of direct electric heating. In any case, because of the higher cost of electric power compared with other energies, the installation of electric heating in old dwellings is always accompanied by improve-

Table 2.20. *Distribution according to energy forms of heating installations in new dwellings* (in %)

	France		U.S.A.		U.K.*		F.R. Germany	
	1971	1978	1971	1978	1971	1978	1972	1976
Electricity	2	50	31	50**	34	6	6	6
Gas	21	22	60	38	46	84	17	25
Fuel-oil	70	15	8	9	8	2	62	49
District heating	–	7	–	–	2	1	14	20
Coal	–	–	–	–	10	7	1	–
Miscellaneous	7	6	1	3	–	–	–	–
References	[35]		[56]		[77]		[7]	

* Figures applying to all dwellings in which a new heating system has been installed.
** Between 20 and 25% of the new dwellings have been equipped with an electric heat pump.

ments on the insulation of the house. In the case of energy substitution for central heating, electricity is never envisaged (this could only be made possible by using heat pumps, which, until now, have practically remained undeveloped in old dwellings). Unfortunately, we have only little information on two countries, Federal Republic of Germany and France, concerning the changes which have taken place since the oil crisis on the market for heating systems for old dwellings. This information however does show that there has been a drop in the use of fuel-oil and a rapid growth in that of gas and electricity. Thus it may be estimated that in these two countries about 100 000 existing dwellings are equipped annually with electricity, which represents a market penetration of electricity of 30% and 40% of Federal Republic of Germany and France respectively. The market penetration of gas can be at present estimated at 40% in France and 60% in Federal Republic of Germany; the rest of the market is shared between fuel-oil and district heating [55, 76].

2. Long-Term Prospects

If we exclude the possibility of a radical and lasting change in the way of life or economic activities of the industrialized countries, then four factors would seem likely to play a determining role in the development of energy consumption in the residential and tertiary sector between now and the year 2000:
– the evolution of the floor area in dwellings, or in professional premises (i.e. increase in the number of dwellings and professional premises)
– the spread of household appliances
– changes in the thermal characteristics of new and old buildings
– changes in final energy use techniques.
It is not our intention in this section to give forecasts concerning these factors in the various countries, but rather to attempt to identify the problems

raised by such forecasts, what we may reasonably consider to be established facts, and what remains as yet uncertain.

2.1. New Constructions

In recent years in most of the industrialized countries there has been a slow-down in population growth, and in some cases a population decrease (Federal Republic of Germany). At present there are no signs that this is not a lasting phenomenon, and in fact all the population forecasts for the year 2000 which have been carried out are based on this continuing trend. Thus although population growth will have only a minor effect on the housing stock, the phenomenon of decohabitation[1] is likely to be a major factor. With the exception of the Scandinavian countries, it is to be expected that the average number of people per dwelling will fall by about 10 to 20%, i.e. from about 3 to between 2.5 and 2.7 (this phenomenon is linked with the fact that families are now smaller, and new social values are emerging).

The resulting volume of new constructions will also depend on the number of houses demolished or put to other purposes in the old housing stock, and, in this case, three main factors will be of importance: the decay of certain dwellings which will have to disappear, the desire to rehabilitate part of the old housing stock and also movements of population within the country. Although the amount of decay in the housing stock is fairly well researched factor, population movements and the number of old dwellings to be renovated are more difficult to project (renovation depending very much on local authority policies).

As far as the average size of the dwellings to be built is concerned, the determining factor will be the breakdown, in new constructions, between individual houses and flats: the increase in the size of dwellings appears to be of secondary importance (see Table 2.5). Although individual house ownership will continue to be strongly motivating, it also however seems likely that the construction of individual homes will continue to be held up, in many cases, by the lack of available land (often linked to local or national town-planning measures), by restrictions related to the distance from the work-place (which can only be aggravated by high-cost fuel) and also by financial mechanisms. Thus, unless of radical changes in the urbanization pattern, the proportion between individual houses and flats will not significantly change compared to the long-term historical trends and the average floor area per dwelling will grow very slowly. It should nonetheless be noted that there is a certain disconnexion between the construction of new individual houses – mainly related to income – and new constructions as a whole: thus, as has recently been observed in several countries, the overall drop in new construction figures was accompanied by a rise in the share of individual houses, which can be translated in terms of a relative stability in the number of new individual houses being built.

We have not considered in this study secondary residences since there in-

---

[1] "Decohabitation" reflects the decrease in the average number of persons per dwelling.

fluence on the overall energy demand is (and will remain) small: indeed for most household appliances, there is not in general a simultaneous utilization in the permanent home and the secondary residence.

The trends concerning floor area in the tertiary sector are related to more complex phenomena, inasmuch as they vary according to the "functions" that these floor areas are to fulfil: thus, in teaching premises, the dynamic element is the population of school-age; in premises used for commercial purposes, the main factor is the level of trade activity, in offices the driving factor is the number of employees etc. Moreover, in commercial activities and, to a lesser extent, in the public services, another question is the way in which the premises are used: thus the increase in working-hours (two shifts for example, or the lengthening of shop opening hours, etc.) results in a proportional decrease in the surface area used per unit of activity. If we use the typology which we applied earlier to the tertiary sector then the following remarks can be made concerning each sub-sector.

As population growth slows down, there will be a correlative ageing of the population which will, of course, result in a relative decrease in the population of school age: this phenomenon, which is however largely offset by the increase in the school-leaving-age, should produce a relative stability of the population of school age, or, more precisely, in most industrialized countries a very slow growth of that population. The abandoning of former teaching premises, either because of decay (and therefore demolition) or because of population move-ments, in itself provides an explanation for some of the new constructions in this field[2]; another explanation would be the tendency for class sizes (or the teacher-pupil ratio) to decrease, which results in a correlative increase in the floor area per person of school age.

Trends in floor areas used for commercial purposes are related to popula-tion growth and to the level of trade. Although, we consider the first phenom-enon to be of only secondary importance, the second one is a determining factor, which however is difficult to quantify: depending on trends in the structure of this trade (food, clothing, or equipment) and sales techniques (supermarket or local retailers) the ratio between the level of trade and the floor area may vary substantially[3]: it is probable that the "productivity of the floor area" used for sales purposes will be an important aspect of this particular problem.

New constructions of premises for commercial purposes will moreover lead to old premises being abandoned, either because of decay (demolition) or because they are not economically viable (through competition from super-markets, or population movements).

The problem of offices is both simpler and more complicated. It is simpler

---

[2] These premises which were formerly used for teaching may be taken over for other purposes.

[3] It should be remembered that in France, in 1973, the turnover per m^2 of floor area for sales purposes varied between 5000 FF/m^2 for domestic equipment goods to 12 000 FF/m^2 in supermarkets [109].

in that the floor area per employee is relatively well known, and fairly homogeneous from one country to another concerning new constructions, and unlikely to vary greatly; it is more complicated in that there is at the present time a lot of uncertainty about trends in labour productivity in the tertiary sector and possible modifications in the work organization in these activities. Nevertheless, it is the number of people employed in offices which will be the main determining factor concerning the development of office floor area. The amount of new constructions will also depend on two opposing trends: on the one hand, offices being used for other purposes or demolished; on the other hand the transformation of flats into offices (in particular in town centres).

To sum up, the factors which we believe will play an important role in determining the volume of new construction are as follows:

— decohabitation, for which the trends can be fairly well outlined and which will determine changes within the housing stock;

— population movements within the national framework, which will mainly be a result of the relocation of industrial and tertiary activities and of developments in the structure of the economy (relative weight of the major sectors: agriculture, industry, tertiary activities);

— the growth of the economy, in terms of volume and structure, which will determine both income growth — and therefore the possibility of house ownership, as well as the increase in the consumption of consumer goods, public and private services — and employment in the various sector of the economy (and therefore employment in offices).

2.2. Household Appliance Ownership

Of all household energy consuming appliances, central heating undeniably has the greatest impact upon household energy demand. Its spread was very important during the sixties and in the early seventies; this led one to expect that almost all homes in most of the countries where heating is required would be equipped with central heating by the mid-eighties. One may wonder if the increase in energy prices will not hinder this development. Indeed over the last few years in certain countries, the installation of central heating in existing dwellings has been reduced in favor of electric or gas room heating. Without being able to give a definite answer to this question, one may nevertheless expect the saturation of central heating at a level below 100% (perhaps around 80–85%).

The installation of hot water and baths or shower will continue in countries where sub-standard dwellings still exist.

The case of miscellaneous electrical household appliances is much more complex. For certain of these, washing machines, refrigerators, television sets, their saturation level may quite easily be foreseen, either because this level has already been reached (U.S.A.), or from the basis of other countries or of the most priveleged classes of the population. On the other hand, for recent appliances such as dishwashers, freezers, or even dryers, it is more difficult to provide an answer. This obviously has an immediate effect upon household specific electricity consumption because of the high specific consumption of these appliances. Large families in particular will acquire dishwashers. Thus one may expect a saturation level at around 50% by taking into account the fact that in industrialized countries, between 50 and 60% of the households consist of two people or less and 20 to 30% of only one person; in addition, these percentages are likely to grow with the increase in decohabitation and in the number of non-active people. The spread of freezers should also be limited to large families and should not affect multifamily buildings for reasons of space; it will also depend upon access to food stores (opening and closing times, distance). The saturation level should thus vary from one country to another in a bracket ranging, from approximately 40 to 60%. However, there should be a spread of two doors fridge-freezers in households without a freezer. The case of dryers is much more difficult; indeed this appliance is very widespread in the U.S.A. (present in 60% of dwellings in 1978, in 20% in 1960) but has had little impact in Europe (so little that there are almost no statistics); in this case, unless one undertakes a thorough investigation of the reasons for the development of this type of appliance in the U.S.A. (income, lifestyle impacts, . . .) it is difficult to anticipate its future development.

Alongside the evolution of needs — more or less related to new constructions — technology, as we have already shown, plays a fundamental role both with regard to the creation of useful energy needs and of final energy demand. After this mainly speculative analysis, we will now go on to a more concrete evaluation of what can be expected from technology over the next twenty years. We will distinguish between the possibilities in this field, and the institution financial and structural restrictions in the countries under consideration.

2.3. Trends in Insulation [1]

Existing Dwellings

It is quite undeniable that the improvement of insulation in existing dwellings represents the greatest potential for reducing useful energy needs in housing. As well as their effects on energy consumption, such improvements also increase the life-span of the buildings and their value. However, despite the attractiveness of insulating old dwellings, there are a certain number of institutional obstacles to be overcome, and this also presupposes the active participation of a great number of decision-makers who may think differently, and even have opposing interests. We will come back to this problem later.

Since the petroleum crisis in 1974, many studies have been carried out which have attempted to evaluate the technical potential of energy-savings represented by the insulation of old dwellings, and also to determine, on the basis of various hypotheses concerning energy price trends and discounting rates, the optimum levels of energy saving (for the community as a whole). We will not describe all these studies in detail, and neither will we compare the costs which they arrive at. They were in fact carried out in various industrialized countries, at different

---

[1]   We include in the term "insulation" the reduction of air infiltration.

periods in time, between 1974 and 1979, and made use of different types of information (some of which was purely speculative, some relying on real experience). What is more, we are not sure that we have at our disposal the most recent and therefore the most relevant studies on each country. Lastly, any comparison between investment costs would only be meaningful if we could evaluate the influence on such costs of the differences obtaining in each country concerning building and insulation techniques, initial insulation levels and labour costs, all of which would lead us too far from the object of this study. Nevertheless, a certain number of general conclusions may be obtained from the studies[2].

– The energy saving potential through insulating dwellings may be estimated on average at 50% of present heat needs; this potential is in no way a technical maximum, and what is more it corresponds to current insulation techniques.

– The insulation of ground floors and roofs are the most profitable type of operation which can be undertaken: double-glazing (and even triple-glazing in the Scandinavian countries) is generally the investment which is less cost effective; the adding of about 15 cm of glass wool is the most frequently proposed solution for roofs which have no insulation whatsoever.

– The cost of insulating outer walls varies a great deal, depending on what method is used: insulation from outside or from inside the dwellings, or insulation injected into cavity walls. Insulation from the outside is by far the most costly solution but it does have the advantage of preventing condensation (compared with the other techniques) and improving the structure of the building (and thus lengthening its life-span)[3]. Insulation from the inside makes it

– The insulation of poorly-heated dwellings (those for example, which do not have central heating) is generally unprofitable because of their lower energy consumption; but it may be worthwhile undertaking major insulation repairs when central heating is being installed (which is already most often the case when electric heating is introduced).

In order to give a more precise idea of the technical and economic possibilities of improving insulation in old dwellings we will briefly outline the main elements of a study which has recently been carried out in France (late 1979) dealing with all dwellings [82]. This study makes a distinction between blocks possible to reduce the thermal inertia of the dwelling and to make it more comfortable heat-wise, however it is difficult to implement (reduction of the size of the dwelling, need to modify the electric system and to rearrange the inside of the dwelling, discomfort for the occupants during repairs) and may cause condensation problems.

---

[2] References of these studies: France [80, 81, 82]; Denmark [13, 28]; U.K. [8, 25]; Federal Republic of Germany [83]; Italy [84]; Sweden [89]; Canada [90]; U.S.A. [56, 72].

[3] In France this type of insulation is considered to cost about 4 times more than insulation from the inside. The cost of a normal resurfacing is about 15 to 20 US $/m² compared with 50 to 60 US $/m² to insulate a building from the outside in 1979 US $ (= 4 F.F.).

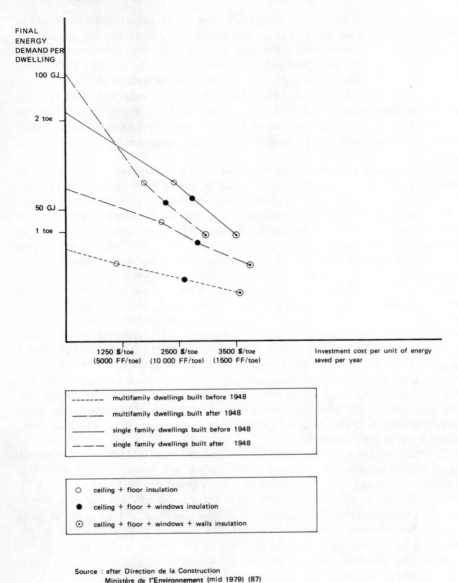

Fig. 2.2. Insulation costs in different types of existing dwellings (France)

of flats and individual dwellings, as well as between dwellings built before and after 1948. Fig. 2.2 indicates the conclusions arrived at concerning the investments necessary in order to obtain different degrees of energy-saving in dwellings with central heating. Several types of insulation-related repairs were envisaged in an order of decreasing cost effectiveness (cost effectiveness measured in terms of investment necessary per unit of energy saved). From this we can observe that the insulation of roofs and ground floors alone, which represents the most cost effective technique, leads to average energy savings of 30% for an investment of about 1000 US $/dwelling (4000 FF), i.e. 2000 US $/toe saved (or 48 US $/GJ). A more ambitious programme of repairs, including insulating the walls and double-glazing would lead to savings of 55% and a cost of about 3400 US $/dwelling (13 500 FF), i.e. 3650 US $/toe saved 30 US $/GJ)[4].

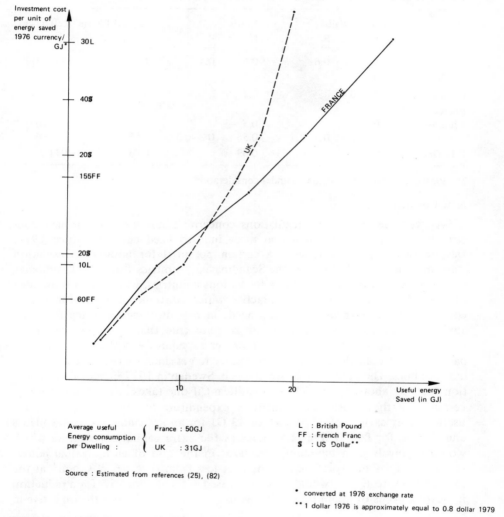

Fig. 2.3. Insulation costs in existing dwellings (France, U.K.)

---

[4] In 1979 price, the price of one toe of heating oil was about 1500 FF in France (375 US $) in late 1979.

Fig. 2.3 indicates for the U.K. and France the run of the curves relating investment costs for insulation repairs and the quantities of energy saved. In both cases it is a matter of average costs for dwellings taken as a whole. Although these curves should be used cautiously, they do nonetheless make it possible to rapidly relate levels of insulation and the approximate investment costs necessary to obtain them.

Table 2.21. *Change in the insulation of new dwellings* (in $W/m^2 \, °C$)

	Outer Walls		Roofs		Ground Floors		References
	N	P	N	P	N	P	
U.K.	1	0.6	0.6	0.4	1		[35, 73]
Sweden	0.3		0.2		0.3		[81]
Denmark	0.3–0.4		0.2		0.3		[28, 29]
France							
houses	0.55		0.5				[91, 105]
flats	0.7	0.4–0.5	0.55	0.2–0.3	0.55		
F.R. Germany	0.81		0.69		0.83		[91]

N = Present standards, P = standards under consideration.

New Constructions

As we have mentioned, regulations concerning heat insulation in new constructions have been tightened in most industrialized countries since 1974. Despite this, there still remains a certain potential for improving insulation standards, in particular outside the Scandinavian countries. Table 2.21 compares the standards adopted since 1974 by various countries, which gives some idea of the differences in insulation practice which continue to exist. Table 2.22 compares the average useful energy needs in new dwellings resulting from the application of the new standards. It is quite true that improved insulation involves heavier construction costs, however expenditure in this case is incomparably lower than the investment necessary to get similar levels of insulation in old dwellings. The tightening of standards in Sweden in 1977 increased construction costs by about 5%, which is insignificant if one takes into account the uncertainty of these costs (supplementary expenditure of about 1100 US $ for useful energy savings of 3500 kWh or 13 GJ for an individual house, 780 US $ and 7.2 GJ for flats[5]). Fig. 2.4 indicates the extra capital expenditure which would be involved in tightening standards in the case of an individual house: the lowering of the coefficient G of heat loss from $G = 1.6$ W°C.h.m³ at the present time, to $G = 1$ would entail increased costs of about 5% for a reduction in heating needs of about 35%[6]. In the long-term (1990–2000) the objective in

[5] In 1977 US $ (1 US $ = 4.5 Swedish crowns).

[6] New houses heated by electricity have an average coefficient of $G = 1.25$. Certain experts disagree with this type of linear relation between extra costs and extra insulation, arguing that improved insulation leads to "technical jumps" which do not involve systematic and proportional cost increases.

France could be to achieve an average *G* of about 0.8–0.85 with techniques which have already been totally mastered.

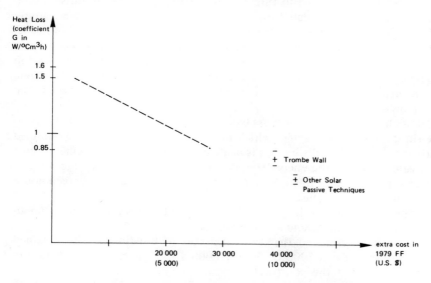

Fig. 2.4. Extra cost of increased insulation standards in new dwellings (France)

Table 2.22. *Heat requirements in new dwellings* (useful energy, around 1979)

| | GJ/dwelling | | GJ/m² | |
	Houses	Flats	Houses	Flats
Denmark	55/65	40/35	0.55/0.5	0.45/0.67
France	37/52	21/28	0.46/0.65	0.29/0.4
F.R. Germany	36/63	25/33	0.43/0.46	0.4/0.47
U.S.A.	61* 48** 57***	36 *	0.42* 0.33**–0.39***	0.42*

dwellings with electric heating / other dwellings

   * F.H.A. standards of 1972 for social dwellings only (usually a reference for all constructions).

  ** Common practice for social dwellings in 1974.

*** Standard recommended by the association of heating installators (ASHRAE, recommendation ASHRAE 90–75).

Source: IEJE (compilation of various sources)

The improvement of insulation in dwellings raises a certain number of problems: selection of new materials both for building and for insulation purposes, thermal behaviour of very well insulated buildings, influence of extra insulation on the heating period, inclusion of free heat when evaluating heating needs (along with extra insulation they cover a considerable share of these needs, which thus makes it possible to turn off the heating in moderate outside temperatures). In very well insulated dwellings a substantial part of the heat supply is used to offset losses through ventilation: thus beyond a certain level of insulation, if one wishes to reduce heating needs even further, it becomes necessary to cut these losses. This may be done firstly by making sure that the windows and doors are airtight, but more particularly by recovering ventilation heat: dynamic insulation, heat recovery on the air extracted by heat exchanger or heat pump (air/air or air/water).

Solar architecture makes it possible in the case of new constructions to achieve substantial energy savings which may be combined with those obtained by insulation. Generally a distinction is made between the two following designs:
− direct gain, in which the energy supply is provided by means of large window surface areas facing South; this system may be improved by adding a green house on the South side of the house.
− the Trombe wall, system in which the South wall is reinforced in order to serve as a heat storage mass, and also double-glazed.

In France it is estimated that the extra cost of building a well designed direct gain house is about 5000 US $ or 20 000 FF[7], i.e. an extra expenditure of about 5 to 10% of the construction costs. The energy saving which results from this type of solution varies, of course, with the level of solar radiation, within a bracket of 6300 to 8500 kWh/year[8] (23 to 31 GJ/year) in the case of France. Compared to conventional dwellings, with normal insulation the rate of energy saving is about 40% to 50% in the North and 70% in the South. The installation of a Trombe wall with reinforced insulation involves an estimated extra cost, in France, of about 4250 US $ (or 17 000 FF). The resultant energy saving (or supply of solar energy) is lower than in the case of direct gain, and varies between 4 to 5000 kWh/year (14 to 18 GJ)[8] depending on the region. The rate of energy saving is also lower, at about 30% in the North of France and 50% in the South. Although apparently less interesting both on the economic and energy level, the Trombe solution does have the advantage of being able to store energy, and thus to carry over part of the solar gain into the night.

A more widespread application of solar architecture would necessitate perfecting new methods of calculating heat needs which take into account weather data, which is seldom the case at present: for example, windows are only considered as sources of heat loss, whereas a double-glazed window on the South side has an identical heat loss to that of a very well insulated wall, and triple-glazing on the South side actually acts as a net heat collector (it receives more heat than it loses). It would also be necessary to demonstrate this solution more widely in order to draw the attention of the general public, and especially of the building professions (architects, building firms).

---

[7] This cost includes essentially extra insulation and extra glazing (1979 price).

[8] These figures are maximum values and should be understood above all as convenient approximations (see reference [94]).

The development of extra insulation and solar architecture could lead to the construction of dwellings which need on average 50% less energy for heating purposes than existing new dwellings. This will affect heating systems which will appear increasingly as back up systems, operating discontinuously, and which will have to be adjustable in order to avoid overheating (and therefore discomfort); moreover, hot water needs will account for the main energy needs in dwellings, and thus particular attention will have to be paid to technical possibilities of reducing these needs (improvement of efficiency).

2.4. Prospects of Space and Water Heating Techniques

In this section we will examine the prospects of developing various heating techniques[1] in the long term. We will not attempt to make any precise comparison of their competitiveness, as this varies greatly from one country to another depending on the relative prices of the various energy forms and on the policies of the national and local decision-makers; moreover, in the long term the conditions of their competitiveness are likely to change radically according to trends in these relative prices and to these policies. We will merely give some general indications, valid for most industrialized countries, on the problems raised by the main heating techniques, as well as the factors likely to slow down or accelerate their development. We will go more thoroughly into new techniques such as solar heating, district heating or heat pumps, since the problems involved in the techniques which are at present applied on a large scale are far better known.

Conventional Systems

By conventional heating techniques we mean essentially central heating by gas and fuel-oil. Direct or storage electric heating, although they do belong to this category, are not discussed here since they would appear unlikely to be improved substantially.

For new appliances the most important improvement as far as energy is concerned will obviously be a result of improving the overall energy efficiency of the heating installations (boiler + heat distribution). It is reckoned that the improvement of conventional heating systems requires greater boiler efficiency on the one hand, and a better balance and regulation in the case of collective heat distribution on the other. The gains which may be obtained on the efficiency of existing boilers are fairly well-known (about 5%), and do however presuppose frequent maintenance with minimum expenditure. The reduction of heat wasting in community heating systems may result in substantial saving — although unfortunately it is difficult to have a global idea of what this may represent on a national level — as well as improving the comfort of the occupants (certain dwellings at the present time are overheated, whereas others remain underheated). The study concerning the potential for energy saving in France which we have already mentioned estimates, for example, that the energy-saving

---

[1] Including water heating.

likely to be obtained from improving the efficiency of boilers and collective
heat and hot water distribution systems is about 27% in return for an average
cost of 1250 US \$ (or 5000 FF) per dwelling, i.e. an expenditure of about
3000 US \$ (or 12 000 FF)[2] per t.o.e. saved (190 FF/GJ)[2]. Among the
technical means which have been considered in order to obtain such savings is
to be found individual metering of heat consumption in the case of collective
distribution. As far as hot water consumption is concerned this is fairly easy to
operate, and, according to recent experiments in Sweden, would lead to a reduction of 40% of hot water consumption [89]. However, with regard to heating,
because of the substantial heat transfers from one appartment to another, this
is likely to penalize badly situated dwellings (those facing North, for example)
and solutions of fair sharing of expenditure must be found (for example, the
payment of a fixed rate calculated proportionately to the number of dwellings,
plus an element taking into account the consumption of each dwelling). The
effect of this type of measure is as yet little known, but it can only reduce
waste by making households more aware of the heat they consume. In our
opinion, it should be seen as a complementary measure to the improvement
of the balance and regulation of these systems, so that the heating temperatures
in blocks of flats and the overall heating efficiencies come closer to those in
individual heating systems.

The new appliances appearing on the market in 1975 in the U.S.A. were far
more efficient than the average existing appliances (74% compared with 50% for
fuel-oil for example) [56]. The aim of the Department of Energy (D.O.E.) is to
achieve the following efficiencies for new appliances: 81% for fuel-oil and 75%
for gas, compared with the average of 61% at the present time. This is to be done
by means of the following measures: automatic closure of chimneys when the
boiler is stopped, improvement of heat exchangers, reduction of distribution
losses by constructing the air ducts inside the houses, installation of spark
ignition for gas heating (instead of pilot lights).

In France and the U.K. the gas companies consider that the present efficiencies of current new boilers are about 75% (in a 65 to 80% bracket in
France). The use of better-insulated boilers equipped with spark-ignition would
make it possible to obtain greater efficiencies, about 80% (bracket 75 to 85%).
It would seem that as far as conventionally designed boilers (without condensation) are concerned, it is not possible to go much beyond an efficiency level of
85%. In order to obtain greater efficiency it will be necessary to develop
condensation gas boilers, in which the smoke is cooled with the water from the
heating circuit in order to recover its latent heat. In this case, efficiencies of
about 95—100% may be achieved. However, the use of this type of boiler does
raise various problems: corrosion of the heat exchangers by gas liquids, size
and cost of exchangers, need to have a space heating system operated on low
temperature water. At present, these boilers are as yet at an experimental stage
and it is difficult to say how they will develop.

---

[2] In 1979 price.

Solar Systems

We are only interested here in collector based solar energy systems ("active solar systems") which serve either to produce domestic hot water or to feed water or air heating appliances. The financial viability and the maturity of solar water-heaters and heating systems varying greatly, we will examine these two techniques successively.

The solar water-heater operates throughout the year and therefore makes the most of the substantial summer solar radiation, which makes it possible to redeem its overcosts over the whole year. It is all the more cost effective if the insolation is intense and well distributed over the year. It is now considered to be competitive, or almost so, in most European countries and in most regions of North America. The cost of installing a solar water heater is at present about 2000 US $ in the U.S.A.[3] (1979). In France it is estimated that the additional cost in relation to conventional hot water installations is 4500 ± 1500 FF (1100 ± 400 US $). The rate of coverage of annual hot water needs (i.e. the percentage of savings of conventional energy) varies, of course, according to the size of the collectors and the weather zone. For a reference size of 4 m^2, which is considered to be standard for an individual house, this rate may reach 75–80% in zones where there is a great deal of sun (for example, the South of France), and is in the 40–50% range in regions where there is less sun (the North of France, for example). The penetration of solar water heaters onto the market for hot water equipment will probably be initially restricted to new construc-tions and existing blocks of flats with flat roofs, for which the integration of collectors raises no problem. Later it may be possible to develop the market of existing individual houses, but in this case the main problem will be inte-grating the collectors on the roof, or near the house (extra cost and eventual aesthetic damage).

On the other hand, active solar heating is generally not very competitive, and its competitiveness varies greatly from one area to another according to the amount of sun and general weather conditions. The most appropriate areas are those where it is cold and where there is a good deal of sun in the winter periods (mountain areas, for example): in this case there may be substantial energy saving. The least appropriate areas are those where heating needs are low and there is little sun (areas with a maritime climate like the West of France and the South of England). In France at the present time there are about 200 solar heating operations being carried out, and their average extra cost varies between 7500 and 20 000 US $ (30 000 and 80 000 FF) [94]. The costs which are generally mentioned in the U.S.A. for this type of heating are in the same range (about 10 000 US $, i.e. about 40 000 FF)[4]. The energy saving which may

---

[3] Collectors of 300 litres (60 °C and collector surface area of about 4 m^2); price range of various manufacturers from 1400 to 2200 US S; in the average cost which is given, the collector itself accounts for about 35% and the installation costs 40% (source: Solar Energy Research Institute, Golden Colorado).

[4] Source SERI.

be expected from this type of system varies of course according to the system used, and the geographical area, as we have already mentioned (ranging between 40 to 70%) [56, 97][5]. Cost reductions are possible, in particular by developing, in new constructions, collectors which are integrated in either the roof or walls (reduction in installation costs). Nevertheless solar heating is likely to remain handicaped by its high cost, and in our opinion it will only be developed if a system of interseasonal energy storage can be perfected.

A recent study discusses the latest developments in solar techniques in the U.S.A. In its conclusions, it draws attention to a certain number of problems which have been met by the systems which are at present on the market. Because of the importance of the American market (about 90 000 existing systems in 1978), it would seem to us to be worthwhile to mention the main difficulties which have come up, in order to better appreciate what has still to be done to enhance the development of solar techniques [96]. The main problems are as follows: collectors not waterproof enough (thus a danger of condensation and corrosion leading to a shortening of the collector's life-span), operating problems in the control and regulation systems, practical efficiency lower than expected and often very low (for solar water collectors the real collector efficiencies are in the 25 to 35% range), high secondary electricity consumption, heavy heat losses in the storage systems, . . . Most of these problems have also arisen in Europe. They may be due to a lack of maturity in solar technology, to the insufficient training and lack of competence or experience of the professionals who design and set up solar systems, and lastly to an absence of technical norms and specifications. The public authorities should aim at developing and organizing a sufficiently large market in order to speed up improvements, and produce more efficient and attractive systems.

Heat Pumps

The heat pump is often presented as a heating appliance of the future, and as a source of substantial energy saving compared with conventional techniques. Indeed this type of heating does have the advantage of returning more energy in the form of heat than it receives in the form of mechanical energy.

Heating by means of heat pumps was developed in the U.S.A. in the nineteen sixties. They most often had a twofold use: space heating in winter and air conditioning in summer, in such a way as to redeem over the year the extra cost compared with other types of heating. Sales of heat pumps dropped substantially between 1965 and 1970 because of the technical difficulties which had arisen on the pumps which were already installed (poor reliability, problem of freezing, etc.). Since the oil crisis, the heat pump market has again begun to develop very rapidly, and it is estimated that between 20 and 25% of new homes begun in 1978 used this heating system. The earlier technical problems would seem to have been solved.

---

[5] These savings can of course be increased by seasonal storage (long lasting) and the use of high performance collectors (70% in the North and 100% in the South of France).

The principle behind the heat pump is exactly the same as that of an air-conditioner or a refrigerator, except that it is used in reverse. Thus a heat pump takes heat from a cold source (outside air, earth, ground water) in order to transfer it to a heating fluid (air or water). The system which has been developed in the U.S.A. uses outside air as a cold source; most often the heat thus obtained is distributed by means of an air heating system, firstly because most American homes use air systems, and secondly because heat pumps are often used as air conditioners during the summer months. In Europe, the heat pump is only beginning to be developed, largely as a consequence of the oil crisis and of campaigns of experimentation and public demonstration carried out by government agencies and electricity utilities. In Europe, air is also the most frequent cold source (either outside air or air from a ventilation system). The disadvantage of air-fed heat pumps is that they necessitate an extra heating appliance in periods of severe cold. If outside air is used the efficiency of the pump decreases concomitantly with the outside temperature, and from a certain temperature downwards it is preferable to use an alternative form of heating. In the case of a heat pump fed by air from the ventilation system, the volume of air of the cold source remains constant (depending on the air flow) and the recoverable thermal power depends solely on the temperature at which the ventilation air is cooled; in general, it is considered that below 5 °C there is a danger of freezing and that alternative heating then becomes necessary. Water pumps however do not necessitate alternative heating since the power may be modulated with the water flow.

The efficiency of a heat pump, or coefficient of performance (C.O.P.), is measured by the ratio of the energy produced to the energy consumed in order to operate it (generally electricity). In the case of air pumps the C.O.P. varies, as we have already mentioned, according to the outside temperature; it is thus necessary to define a coefficient of efficiency which will give some idea of the average efficiency over the period in which the heating is used (S.P.F. or Seasonal Performance Factor). In the U.S.A. it is considered that the S.P.F. varies between 1.6 [18] in the North of the country and 2.5 in the South (Texas); the average is between 2 and 2.25. In France, the performance would seem to be lower (in identical weather conditions) with a S.P.F. of about 1.6 when the cold source is ventilation air, and from 1.5 to 2.3 when using outside air. The heat pumps using water or earth as a cold source have the highest S.P.F., of between 2 and 3. Although until the present time electric heat pumps alone have been developed, other sources of energy may be used. In this case the fuel (gas, diesel-oil, . . .) feeds an engine which drives a compressor: exhaust gas may even be recovered in order to improve the overall energy efficiency (S.P.F. of between 1.2 and 1.5).

Whatever the type, air/water or water/water heat pumps are not compatible with the heat distribution techniques using water heated to 70–90 °C which are at present in most widespread use in Europe. In particular, this may be a constraint to their development in existing dwellings in place of conventional space heating techniques. Their development pre-supposes adopting new solutions (low temperature floor heating, distribution by air, . . .) and a better overall

optimization of the heating installation (extra heating appliances, regulation, . . .). Besides their use as main heating mode, heat pumps can also be combined in an interesting manner with other energy techniques or sources:
− either in homes which are already centrally heated to replace boilers when outside temperatures are moderate; the boiler being used in addition to the existing appliances at low outside temperatures (generally, temperatures < 3 − 4 °C). This solution makes it possible to save fuel, in the region of 70%, and to make better use of the heat pumps (which then operate regularly within a power range which reduces the work done by the pumps and results in high efficiencies),
− or in combination with energy sources of low thermal levels in order to make the most of them (solar energy, geothermal energy, waste water, . . .), the heat pump, in this case, being used to increase the temperature of the energy vector (the SOLPAC system, for example, which operates with solar energy), or to recover a maximum of energy from this vector (this is the case for geothermal energy for example, whereby it is possible to increase the thermal power of the well by reinjecting the water at a lower temperature).

The development of heat pumps at the present time, and in particular in Europe with regard to the more recently designed water pumps, raises the same type of difficulties as those already mentioned in the case of solar energy: practical efficiency far lower than expected, poor design, . . . Here again the difficulties are largely due to a lack of competence among the professionals involved, and a lack of knowledge about the best solutions to adopt (all the more so since several energy forms may be used together). There is no reason why the use of heat pumps should not be envisaged for heating and hot water purposes in any type of dwelling, no matter how old it may be, since this diversity can be met by the variety of solutions which make use of the heat pump. We have not attempted to compare the various possible solutions, either with each other, or with conventional heating techniques, simply because this type of comparison may vary in time and from one country to another.[6]

One interesting conclusion which may be drawn from a study [98] is worthwile stressing: as opposed to what might have been thought, the improvement of insulation in homes does not work to the disadvantage of the heat pump, and this is because extra insulation costs are offset by the reduced size of the pump and the improvement of the C.O.P. (by reducing the need for extra alternative heating during cold periods). According to this study, heating costs are relatively independent of insulation levels (flat optimum), whatever the climate and the type of pump used. We believe this to be an important conclusion, as it means that it could well be possible to combine savings from extra insulation with those obtained by using the heat pump without being economically penalized.

District Heating

The term "district heating" covers all heating systems in which heat (hot

---

[6] The reader seeking more information on such comparisons should consult the following studies: France [38, 94, 98]; U.S.A. [56], and U.K. [25].

water, over-heated water or steam) is distributed through a network; the heat may come from a boiler, an electric power station (combined production), a geothermal well, or lastly from thermal waste from industrial installations. This type of heating is widespread in the Scandinavian countries and Eastern Europe. Its high degree of penetration in these countries compared to countries like France or the U.K. is due to two factors: firstly to the existence of local energy utilities, which has facilitated the financing and planning of this type of heating; secondly to the national decision-makers' attempt to save energy and make the most of existing national energy sources (coal in certain Eastern European countries) by developing combined production installations of heat and electricity, and therefore district heating.

The value of district heating is a subject under debate, and experts are often in disagreement over this. This is due to several facts. Firstly the cost effectiveness, stricto sensu, of this type of heating, which necessitates heavy investment, is closely related to the interest and discounting rates which are used. Moreover, economic calculation is unable of taking into account certain advantages of district heating (better pollution control, use of low quality fuels). Lastly, the acceptable density level in terms of dwellings per km^2 which can be connected on to the network has not yet been accurately determined: the level, which is often put forward, of 35 $MWth/km^2$ or about 50 dwellings/ha, is not, in our opinion, based on any serious investigation. Besides the economic aspect, district heating has also been accused of causing discomfort because it is difficult to regulate, and moreover of not being sufficiently energy-saving because of high transport and distribution losses. Although this was often the case in the systems installed in the past, the use of better regulation systems and insulation techniques for the pipes could largely do away with this disadvantage in the future; the extra cost of these improvements being justified by energy price increases (except, perhaps, in the case of combined production).

What about the future development of this type of heating? Firstly, it may be considered to have been completely mastered on a technical level, which is not the case for the techniques we have previously discussed. Moreover, because of the continuing tension on the hydrocarbon market, district heating should mainly be developed through combined production, or the use of geothermal energy or low quality fuels (waste, coal, . . .). This will represent far heavier investments than for conventional district heating systems. Because of this, the orientation will be towards mixed systems in which the electric power station or the geothermal well will operate as a base (5 to 6000 hours) in order to amortize the investment over a longer period; the rest of the output (20 to 30% will be obtained from back-up conventional boilers.

In those countries in which district heating is already well implanted, the growing cost of energy should act as an incentive to extend this type of heating, in particular by developing combined production. In other countries the development of district heating will depend essentially on the policies of the public authorities in this field. The high investment costs involved in this type of heating together with the uncertainty concerning its financial viability (random character of the connections) are unlikely to draw private investors into this line of production without government intervention. This invervention may come in the shape of subsidies (as in the case in Federal Republic of Germany), preferential loans or a mandatory system of connections on to the heat network developed in such a way as to guarantee a certain market (measure taken in Denmark). Once again combined production would seem to us to be the most promising option. From the various studies which have been carried out up until now, we may draw the following conclusions: firstly, the development of combined production is only of economic interest if there already exists a district heating network, and thus this presupposes developing a network progressively and supplying it through a combined production plant only one it has reached a certain size; secondly, the minimum level at which combined production may be envisaged is for towns of about 20 000 to 50 000 inhabitants.

All future developments of district heating are likely to conflict with improvements in housing insulation. The insulation of dwellings which may be connected onto a heat network firstly involves very heavy overall investment (insulation + district heating), and secondly makes district heating less economically attractive since it reduces the density of energy consumption. In particular, it may appear worthless to insulate dwellings in order to arrive at energy savings when the heat is produced by combined production and therefore at very low costs (almost free energy).

New Heating Techniques: Conclusions

By way of a conclusion on new heating techniques we can come back on two characteristic features of these techniques: the use of flow energy (electricity, solar energy, geothermal energy, . . .) as opposed to storable energies such as oil and even gas on the one hand, and the use of energy distribution vectors at lower temperatures than in conventional systems on the other.

The use of flow energy, of course, raises the problem of adapting supply to demand. This problem may be resolved in two complementary ways; storage (hot water storage, for example) and the use of back-up storable energy (in this case the systems are said to be "bi-energy"). Because of this, the implementation of new heating techniques is, in fact, far more complex than that of conventional techniques, since it involves the combined use of several systems for which an optimal combination must be found: energy production from flow energy, storage and back-up energy source. Automation and regulation will therefore play an increasingly important role if these flow energies are to be used to the full. It must be said that, for the time being, the specialists are still hesitant about the various possible combinations, because of the uncertainty surrounding future energy prices and the cost of the different types of necessary equipment (geothermal energy + boiler + heat pump, solar energy + storage + heat pump + + boiler . . .). The present trend is nonetheless to operate for as long a period of time as possible with a flow energy base, attempting to cover most of the energy consumption (70%) in this way, and leaving the storable energies to cover the peak periods: this makes it possible to amortize in a more satisfactory manner the heavier investments involved in flow energies. It should also be noted that improved insulation in homes, by levelling off the heating load makes it possible to use flow energies more efficiently.

Conventional heating systems have been designed to operate at fairly high temperatures (70–90 °C). By using new heating techniques it is not generally possible to reach such high temperatures — which are not actually necessary — and thus they must be used in association with low temperature heat distribution systems (convectors, new design floor heating, larger radiators, . . .). The choice of heat distribution temperatures and of the mode of distribution should not be made irrespective of heating techniques or rather of the combinations "flow energy, storage, storable energy" which we have just discussed. In fact, in each case it is necessary to envisage heating as a system in which an optimal role should be played by each of the various components. This also involves the profession adapting itself to the new situation: training, the use of computer programmes, . . .

2.5. Technical Changes with Electrical Household Appliances

The development of the specific energy consumption of household appliances will result from two phenomena working in opposition to one another: the improvement of their energy performance on the one hand, their increased size on the other. For an identical service rendered (identical size of refrigerator/freezer, or same cycle of a washing-machine or dish-washing machine) it is quite remarkable that the annual electricity consumption indicated by the manufacturers varies considerably. Thus, for example, the energy consumption of refrigerators of 200 litres capacity which are at present on the market in France may vary by 100% (ranging from 0.75 kWh/day to 1.5); the consumptions of freezers vary even more (from 1.1 kWh/day to 2.7 kWh/day for freezers of about 200 litres capacity). These differences are mainly due to different designs: until now there has been no incentive for household appliance manufacturers to improve the energy performance of their products, and more important criteria have predominated (cost, outward appearance, . . .). Two studies which have been carried out in France and Denmark give some idea of the technical possibilities of reducing the energy consumption of the main household electrical appliances (Table 2.23). American estimates are of little interest here because of the much higher consumptions of American refrigerators and freezers. On the other hand, Danish and French estimates may be applied to any European country because of the standardization and concentration of household appliance production in Europe.

As far as the refrigerators and the freezers are concerned, the main sources of energy-saving are their insulation (thus making them increasingly cumbersome) and the improvement of the C.O.P. of the refrigerating plant. The dishwashers and washing machines can save energy by reducing their water consumption. A possibility of energy-saving which is often mentioned is to connect the dishwashers and washing-machines directly onto the hot water supply; a common practice already in the U.S.A. In fact, energy saving depends on the manner in which the hot water is produced, and is therefore of particular interest if the water is heated by solar energy or district heating (combined production, hot water). In the case of these machines being directly connected to the hot water tap there is an estimated reduction of electricity consumption of about 80% (in comparison with the consumptions shown on Table 2.15).

Table 2.23. *Energy saving possibilities for the main household electrical appliances* (unit: kWh/dwelling)

	France		Denmark*			
	Present consumption	Possible reduction	Present consumption	Moderate reduction	Strong reduction	Radical reduction
Refrigerator	300	230	550	345 (8 $)	200 (20 $)	90 (100 $)
Freezer	800	500	800	480 (13 $)	270 (38 $)	145 (120 $)
Washing machine	450	300	575	460 (0)	200 (27 $)	71 (27 $)
Dishwasher	1000	800	650	480 (0)	285 (30 $)	95 (30 $)
Television black and white	180	100	165	120 (0)	120 (0)	120 (0)
color			275	130 (0)	130 (0)	130 (0)

* Figures between brackets: cumulated extra-costs of the appliance (in dollar 1975).
Sources: France: [35]; Denmark: [95].

2.6. *The Conditions of Technical Change*

Now that we have examined the range of technical options, it remains to look at the conditions in which these changes can be carried out. In general, technical change in the residential and tertiary sector results from two phenomena:
— changes in the housing stock and energy equipment as a result of demolition of old houses and the building of new ones (this phenomenon has an increasingly marked effect if the share of new constructions is high);
— technical choices made at all levels in old or new houses, by the various decision-makers.

The question of the technical choices is posed in the following terms: Who chooses? Between which available techniques? For what reasons? Under what constraints and in what context? Now that the range of technical options has been dealt with, it is necessary to identify the main actors in this process, their behaviour, their relations (be they conflictual or complementary), and the information they receive.

The Actors and Their Behaviour

The five main actors operating in the residential and tertiary sector are:
— industrialists who develop techniques and equipment (manufacturers of insulating material, boilers, . . .);
— public authorities who determine the regulations concerning their use and financial arrangements;
— energy utilities who attempt to orientate these techniques in relation to their own energy products;
— private property developers[1] who decide, for the building under construction or renovation, on its technical characteristics (insulation) and also some of its inside equipment (heating installation);
— the banking establishments and financial institutions which determine the volume and some of the conditions of financing the techniques.

In the case of the residential sector two other actors should be considered:
— households, of course, who, when they are building their own home, decide both on its technical characteristics as well as those of all the domestic equipment; and who, in other cases, choose only part of that equipment (cooking, household, electrical appliances);
— public property developers[1] (the H.L.M. in France, local authorities in the U.K. for example).

Lastly, in the tertiary sector, the various private entrepreneurs of service firms, banks, the hotel trade, businesses, etc. are actors deciding on all or some of the technical characteristics of their premises, and their inside equipment.

In general, all the actors of the private producing sector will attempt to maximize their profits in the short term, while attempting to ensure their own survival in the long run. Thus they will tend to market and finance the most "marketable" products and to ensure maximum immediate profits. Thus the private developer will tend to prefer low investment cost equipment and techniques (the case of electric space heating). On the other hand, in a context of high-price energy, the strategy of the private actors may lead to the development of energy saving techniques.

The actors belonging to the public sector (public authorities, public property developers) in general make their decisions in keeping with the public interest. Thus, they will make technical choices and determine the terms of finance by applying criteria which should lead to an "optimal" solution for the community — this, of course, is carried out within the fixed framework of public finance by taking into account possible constraints (e.g. maximum house prices in the case of public property development).

Lastly, households whose objective is to obtain maximum satisfaction at minimum cost, will behave very differently according to their financial constraints, their aspirations and their system of values.

The way in which each of the actors pursues his objectives and makes his

---

[1] We consider that private or public landlords behave in a similar way to property developers.

decisions will be determined both by the attitudes of the other actors and the information he receive.

Institutional Structure and Relations Between Actors

These various actors are not all equally powerful, and do not have the same degree of freedom in the decision-making process; the nature of their relations with one another will determine both their relative power and the scope of their decisions. It goes without saying that from this standpoint each country represents a particular case. Nevertheless, it remains the case that the development and marketing of a technique will be the result, at one moment in time, of the converging objectives of the main actors. Thus, it is worthwhile to attempt to delimit the main typical situations which may arise.

The first case is that in which the public authorities either at a national or local level are structurally powerful and attempt to orientate the market; such a situation, in which the banking and energy sectors have often been largely nationalized, will lead to the rapid spread of techniques which promote the energy policy of the authorities, either at the supply level (electric heating in France, cogeneration and gas in Denmark, for example) or at the consumption level (insulation): the actors in the private sector will be encouraged to follow — or anticipate on — the desires of the public authorities, since in this way they will be sure of a market: households will be obliged to choose within a reduced range of techniques and will be orientated in their choice as much by various types of incentives (financial, and others) as by the economic advantages of certain techniques.

The second case corresponds to the classical conditions of the market economy: here the combined interrelations between private manufacturers and households will determine which techniques are to thrive on the market. As far as properly so called energy equipment is concerned, the most frequent situation is that in which an alliance is formed between the energy producers and the equipment manufacturers which results in the marketing of a limited range of equipment which meets the aims of the two types of producer. As far as more specifically domestic techniques are concerned, there may be some conflict between the energy producers and those who elaborate these techniques: in this case it depends on the property developers — private, public and households — which techniques are to be developed in relation to market conditions and the aims and behaviour of each participant. Lastly, in some cases, households organized in consumers' associations, as well as local authorities (town councils, etc.) may have a greater or lesser say concerning which techniques will be promoted or developed (district heating, for example).

The decisions which the various actors will have to take will be influenced, in one way or another, by the information they receive from their social environment, concerning prices, investment costs and financial outlays. In a word, one may consider that all these choices are the result of weighing up present and future expenditure, and that from this standpoint the cost structure of a technique will often be a decisive factor in whether it is to be developed or not. Thus it is likely that any real increase in the price of energy or any anticipated increase, as well as any decrease in the real cost of financing investment will orientate the market towards more "capital-intensive" and energy-saving techniques: on the other hand, such a movement would be slowed down considerably by a reduction of credit or an increase in the cost of financing investment. However, these phenomena are in fact more complex:

— the present and future expenditure is weighed up differently from one actor to another and the decision-making structure may in this case considerably distort the market mechanisms: this is particularly true, in the case of existing housing for private and public landlords and their tenants, since, unless adequate correcting mechanisms have been introduced, there is a complete dissociation between the person who invests and the person who benefits from the fruits of the investment.

— the financing mechanisms for housing are quite complex, and ensure a perequation between household income and the volume to be financed at preferential rates; any extra investment due to a choice of "capital-intensive" techniques is thus likely to surpass this volume and makes it necessary to use complementary financing at high interest rates.

As a conclusion, let us examine what could be the policy of the main actors — public authorities and energy firms — in the case of anticipating energy price increases.

Energy firms will generally attempt to orientate the choices of heating appliances, through publicity to decision-makers and households, by stimulating research and development of new techniques and supporting demonstration operations (solar energy, and heat pumps, for example). On observed post oil-crisis trends since 1974, it may be assumed that in this field the gas and electricity producing and/or distributing companies will continue to occupy a dominant role. The oil companies, whose market is at present declining in all countries, could play a role at a later date on the new energy market (solar energy). The role of the district heating companies is more difficult to apprehend, and depends on how well they are implanted. Particularly in Denmark and, to a lesser extent, in Federal Republic of Germany, where district heating has been well developed most often in terms of combined production, the district heating companies are likely to become more powerful. In other countries, their importance will depend on the one hand on the policies of the public authorities and on the other hand on the attitude of the electricity companies towards combined production.

Energy firms may also intervene in the field of energy saving. Thus, in certain countries, energy firms have attempted to encourage their customers to save energy: by taking the responsability themselves for the necessary expenditure and then including in their customer's bill a monthly reimbursement charge; by applying different rates by taxing those customers who increase their consumption and subsidising those who reduce it (this policy has been adopted in several states by gas and electricity utilities in the U.S.A.); by carrying out technical visits at their customer's home and advising them on energy saving; or lastly by recommanding and controlling norms in new constructions (or even old constructions) which are heated by the energy form which they distribute (this is the case for the national electricity utility E.D.F. in France).

Since 1974 the energy policies carried out in the industrialized countries have been largely dictated by trends on the oil market and the degree of tension existing on this market. The public authorities have thus tended generally to react to short-term difficulties (trade balance) rather than in a long-term perspective (possibility of new energy sources). The nature of the decisions which have been taken, in particular in the field of energy saving, reflect to a great extent the predominance of short-term preoccupations: thus these decisions have tended to give preference to energy-saving measures which are easy to implement to the detriment of measures whose effect would be felt only progressively but which in the long-term would have a greater impact on energy demand.

These policies will also depend on the manner in which the public authorities weigh up the respective advantages of increasing output (supply policy) and saving energy (conservation policy); this choice will determine the financial support to be given to energy saving programmes on the one hand, and to the development of new sources of energy (nuclear, solar energy) on the other. Theoretically this should be done by taking into account economic factors (minimum overall cost to the community) but also more qualitative factors (such as security of supply, impact on the trade balance, harmful effects, . . .). In practice, the community interest is most often relegated to second place, and the policies which are adopted represent the choice of the line of least resistance and the interests of the major firms. Thus a supply policy appears, when applicable, as the most attractive solution simply because it is the easiest to put into practice; the practical application and financial support are left largely to the energy firms. On the other hand, a conservation policy comes up against the difficulty of having to cover a very heterogeneous field of activity (housing, heating, . . .) and to take account of the behaviour and reactions of a multitude of decisionmakers with conflicting objectives (tenants, landlords, private housing companies, . . .). For this reason, the effects of an energy conservation policy may appear far more uncertain to the authorities than an increase in energy supply (line of least resistance). Moreover, there are powerful and well-established firms in the energy field whereas energy conservation is carried out by new industries (e.g. solar industry, insulation of homes) which are less well positioned to influence government decisions.

III. Energy Demand in the Transport Sector

1. Historical Survey

In the last thirty years, the transport sector has been characterized in all industrialized countries by three interdependent phenomena: the oil boom, the spread of car ownership and of road transport and a very rapid economic growth. This has, in general, resulted in a sustained increase of the energy consumption in the transport sector: between 1950 and 1975, this consumption doubled in the U.S.A. and in the U.K. and underwent an eight-fold increase in Japan; in most European countries, the increase was three-fold or greater[1]. It is also worth noting the disparity in the growth rates of the energy consumption between the various countries. Per capita transport energy consumption presents, from this point of view, various aspects which deserve to be emphasized (Table 3.1):
- firstly, per capita consumption was widely different in 1950, with a maximum range of 1 to 20 between Japan and the U.S.A., European countries having a per capita consumption approximately five times lower than that of North America;
- in the 1950–78 period, one may observe a narrowing of the gap between the various countries, with the exception of the U.S.A.;
- finally the energy consumption of the transport sector developed along very similar lines in all countries, though the timing was different, and regardless of their geographical dimensions (the comparison between Belgium, France and Japan is, from this point of view, most revealing); here also, the U.S.A. play a quite distinctive role.

Consequently, the disparity in the growth rates of the various countries seems to derive mainly from differences in the levels of consumption at the beginning of the fifties. The homogeneity of the dynamics of development on the one hand, and the particular development of the U.S.A. on the other, suggest the existence of a relative autonomy in the growth of the transport sector's energy consumption, according to a kind of logistic curve, with a very rapid growth phase (the 1960's for Japan and Europe) followed by a gradual deceleration (as in the U.S.A). The question that remains is whether the present

---

[1] See Appendix 2 for the statistics used (Table T.1).

Table 3.1. *Per capita transport energy consumption* (GJ/capita)

	1950	1960	1970	1975	1978
U.S.A.	52	55	72	81	84
France	9	11	17	23	24
F.R. Germany	9	13	20	23	26
U.K.	14	17	21	22	24
Italy	3	6	13	15	16
Netherlands	7	11	21	23	25
Denmark	7	12	26	29	29
Belgium	10	13	20	22	24
Sweden	9	19	27	29	31
Japan	3	5	13	16	17

1 GJ is approximately equivalent to 30 litres of petrol.

Source: Appendices 1 and 2.

U.S. level — three to five times higher than in the other countries — is likely to be reached by the other countries or whether the singularity of the U.S.A. has its roots in its exceptional geographical dimensions or in a particular relationship between the transport sector and the rest of the economy.

By drawing a comparison between the evolution of energy consumption and that of economic activity[2], a major disparity becomes apparent both in the historical development of one country and in that of the countries amongst themselves. Nevertheless, small groups of quite homogeneous countries do exist: the U.S.A., France and Federal Republic of Germany, on the one hand; the U.K., Belgium and Japan on the other. These differences indicate the existence of very complex links between economic growth and the development of the transport sector's energy consumption. Whatever the case may be, it is impossible to arrive at any sort of general rule as regards the way in which economic growth generates an energy demand for transport activities. Here again, the size of the country seems to be of no influence. In addition, it is surprising to note that the countries which have no transport vehicle industry did not develop any differently.

However let us get back to the acceleration of the 1960's, which varied from country to country, but was present everywhere. It is impossible not to refer this observation to the fact that this period was characterized, on the energy level, by the exploitation and the commercialisation, on a wide scale, of very cheap Middle-East oil, and by the invasion of the energy market by this source of energy. Transport and oil are interdependent; if the modes of transport at first ensured a significant (and quite profitable) outlet for oil — from 30 to 60% of oil products according to the country — oil rapidly became the exclusive source of energy of the transport sector (from 1970 onwards oil generally represents more than 95% of the energy consumption in this sector[3]). Put onto the market

---

[2] See Appendix 2 (Table T.2).

[3] See Appendix 2 (Table T.3).

in enormous quantities and at a low price, oil engendered and sustained the explosion of road transport, private cars and goods vehicles of all sizes, which could hardly have been conceived with other forms of energy. There is no doubt that this explosion in turn sustained high rates of economic growth and that it generated a large increase in passenger and freight movement by rendering the development of transport activities independent of the infrastructure and network constraints.

This rapid comparative historical analysis of the Energy consumption of the transport sector in the principal OECD countries leads us to the following conclusions:
— on the one hand, it appears impossible, on the aggregate level, to determine any kind of relationship explaining in a satisfactory way, from the basis of geography or of economic growth, the development of the transport sector's energy consumption;
— on the other hand, the discovery of Middle-East oil considerably modified the development of the transport system, leading to a rapid growth of road transport and a significant increase of the transport sector's energy consumption.

These conclusions make all the more necessary to apprehend the evolution of the transport sector's energy demand on a sufficiently detailed level. This will make it possible to identify the different determinants of this demand, and to analyse their respective roles in the evolution of the demand and also the mechanisms which govern their own evolution. First of all, we shall consider passenger transport, then that of goods.

2. Passenger Transport

Any trip done by an individual by means of a vehicle generates an energy consumption; either directly, if the vehicle is used on purpose to allow the individual to travel, or indirectly if the vehicle is used in any case to meet a collective demand. The level of this consumption, and the type of energy required, depend directly on the length of the journey, on the mode of transport used and on the conditions of use of the latter.

On a national (or regional) level, the energy demand for passenger transport is thus directly determined by the number of individuals travelling (the population of the country), by the frequency and length of their journeys, the distribution of these journeys among the various modes of transport and the technical characteristics of the vehicles and their conditions of use (Fig. 3.1).

Certain of these determinants may be subjected to a continuous or discontinuous, total or partial, statistical measures, the other only being known through studies or surveys. Whatever the case may be, prior to any historical analysis, it is appropriate to comment upon the data used.
— There is no real statistical observation of the energy consumption of passenger transport. This consumption is derived from the general transport statistics: on the one hand, on the basis of reliable information disclosed by rail, sea or air companies; on the other hand, on an estimate of the allocation of oil products (petrol and diesel oil), between private cars, public road transport (buses and cars) and goods road transport.

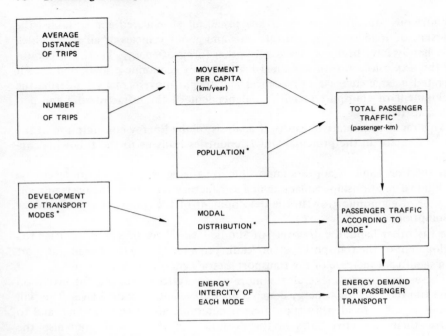

* Variable usually subjected to statistical observations

Fig. 3.1. Energy demand determinants for passenger transport

— The evaluation of traffic is reliable when it is derived from fares based on the distance travelled; it is less reliable when this fare is independent of the distance covered (urban public transport); it becomes much less reliable when it concerns the private car since, in this case, it always results from an estimate based on the petrol consumption (which in itself is an estimate), the average specific petrol consumption of cars (which is itself estimated from the car population) and the average car occupancy (here again this is an estimate[1]).

In the wake of these warnings, we shall emphasize first of all the predominant features of the last 30 years, such as they may be appreciated through usual statistics; we shall then carry the analysis further to consider both, the formation and evolution of the needs for mobility and the technical and economic characteristics of the different transport modes. Finally, having shown the major consequences of the 1973/74 crisis on this sector, we shall try to determine some of the main future trends.

---

[1] The total petrol consumption divided by the number of cars gives the annual consumption per car, which divided by the specific consumption per car allows for the calculation of the annual distance covered per car (km/year); this distance may also be obtained through household surveys which allow for the verification of the first estimate. This distance multiplied by the number of cars indicates the car traffic, expressed in car-km, which, if in turn multiplied by the average car occupancy, indicates the passenger traffic (expressed in passenger-km).

2.1. Main Historical Trends

The major characteristic of the last three decades in all industrialized countries, has been the spread and the generalization of the private car; an observation which through repetition becomes banal, but without which it is impossible to proceed to any serious analysis of the evolution of passenger transport. Thus, in the wake of the Second World War, the private car was almost an inaccessible luxury and only concerned a marginal fraction of the population: 1 to 5% in Europe, depending on the country, 0.05% in Japan; the U.S.A. alone proved to be an exception since by 1950 almost 60% for households owned a car. Today, two-thirds or more of households in all industrialized countries have a car, and more than 10% of them have two or more cars[1].

More than a simple means of locomotion, instrument of freedom and of individual initiative, the car has removed the spatial constraints on which social life until then was organized and has generated new types of needs. One may especially perceive this phenomenon through past urban development, characterized by the predominance of large urban concentrations, the spread of the towns and their partitioned and "functional" spatial organization (residential areas, commercial centres, etc.), the development of new cities almost completely organized in a functional way for the car (Brazilia, several cities in the U.S.A.). It may also be perceived in the development of new modes of life and new behaviours, in which the car plays a predominant social role and where travelling is sometimes a leisure in itself (Sunday outings).

The development of per capita passenger movement and the role of the car in this evolution (Table 3.2) give an indication of the breadth of this phenomenon and of its generalization in all western countries. From this table, one may derive conclusions analogous to those made in the introduction of this chapter, concerning the influence of the geographical dimension of the country or of its economic growth, or finally those concerning the special situation of the U.S.A.

By drawing a parallel between this table and the evolution of the cars' population in the same countries[2] one may notice that, between 1960 and 1977, the increase in passenger movement can be explained almost completely by the growth of the car population, the mobility associated with other modes remaining approximately constant and surprisingly similar from one country to the next (in 1975, between 1700 and 2100 km per capita). This would tend to confirm the fact that the acquisition of a car generates new travel needs; the American example would tend to show that these new needs continue to appear for as long as the car population increases, even when households acquire a second or even a third car. We shall come back to this point further on.

The spread of the private car favoured a type of urbanization where reliance on public transport networks was no longer necessary; developing, as it did, in

---

[1] See Appendix 2 (Table T.4).

[2] See Appendix 2 (Table T.4).

Table 3.2. *Per capita passenger movement* (km/capita/year)

	1955	1960	1970	1975	1977
U.S.A.		11050	14520	16320	
	(7300)	(10130)	(13160)	(15500)	(16600)
France	.	2970	6870	8750	
		(1670)	(5400)	(6900)	(7900)
F.R. Germany	.	4550	7500	8430	8850
		(2920)	(5780)	(6560)	(7000)
U.K.	4020	4870	7210	8000	8220
	(1705)	(2740)	(5510)	(6380)	(6640)
Italy	1880	2450	5750	6620	
	(820)	(1190)	(3950)	(5000)	(5100)
Japan	.	3840 (1965)	5560	6250	
		(400) "	(1730)	(2200)	(2330)
Netherlands	.	3050	7080	8970	
		(1380)	(5630)	(7530)	

Figures in brackets: per capita movement with private cars.
Source: Tables T.15, T.24, Appendix 2.

a period of rapid urbanization (or accompanying it) and often in a period of massive reconstruction (following the Second World War), this contributed to a rapid re-modelling of the urban structures into their present shape. Organized by and for the car, modern towns have most of the time become unsuited for public transport and could probably only adapt again to it in a much slower way. This gradual inadaptation of public transport in modern towns has resulted concretely in a "vicious circle" often described as follows:

spread of the car → increase of car traffic → reduction in the speed
and quality of the services provided by public transport → loss of
their attractiveness → increased reliance on the car → new increase
of car traffic, etc.

With the exception of certain towns which have been able to preserve appealing and efficient public networks (tramway or underground), this phenomenon has finally reduced public transport to a minimum public service, economically quite non-viable and thus heavily subsidised.

It is nevertheless striking to notice that, on the whole, the movement by public modes of transport has not been affected by the individual car (Table 3.2): its progression has certainly been slow, but there has been a definite progression. This can be explained by the existence of several trends with opposite effects. Reliance upon the car has, of course, been the important phenomenon, but simultaneously, the setting-up of new urban structures and the development of new ways of life encouraged by the car have influenced the whole of the population, including those who did not have a car; on the one hand, this led to an increase in the overall travel needs and on the other hand, to a substitution of public transport trips for walking or bicycle trips. Similarly, the increase of professional and commercial exchanges, related to economic growth, has led to an increase of travel needs, some of which were hardly compatible with the car (business trips).

In order to better understand these different phenomena and to draw information from them which will prove useful for the future, it becomes necessary, at this stage, to broaden the analysis; firstly, by trying to define how the travel needs have developed, secondly by looking at the modes of transport made available to consumers, whether on the social, economic or technical levels.

2.2. Travel Needs

The need to travel originates in the distance between the place where one is (the home for instance) and the place where, for whatever reason, one has to go to. The notion of "travel needs" thus covers the notion of the purpose of the journey and the distance to be covered. One speaks of motorized mobility whenever the distance or purpose of the trip, justifies the use of a vehicle[1].

On the basis of this definition, travel needs can be classified in two categories:
— the first, based on the main trip purposes, brings into focus the trips which have as destination the place of work (home/work trips), those aiming to satisfy different kinds of social needs (shopping, leisure, health, etc.) and finally those done in the course of work (professional),
— the second, based on the notion of distance, brings into focus those trips done within urban zones (in their widest meaning), those done on the periphery (regional trips) and finally long-distance trips.

Depending on which studies, surveys, even statistics are used, it is possible to find one or the other of these classifications or a combination of both; because of this, it is often difficult to draw meaningful comparisons and the choice of one classification rather than of another is difficult to justify. Thus, for the purposes of our analysis, we shall define our own classification which will combine the two classifications and which will attempt, on the one hand, to deal with homogeneous physical contexts in relation to the energy demand (distances) and on the other hand, with needs, the dynamics of which is homogeneous. We shall thus distinguish between
— private urban trips, themselves divided up into "home/work trips" and "other urban trips;
— private inter-city trips corresponding to three purposes: holidays, week-end leisure, visiting of friends or family;
— professional trips divided up into two main categories: commercial trips (salesmen) and other trips.

---

[1] By vehicle is meant motorized vehicle.

Home/Work Trips

Simple common sense shows that any person who works must travel two or four times per working day in order to go to work (depending where he/she takes lunch). According to the distance to be covered, this person will or not use a vehicle and will be more or less encouraged to have lunch on the premises. The mode chosen, among the existing alternatives will be that giving the most sought-after service (speed, comfort) within this person's financial constraints.

    The joint phenomenon of the spread of the private car and the mushrooming of urban structures led to the following consequences with respect to home/work trips:
— a sustained tendency to live further away from one's place of work, well highlighted by the constant increase in the average car mileage corresponding to home/work trips[2];
— similarly, a progressively increasing reliance upon vehicles and a decrease in walking and bicycle trips: this trend appears most clearly both in the historical analysis of one country (for example, France, U.K. and the Netherlands[3]) and

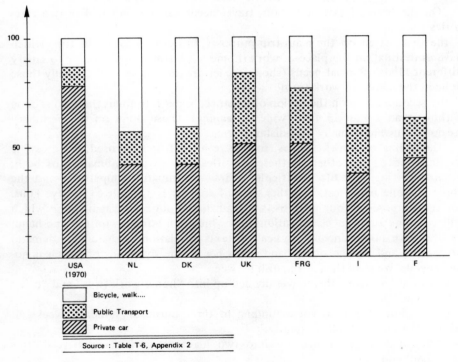

Fig. 3.2. Distribution of home/work trips by mode in 1975

---

[2] Mileage = annual average distance driven by car, see Appendix 2, Table T.5.

[3] See Appendix 2, Table T.6.

in the comparison between different countries (especially the comparison between Europe and the U.S.A);
— although the choice between different motorized modes of transport, varies
from one country to another (Fig. 3.2), the first option is the private car whenever the density of the population and the size of the town allow for this particular choice (non-saturated road infrastructure); however, when saturation phenomena appear, the choice seems to be in favour of public transport, especially
at rush-hour times (for instance, in all major European cities: Paris, London,
Frankfurt, . . .). It is of interest to note, at this stage, that the role of the private
car in home/work trips in European countries seems to have reached saturation
level at around 50%; the substitution of motorized for non-motorized trips
almost exclusively benefits public modes of transport. The U.S.A. here stand
out as the exception; an exception which, it would seem, is entirely due to
historical and geographical reasons.

Further analysis reveals important differences between towns of different
sizes. Not that the actual number of home/work trips varies to any significant
degree from one town to another but in so much as their average distance and
their distribution between the various modes of transport are subject to numerous variations. Thus, in France, this average distance varies from 7.5 km in the
Paris area, to 3.1—3.5 km in regional cities (of more than 500 000 inhabitants)
and to 1.4—2 km in the towns of less than 100 000 inhabitants[4]. The share of
public transport, substantial in large cities (45% in Paris [25], 46% in London
[21], 66% in Rome and Milan [8]),drops rapidly as the size of the town decreases; it falls below 15% in towns of 500 000 inhabitants or less[5].

The reason for this disparity between towns originates, it would seem, in
the particular characteristics of this kind of travel: bound as they are to the
opening and closing hours of work premises, home/work trips are indeed concentrated in time and are thus generators of the rush-hour phenomenon: a study
[26] shows, for example, that in New York the train load is multiplied by 4 in
a 20-minute interval between 8:30 and 9:00 a.m. This rush-hour phenomenon
affects, first of all, private car trips and results in heavy congestion of the town's
road networks (the point of congestion depending upon the state of the towns'
development [26]); any increase in traffic beyond this saturation stage can obviously only be guaranteed by public transport with a separate infrastructure.
Thus, is it possible to explain both the success of public modes of transport for
home/work trips within large cities (the population increases much faster than
the roadway capacity) and the fact that beyond a certain development threshold
of the private car, any substitution occurs exclusively between non-motorized
trips and public modes of transport.

Other Urban Trips

There is much less information on the other urban trips than on home/work
trips. Corresponding to different current household activities (shopping, leisure,

---

[4]   See Appendix 2, Table T.7.

[5]   See Appendix 2, Table T.9.

sport, outings, . . .) they reflect at one and the same time, ways of life, modes of consumption and living conditions. Contrary to the trips analyzed above, other urban trips may considerably vary in frequency. The fundamental element is no longer the need to travel but the possibility and the wish to do so. The new phenomenon is thus the link between the frequency and the conditions of the trip; the time factor, absent in the analysis of home/work trips, in this case plays an all-important role. The significant disparities in the frequency of trips of this kind between different-size towns are, from this point of view, most revealing. As shown for France in Table 3.3, the average number of motorized urban trips other than home/work trips, per year and per household, goes from 490 for the Paris area to more than 1100 for small towns; thus the multiplication factor from one to the other is approximately 2.5. By multiplying this frequency of trips by the average distances in the different town categories, one notices a significant reduction in the disparity which would tend to show that the time allocated to these trips is not significantly different from one town to another. These findings are, in any case, backed by the comparative analysis of urban trips in other countries and more particularly by the comparative analysis of the uses of the private car[6]. If we admit the basic assumption that the time factor acts as a rigid constraint in the formation and evolution of trips other than home/work trips, it then follows that any increase in subsequent traffic originates in the increase of their average speed.

Table 3.3. *Motorised urban trips other than home/work (France, 1974, 2. wheels vehicles excluded)*

	(number of trips/household/year)
Paris area:	490
Cities with more than 500 000 inhabitants:	760
Cities with 200 000 to 500 000 inhabitants:	840
Cities with 100 000 to 200 000 inhabitants:	960
Cities with less than 100 000 inhabitants:	1120

Source: [36].

In this case also, the car phenomenon has played an all-important role in the evolution of the traffic associated with these trips; but contrary to home/work trips, this role does not seem significantly different from one town to another. The private car obviously benefits from intrinsic advantages for these kinds of trips: it is faster, more comfortable and more flexible in its uses. Thus, it is not surprising that car ownership (whether it be of one or two cars) has resulted everywhere both in the replacement of walking or bicycle trips by car trips — thus increasing the corresponding motorized traffic — and by a move away from public modes of transport towards the private car. This substitution, favouring a relatively faster mode of transport, has also contributed to the increase in traffic.

---

[6] See Appendix 2, Table T.10.

The analysis of the use of cars reinforces this observation, in so much as it shows that on average a household with a car travels 2.5 times more than a household without a car, and that the ownership of a second car increases the travelling by 4[7]. Much more evenly spread out over the day, these trips do not generate, in themselves, rush-hour phenomena; at the most, they contribute to reinforcing those generated by home/work trips.

Holiday Trips

Holidays are both the expression of a certain kind of urban life — widespread in all industrialized countries — and a reflection of economic growth: thus, in most countries, there exists a close correlation between household income and the rate of holiday departures [27] (Table 3.4). Nevertheless, it does appear that income is not the only factor responsible for holiday departures. As shown by a French survey, there also exists a correlation between the size of the towns in which families are living and their rate of holiday departures (Table 3.5).

Table 3.4. *Holiday departures (OECD average, 1975)* (per year and per capita)

Income (FF)*	Under 10 000	10–20 000	20–30 000	30–50 000	Above 50 000
Households with a car	1.32	1.71	1.93	2.08	2.83
Households without a car	1.38	1.21	1.40	1.77	3.39
Average	1.36	1.50	1.77	2.02	2.88

* 1 FF = 0.21 US $ (1973).
Source: [27].

Table 3.5. *Rate of holiday departures according to the place of residence* (percentage of people going on holiday)

	France 1968	1974	1977	F.R. Germany 1977
Rural areas	18	26	30	27
Towns with less than 20 000 inhabitants	36	40	44	39
Towns with 20–100 000 inhabitants	48	51	57	46
Towns with more than 100 000 inhabitants	54	59	63	51 (under 500 000)
Paris area	74	77	84	57 (above 500 000)
Overall	42	48	53	
References	[31]	[31]	[51]	[71]

[7] See Appendix 2, Table T.11.

The comparison between like-size towns or towns with similar living standards, situated in different countries reveal specificities in each country which may not be attributed to either one of the two afore-mentioned factors[8]. It is likely that one of the causes for this disparity stems from the differences in the level of car ownership, since for an identical income level, car ownership apparently encourages holiday departures.

Beyond the traditional summer holidays, new kinds of holidays are becoming increasingly popular, such as winter sports and package deal holidays. Each kind of holiday has its own characteristics, which favour a particular mode of transport. Let us merely say that package trips are closely restricted to certain particular modes of transport such as the coach or the plane; the private car remains the privileged vehicle of family holidays and public modes of transport (train, coach, plane) have the edge whenever the time of absence is short or if the presence of a car during the holiday is useless or even undesirable (winter sports for instance).

As regards the modal distribution of holiday departures, there are significant differences between countries, partly linked to the distances involved in reaching the holiday resorts[9]; thus the private car only accounts for 61% of holiday departures in Germany as against 76% in France; similarly the plane accounts for 20% of holiday departures in Denmark as against 8% in the Netherlands and 1% in Italy.

Finally, let us note that the distances entailed by these trips are only moderately linked to household incomes: the range estimated in an OECD study [37] goes from 500 to 670 km with 570 km as an average (distance from home to the place of holiday).

Week-End Trips

Week-end trips (short leisure trips) have particularly increased with the spread of the car. Corresponding mostly to the need for "getting-away", they have entertained with the private car a very close relationship, and it is reasonable to consider the car as a mode of transport quite specific to this kind of trip. It is striking to note, in this respect, that the traffic per household resulting from week-end trips has, on the whole, no connection whatsoever with the income level, whether it be for France or a sample of OECD countries [24, 27]. In addition, a transport survey of France [24] shows that 91% of the car-owning households use their car at the week-end, as against 41% for home/work and 63% for holiday trips.

In a way responsible for the creation of this need, the car also imposes its own spatial limits; the time factor is here at least as important as in urban trips other than home/work, and the speed constraints, on leaving and entering the place of residence, will determine the acceptable distance to be covered[10]. In

---

[8] See Appendix 2, Table T.12.

[9] See Appendix 2, Table T.13.

[10] The increasing distance of week-end homes with the construction of a motorway well illustrates this phenomenon.

addition, these trips are characterized by rush-hour phenomena, at least in large towns where the exit roadway capacities are relatively less developed, in comparison to the population, than in towns of lesser importance. One of the effects of rush-hour periods is to diminish average traffic speeds; it is therefore not surprising to find an inverse correlation between the overall traffic resulting from these trips and the size of the cities.

Social Trips

We shall only briefly consider this kind of trip, in so far as it is often difficult to differentiate these trips from holiday or week-end trips. We shall emphasize two principal characteristics: on the one hand, population migrations within the territory tend to increase, if not the frequency, then at least the length of these trips; on the other hand, when the distance increase, the income factor becomes increasingly influential as regards the frequency of these trips. In the U.K., in 1975, the difference between low and high income families was of 16 km per annum and per capita, as against an average traffic of 85 km per annum and per capita for households with higher income levels [21].

Professional Trips

The term professional trip applies to any trip done within the framework of one's professional activity, excluding home/work trips. They include everyday commercial trips (salesmen), business trips, trips to attend congresses, conferences, etc. and work trips done on behalf of administrations or companies (postal vans for example). Accounting for most of the domestic air traffic, in the majority of countries, and a great deal of the international traffic, they are equally important as regards fast "inter-city" trains; in addition, a significant proportion of car traffic, either in private or in commercial cars, may also be attributed to professional trips (23% in France, 29% in the Netherlands and 24% in Federal Republic of Germany) [20, 22, 28]. It is important to note, at this

Table 3.6. *Use of car for professional trips*

		1963	1965	1970	1976	References
Netherlands	distance travelled by car* (km/year)	18 400	18 000	17 200	14 000	[22]
	percentage of professional trips (%)	58	51	38	29	
F.R. Germany	distance travelled by car* (km/year)	15 400	15 400	14 800	.	[7] [20]
	percentage of professional trips (%)	44	.	24	.	

* Figures for all cars; the annual distance travelled by commercial cars only was 22 200 km in 1970 in F.R. Germany; in the Netherlands, it remained quite stable: 22 300 in 1963, 22 500 in 1965, 21 300 in 1970 and 22 800 in 1976.

stage, that in certain countries (Federal Republic of Germany or the Netherlands for instance), professional trips played a dominant role in car traffic at the beginning of the spread of the private car, and that now this role is decreasing: this resulted, as shown in Table 3.6, in a very high annual average mileage with a significant proportion of professional trips in this mileage, at the beginning of the 1960's, followed by a regular decrease of these two indicators ever since. Once again, the study of this table allows one to notice that the geographical size of the country has no bearing upon professional car trips and that the annual average mileage of commercial cars is remarkably similar from one country to another (also true of France).

As we have already seen, on several occasions, technology often does not play an altogether passive role in relation to travel needs, and the vehicles are not merely the means for converting an energy product into a useful mechanical energy. Thus, shall we approach the study of transport modes from two points of view, socio-economic on the one hand, technical on the other.

2.3. The Private Car

The private car would, alone, justify several volumes. We shall only emphasize here what directly concerns the problem of energy demand, by successively determining the pattern of utilization of the car, its social, economic and technical aspects.

Patterns of Use

One of the most characteristic features of the use of the private car is probably that the average annual distance travelled (Fig. 3.3) is very similar from one country to the next; the saturation limit being approximately 15 000 km/year[1]. Indeed, one may notice, in the case of the U.S.A., where car ownership is a long-established phenomenon, that the annual distance travelled by cars remained almost unchanged in the period from 1950 to 1974 (14 800 km/year in 1950, 15 700 in 1970, 15 000 in 1975). Similarly, after correction of the bias introduced by commercial cars[2], the maximum difference between the European countries under review was 1700 km/year in 1965 (12 100 km for France, 13 800 for Federal Republic of Germany). In 1970, the most recent date for which we have sufficient and reliable information before the oil crisis, the average annual distances travelled by cars in most industrialized countries settled between 13 000 km and 14 000 km with a dispersion of 7% which is small in relation to the uncertainty of the figures[3] (except for the U.S.A., where the average annual distance was a bit higher: 15 000 km).

---

[1] See Appendix 2, Table T.4.

[2] The distance travelled by commercial cars is much greater than that travelled by private cars and averages around 22 000 km/year for Federal Republic of Germany [20] and for the Netherlands [22].

[3] In the INSEE study concerning France [30], an uncertainty is implicitly admitted regarding the average distance travelled by cars, of approximately 1800 km (11 700 according to the interviews, 13 500 after correction) or approximately 15%.

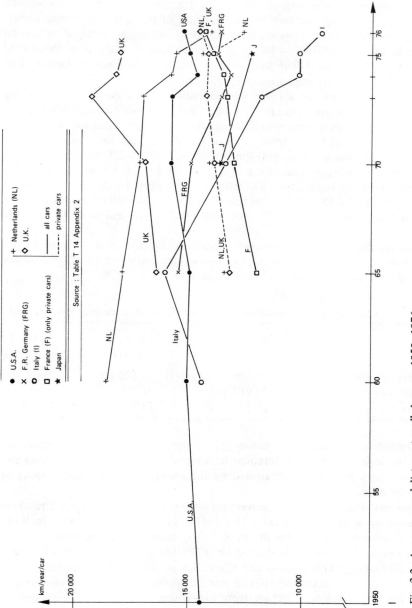

Fig. 3.3. Average annual distance travelled per car 1950—1976

The existence of a limit upon the annual distance travelled by cars seems to be confirmed when one analyses the distribution of this distance among different income classes or different socio-professional categories: thus, according to a survey in France in 1973/74 [30] the average mileage varied from 9000 km/year/car to 17 000 km[4] for high income households (income higher than 100 000 FF[5], with an average around 13 500 km.

The comparison of the average annual distance travelled per car according to the size of the towns, either in France [30] or in the Netherlands [22] reinforces the notion of a certain independence between the land use pattern and the annual average distance driven by car. In France, this distance in 1973/74 varied from a minimum of 11 800 km for towns of 10 to 20 000 inhabitants to 13 100 km in rural areas, reaching a maximum of 14 000 km in the Paris area (a dispersion of approximately 8% from the average). In the Netherlands, it varied in 1974 from 13 400 km for towns of 30—50 000 inhabitants, to 14 100 km in rural areas and towns of 50—100 000 inhabitants, and to 15 000 for the suburbs.

Similarly, the comparison between the annual average distance travelled per car by households owning one car or several cars indicates an analogous use whether it is a first car or a second car (Table 3.7).

Table 3.7. *Annual average distance travelled by car according to car ownership* (km/year/car)

	France (1973—74)	Denmark (1975)	U.S.A. (1969)
Households with one car	12 850	16 500	17 400
Households with two cars	13 910	16 900	19 300
References	[30]	[33]	[5]

Nevertheless, the apparent uniformity of annual average distances travelled by cars conceals significant differences in the real conditions of use of cars and the services they provide, as illustrated by the evolution in time and in space of various ratios linked to car traffic.

In the first place, individual movement per car varied greatly from one country to another at the beginning of the 1960:s (1200 km/year/capita in Italy, 3300 in Denmark and 10 100 in the U.S.A.); these differences tended to diminish towards the end of the period (in 1975 the gap was of 1 to 3 between Italy — 5000 km/year/capita — and the U.S.A. — 14 800 km/year/capita[6]. In spite of these differences, the overall trend in personal movement per car presents a quite homogeneous picture from one country to the next, with the exception of the U.S.A. (Fig. 3.4).

---

[4] Of which 1800 km/year were done for professional reasons.

[5] 1974 FF; US $ = 4.5 FF (1974).

[6] See Appendix 2, Table T.15.

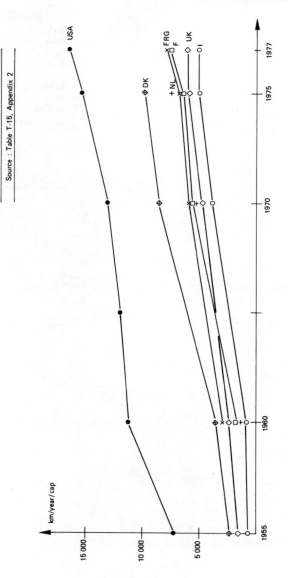

Fig. 3.4. Individual mobility by car 1955–1977

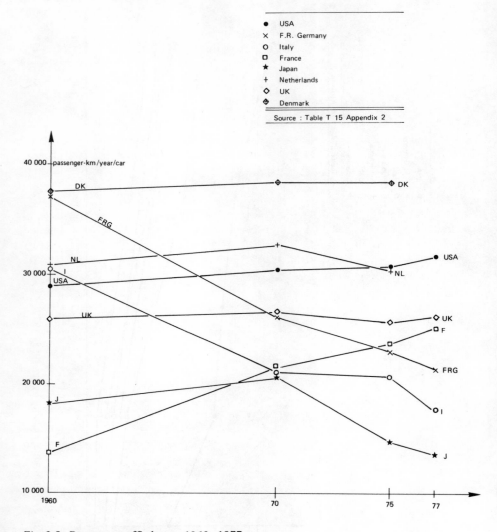

Fig. 3.5. Passenger traffic by car 1960–1977

The same cannot be said of passenger traffic by car, or, in other words, of the real contribution of the car to the overall passenger traffic[7]. In Fig. 3.5 one may notice both a very great heterogeneity in the situations for all the reference years, and also evolutions presenting notable contrasts among the various countries. This is due to two factors:
— to the differences in the average distances travelled by cars, although, as we

_____

[7] See Appendix 2, Table T.15.

have noted these differences are minimal towards the end of the period;
— to the way cars are used, and namely car occupancy.

In order to examine more closely the present uses of the car, it is necessary to determine the main "services" it provides; this is what we have done for three reference years and five characteristic countries on the basis of the mileage structure of the car (with and without professional trips)[8]. At the outset, one may deduce a relative homogeneity in this structure between countries. Some additional points, however, deserve to be made.
— The car mileage for commuting trips seems to be more important in countries where single family dwelling is a widespread phenomenon (the U.K., the U.S.A.), and this all the more so when urban structures have spread further afield and dispersion of the homes is greater (the U.S.A.).
— The role played by holidays in car mileage tends to regularly diminish as the standard of living rises, probably as a result of the two-fold effect of multiple car ownership (only one car is used to go on holiday) and the increased reliance upon modes of transport such as the train or the plane for long-distance trips (an observation which is valid in the case of one country alone or in the case of a comparison between countries[9]).
— Generally speaking, the development of the economies and of the land use pattern generated by the car have led to an increase of the proportion of urban and suburban trips in car mileage.

Table 3.8. *Average car occupancy* (persons per car)

	Netherlands (1976)	U.K. (1975–76)	U.S.A. (1971)	France (1975)
Home/work trips	1.5	1.24	.	.
Professional trips	1.6	1.15	.	.
Holiday, week-end trips	3.0	2.12	.	.
Urban trips	.	.	1.9	1.3
Intercity trips	.	.	2.2	2.0
Average	2.0*	1.62	2.05, 1.9	1.7
References	[22]	[21]	[35, 38]	[36]

* This average car occupancy increased from 1.7 in 1960 to 1.8 in 1965 and 1.9 in 1970.

Thus, it does not seem that the structure of car mileage can, alone, satisfactorily explain the disparities in car traffic. It is therefore necessary to pursue this analysis yet further by comparing average car occupancy according to trip purposes (Table 3.8). This seemingly leads one to highlight behaviours which are relatively different from one country to the next, and this for each particular

---

[8] See Appendix 2, Tables T.5, T.10.

[9] One may notice the same phenomenon by considering car uses according to income levels [28, 30].

purpose; one may, in general, observe an increase in car occupancy according to the distance to be travelled (urban versus interurban), or according to the purpose of the trip (the increase being small in the case of professional and commuting trips, and large in the case of leisure trips). The significant differences which appear between countries, for both average car occupancy and for the occupancy related to different trip purposes, cannot, it would seem, be explained by differences in car ownership or in housing conditions; the question remains to know if these differences really do exist and reflect behavioural differences or if they come from biases introduced in passenger traffic estimates, on the one hand, and vehicle traffic, on the other.

Socio-Economic Aspects

From all that has been said so far, one may derive the notion of quite a great uniformity, at least nowadays, in the way the car is used in the main industrialized countries of the OECD. Significant differences have, however, appeared in the mobility by car, the causes of which we shall now attempt to analyze.

First of all, it is obvious that if the average mileage per vehicle and per year does not considerably vary from one country to another the number of cars in use becomes the determinant element of the total traffic; in other words, the car ownership ratio is the determinant element of mobility. This is, indeed, what one may observe by comparing the level of car ownerhip per household and the distance travelled every year with a car, by average households, on the one hand, and car-owning households, on the other (multiple car ownership effect)[10].

The differences in the car ownerhip levels apparently stem from three principal causes: income, housing conditions and purchasing and utilization costs of the car.

The influence of the income level upon car ownerhip may be determined on one country alone or by comparing various countries: Fig. 3.6 compares three countries (1973/74): France, the U.K., the U.S.A. The curves of the households' first car ownerhip in relation to income are remarkably similar for the U.S.A. and France, which would encourage one to think that the differences in the car ownership levels between these two countries are solely due to differences in the average income levels and in their distribution. The example of the U.K., however, would suggest slight differences: even taking into account inflation and the change in exchange rates from 1973 to 1976, it seems that in the U.K. the car ownership/income level ratio developed a little slower than in the other two countries, and more especially in those classes with average or high income levels. Multiple car ownership curves, on the other hand, indicate substantial differences between the countries: in the U.S.A. the progression as related to the income level is much swifter than in France or the U.K. This two-fold observation — similarities in the case of the first car ownership, and differ-

---

[10] See Appendix 2, Tables T.16 and T.17.

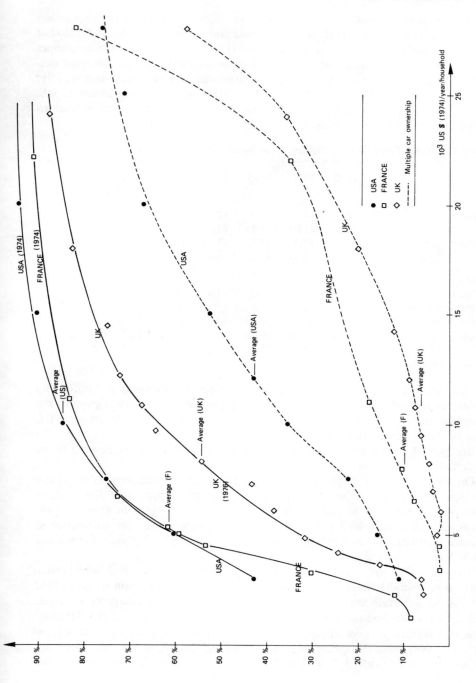

Fig. 3.6. Car ownership according to household income: comparison between U.S.A., France, and U.K. (1974)

ences as regards multiple car ownership — seems to indicate that the acquisition of a second car rests on a certain type of logic and behaviour, different from that leading to the purchase of the first car, and that according to the circumstances (geography, type of urbanization, level of development of public transport networks) multiple car-ownership develops differently and more or less rapidly; thus we could explain the high level of multiple car ownership in the U.S.A. by the space available in this country, the scattering of urban agglomerations and finally the relative meagreness of public modes of transport.

Table 3.9. *Share of transport expenditure in the budget of households* (in %)

	1960	1965	1970	1974	1975	1978	References
France							
Total	8.1	8.9	9.5	11.2	11.2	12.2*	[39]
(Public transport)	(2.0)	(1.8)	(1.7)	(1.7)	(1.7)	(1.8)	
(Purchasing of car)	(2.2)	(2.7)	(2.7)	(2.7)	(2.8)	(3.2)	
(Use of car)	(3.9)	(4.4)	(5.1)	(6.8)	(6.6)	(7.2)	
U.S.A.							
Total	13.0	13.5	12.6	12.9	12.9	14.3**	[5]
(Public transport)	(1.0)	(0.9)	(0.9)	(0.8)	(0.8)	(0.8)	[38]
(Purchasing of car)	(5.2)	(6.2)	(4.9)	(4.6)	(4.7)	(6.0)	
(Use of car)	(6.8)	(6.4)	(6.8)	(7.5)	(7.4)	(7.5)	

* Preliminary figures, ** 1977.

Moreover by comparing the budget allocation for transport in French and American households (Table 3.9) and more especially that which is given to the purchase and use of cars, one does indeed notice much greater allocations in the case of American households (especially as regards purchasing), and this for the entire period stretching from 1965 to 1975. Two other points deserve to be underlined in this table.

— On the one hand, the growth of average incomes does not seem to entail any notable alteration in the allocation given over to transport in the budgets whether in France or in the U.S.A. (a survey done in France in 1966/67 [24] confirms remarkably well this observation); in other words, the difference in average incomes does not explain the budgetary disparities between France and the U.S.A.

— The allocation for current transport expenses (use of the car and public transport) is very similar in the U.S.A. and in France[11] and once again seems to bear witness to a certain budgetary rigidity concerning current transport expenses and of a certain homogeneity in the behaviour on either side of the Atlantic. This last remark is most important if we refer to the mobility indicators mentioned above: from this point of view, the French and American situations are rather different (Table 3.2) and it does not seem absurd, in the wake of the

---

[11] Maximum gap of 0.9% in 1970, 0.1% in 1974 and 1975.

above remark, to attribute these differences, at least partly, to the differences in the cost of the average kilometre travelled[12]; on the whole, these differences arise from the different fuel taxation levels (a one to three ratio in the price of a litre of 4 star petrol in France and in the U.S.A.)[13].

Thus we may argue that the price of fuel has a permissive influence upon mobility (a certain price allows for a certain mobility) and therefore, on multiple car ownership (following the saturation of mobility ensured by the first car). We may however question the fact that this cost plays an active determinant role in multiple car ownership: the comparison of fuel prices and car owner-ship in relation to income, in France and the U.K., would rather seem to prove the opposite.

Technical Characteristics and Specific Energy Consumption

In spite of slight technological differences, today's cars offer a great range of fuel consumption levels (scale stretching from 1 to 4)[14].

Weight is one of the first explanations for this diversity, especially in urban zones where one frequently has to stop and start, and change gears. The materials used are generally the same from one car to the next; the differences in weight principally depend upon the size of the car and the thickness of the bodywork (security); both factors often being found together.

The second explanation of the differences in fuel consumption, also linked to the weight factor, is the power of the engine. Since the increase in the engine size allows for more rapid speed changes, makes it possible to reach higher speeds and more generally makes it difficult to achieve optimal running condi-tions (thus a lessening of efficiency), it almost invariably leads to an increase in the fuel consumption level.

Apart from these technical factors, the way in which the cars are driven greatly influence their fuel consumption. Speed, first of all, is an important factor in the increase of this consumption: the curve of fuel consumption in relation to speed established for several kinds of cars, shows that from a certain speed upwards, the fuel consumption increases almost exponentially (in fact it increases with the square of the speed)[15]. Aerodynamics can certainly limit the influence of this factor, but only in a secondary way.

Changes in driving speed, stopping and starting, engine speed — may also greatly influence the fuel consumption; it is generally thought that fuel con-sumption increases by 30% from an average inter-city trip (on a flat country road) to an average urban trip (9 litres/100 km as against 12 litres/100 km in

---

[12] See Appendix 2, Table T.18.

[13] See Appendix 2, Table T.19.

[14] In this whole paragraph, the fuel or petrol consumption of cars pertains to their specific consumption measured in litres per 100 km (1/100 km).

[15] One should notice here that speed limitations was one of the first energy saving measures taken by governments.

France in 1975 [41], 14 litres/100 km as against 20 litres in the U.S.A. in 1970 [35]).

As previously stated, there is no statistical observation of the real average fuel consumption of cars; nevertheless, there do exist measures taken according to normalized conditions for most new cars (for example the brochure published by "L'Agence pour les Economies d'Energie" – France [19] which gives the fuel consumption of all private cars used in Europe in 1979, for urban and non-urban driving). In comparing these figures, we notice a very great homogeneity within the European car fleet with a fuel consumption averaging around 10.5 litres/ 100 km (12 in urban, 9 in non-urban) and a difference of 1 to 1.7 between Europe and the U.S.A. which is not surprising in view of the differences in size, weight (average for American cars is 1.5 t) and engine power. With a view to an ulterior comparison with other modes of transport, we have related in Table T.5 (Appendix 2) the fuel consumption of cars, expressed in GJ per passenger-km, to different rates of occupancy.

If we roughly divide the total fuel (petrol and diesel) consumption by the traffic expressed in vehicles-km, we obtain relevant ratios on the real consumption of the car population. The Table 3.10 shows that despite a certain homogeneity, Europe also experiences slight differences in the consumption of private cars; these differences probably reflect differences in the structure of the car population between cars of different power.

Table 3.10. *Statistical average petrol consumption of private cars* (in litres/100 km)*

	1965	1970	1975
France	.	9.5	10.3
F.R. Germany	9.5	10.2	10.7
U.K.	.	9.5	8.5
Italy	.	8.6	.
Netherlands	11.4	10.3	8.7
U.S.A.	17.0	18.0	17.3

* Obtained by dividing the total petrol consumption by the number of cars.
Source: Appendix 2.

With a radically different engine design, diesel engines differ from petrol engines in that their efficiency is noticeably higher, and the fuel consumption, for a similar weight and driving, as approximately 25% lower [24]. The spread of diesel cars is as yet insignificant in all countries as shown in Table 3.11.

Table 3.11. *Percentage of diesel cars in the car population (1973)*

France	F.R. Germany	Netherlands	Italy	U.K.
1.4	3.3	1.3	0.6	0.1

Source: [42].

2.4. Public Modes of Transport[1]

Public modes of transport are bound to networks in so far as their operation requires an infrastructure (railroad, station, airport), vehicles (the train, plane, bus, . . .) and an organization. This results, as concerns the passenger, in constraints both on the places and times of departure and arrival, on the routes and their length; constraints which, of course, do not exist with the car.

In terms of energy consumption, road and rail public modes of transport are characterized by a generally lower energy intensity per passenger-km than the private car (Fig. 3.7). Thus substitutions between the car and these modes of transport have, in the past, been influential, and will continue to be so, in the evolution of the energy consumption of transport. For this reason, before analyzing the technical aspects of public modes, we shall consider their conditions of supply and use, which will determine the phenomena of substitution.

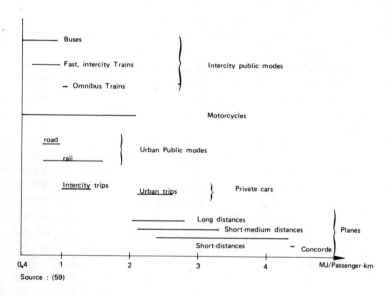

Source : (59)

Fig. 3.7. Specific energy consumption of passenger transport modes

Supply

The indicator which can most clearly reflect the supply of public modes of transport is without doubt the number of vehicles-km or of seats-km available for the public. This indicator also directly determines the energy consumption of public modes of transport. However, it only provides an overall view of the supply and gives no indication as to the underlying reality (the networks); more particularly, it is insufficient to analyze future expansion (or recession) possibili-

---

[1] In this context public modes of transport (or public transport) refer to mass transport (i.e. buses, trains, planes) as opposed to individual transport.

ties and their causes. It is thus necessary to complete this view of the supply, more especially by an analysis of the networks, seen from the view-point of the infrastructures and vehicles made available to the passengers. Since they are apt to change slowly, the infrastructures determine the range of possibilities of medium and long-term supply. The stock of vehicles, which characterizes the degree of use of these infrastructures, indicates the actual level of supply within the range of possibilities, and thus the possible modifications in supply in the medium and long-term. We shall emphasize these different aspects of supply for road, rail and air transport.

Road Transport. Public road transport relies upon the road infrastructure, which it shares with private cars and goods vehicles. In general, this infrastructure is greatly over-expanded in relation to the real needs of public modes of transport, and thus does not hinder their development; however, the very rapid development of road transport as a whole, which resulted, in some cases, in the appearance of saturation phenomena in the infrastructure, was able in certain cases (and will be able to do so in the future) to restrict this development (notably in certain towns).

The vehicles made available to passengers consist of three main categories: urban buses, able to contain an average of 90 people, standing or sitting; inter-urban buses, able to contain up to 60 or 70 seated passengers (50 on average); and trolleybuses, differing from buses by their traction energy (electricity) and their subjection to fixed routes.

The number of available buses and coaches per thousand inhabitants varied according to the country, in 1975, from 0.72 (Netherlands) to 2.17 (U.S.A.); in Europe this range was notably narrower — between 0.72 (Netherlands) and 1.38 (U.K.). Development varied from one country to the other between 1960 and 1975 from a slow decrease (U.K., Netherlands) to a rapid increase (+ 50% in 15 years in the U.S.A., in France, in Italy and in Japan). A quite remarkable fact is that everywhere these developments were independent of the level of supply at the beginning and at the end of the period.

As regards the supply itself (service offered, expressed in vehicle-km, per year and per person), one can notice in Fig. 3.8 a generally slow increase from 1960 to 1975 (except in the U.K.) and a much narrower dispersion in 1975 than that observed for the vehicles (in most countries the service offered varies between 30 and 40 vehicle-km/year/capita except for Japan and the U.K. which stand out with 49 and 64 vehicle-km/year/capita respectively).

The divergence between these two indicators comes from differences in the average annual distance travelled per vehicle[2]: relatively homogenous in Europe (ranging from 38 000 km/year in France to 57 000 km/year in the Netherlands), this distance is noticeably smaller in Japan (25 000 km/year) and smaller still in the U.S.A. (17 500 to 18 000 km/year). One may also note an overall trend, since 1960, towards a reduction in these average distances. The differences in

---

[2]   See Appendix 2, Table T.20.

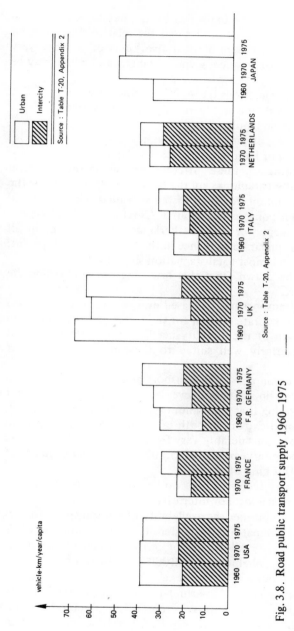

Fig. 3.8. Road public transport supply 1960–1975

the annual distances per vehicle may be explained by the heterogeneity of the services ensured by public road transport modes and the relative share of their various uses. Indeed, these modes ensure at least five kinds of services, very different from the point of view of frequency and distances, and which may be classified in the following way:
— public transport in urban agglomerations (generally a public service)
— local transport, in rural or suburban zones (generally a public service)
— long-distance public transport on regular routes
— occasional services (generally by private transport companies)
— special services, such as school or factory buses, etc.

It is often difficult to distinguish these different services on the statistical level: the first two are often inseparable, as are the next two. By regrouping the supply of vehicle-km per inhabitant for long distance regular and occasional services, we notice a very high convergence around 22 vehicle-km/capita/year, for almost all countries (except for the Netherlands). In addition, in all European countries, there is a similar convergence in the historical development; in the U.S.A., we can observe an almost total stagnation since 1960.

Several conclusions may be drawn from this brief analysis concerning the supply of public road transport.

The supply of inter-city transport has increased everywhere in the last two decades and often at quite a similar rate (except for the U.S.A.); this would seem to come from a general growth of the mobility needs, and more especially of mobility needs which are relatively well suited to these modes of transport (group tourism, for example).

Similarly, the supply of urban and local transport and passenger collecting has undergone everywhere a certain stagnation, even a slight decrease (significant in the case of the U.K.) indicating that a minimum service has been maintained, in the midst of a period of rapid expansion both of mobility and of the private car. This supply, however, does considerably vary from one country to the next (from 10 to 40 vehicle-km/capita/year in 1975), thus showing the range of development possibilities for this kind of service.

Lastly, the size of a country seems to have no bearing upon the supply of public road transport, whether on a local or interurban level.

Rail Transport. Let us now consider the availability of rail transport, firstly, in terms of infrastructure. The comparison of the density of the railway network (track mileage per thousand square kilometres of territory) and of the infrastructure at the disposal of each inhabitant (km/1000 inhabitants) shows most disparate situations from one country of the next[3]. The U.S.A. and Sweden, countries with low population densities, have similar and relatively low network densities (30 to 40 km/1000 km^2); their infrastructure, per inhabitant, however, is most developed and also similar (approximately 1.50 km/1000 inhabitants in 1975). Another group of homogeneous countries is the U.K., the Netherlands, Japan and to a smaller extent, Italy; this group presents network densities which

---

[3] See Appendix 2, Table T.21, for all indicators concerning rail passenger transport supply.

are approximately twice as high as those of the previous countries (70 to 80 km/ 1000 km²) but infrastructures which are 5 to 7 times lower per inhabitant (0.20 to 0.30 km/1000 inhabitants in 1975). Lastly, the particular features of Federal Republic of Germany and France set them aside: Federal Republic of Germany heads the list as regards density with 116 km/1000 km² in 1975; France, however belonging to the previous group as regards density (63 km/ 1000 km² in 1975), is, in terms of infrastructure per inhabitant, ahead of Federal Republic of Germany (0.65 km/1000 km² as against 0.47 in 1975) and of course of all the previous countries. These differences between countries, which seem independent of their respective sizes, apparently have two causes:
— population density (U.S.A. and Sweden on the one hand, France on the other, and lastly other countries),
— the policies adopted in the past, concerning transport and the development of the infrastructures, well illustrated by the comparison between the U.K. and Federal Republic of Germany, two countries sharing similar population densities and sizes.

Two phenomena are striking as regards the historical development: the general and regular reduction of rail infrastructures, partly offset by the doubling of heavy traffic routes, and the development of electrification, of particular importance in European countries. In 1975, 50% or more of the net-work was electrified in the Netherlands, in Italy and in Sweden; in 1960 less than 15% of the German network was electrified but by 1975 this figure had increased to one third; in France 10% of the tracks were electrified in 1950 as against 30% in 1975; in the U.S.A. electrification has remained negligible (less than 1% of the tracks).

If we consider the vehicles made available for the passengers (rail cars, trains, etc.) we may notice major differences in the way the rail infrastructures are used for passenger transport: significantly decreasing from 1950 to 1975 in the U.S.A. (0.03 cars/1000 inhabitants in 1975), small in Italy and in the Netherlands (0.15 to 0.20 cars/1000 inhabitants), the number of passenger-cars may be estimated at 0.30 to 0.40/1000 inhabitants for other countries and has been experiencing, ever since 1950, a reduction similar to that of the infrastructure (reduction reaching 50% in Sweden over a 25-year period; 25% in Federal Republic of Germany over a 15-year period, etc.; in Japan alone, the number of cars offered has been increasing).

Paradoxically, however, the almost general reduction in the infrastructures and vehicles has not led to any similar reduction of the service offered to pas-sengers (Fig. 3.9); in fact this service, expressed in seat-km supplied (or in gross ton-km hauled per inhabitant and per year)[4], has stagnated to a certain extent in Italy, the U K., and Sweden; it has however, regularly increased in France and Germany. In the U.S.A. alone, supply has substantially decreased. This apparent contradiction in the evolution of rail transport supply may be ex-

---

[4] The gross ton-km hauled for passenger trains are not always available in statistics; in this case, they must be estimated from the basis of train-km or car-km which necessarily intro-duces biases. This indicator, however, does reflect quite accurately the seat-km offered.

plained by a modification of the structure of the services offered by the train: a trend towards the disappearance of small local and omnibus services (replaced by road transport) in favour of long-distance trains (inter-city trains, fast trains, etc.), with higher rates of occupancy.

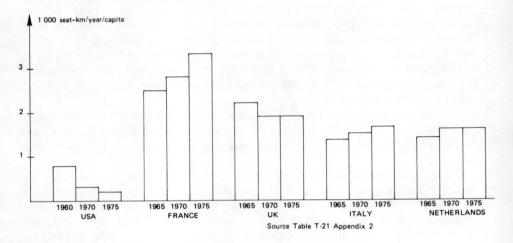

Fig. 3.9. Rail passenger transport supply 1960–1975

Domestic Air Transport. The supply of domestic air transport is often difficult to apprehend since the statistics usually include long-distance international travel. Nevertheless, it is obvious, that there is a close relationship between the size of the country, the distances travelled and the development of the supply of air transport. In 1975, in Europe, the domestic supply was approximately 70 seat-km offered per inhabitant and per year whereas in Japan it reached 280 and in the U.S.A. 990. In all cases, the progression of this supply has been very rapid (three or four-fold between 1960 and 1975), except in the U.K., where it has remained fairly constant; as for Japan, the progression there was tremendous since the supply was multiplied by 20 between 1960 and 1975 and doubled between 1970 and 1975.

Passenger Mobility by Public Modes

The major trends characterizing the supply of public modes of transport can also be observed in passenger traffic and in the individual mobility met by these modes, with however, slight differences brought about by the conditions of use of these modes. Nevertheless, by considering the mobility by different modes, and comparing it to the mobility by car, one may emphasize certain phenomena, worthy of attention, whether on the level of historical developments or on that of substitutions. Firstly, as shown by Fig. 3.10, the individual mobility by all public modes, in 1975, differed very little from one country to the next (approximately 1600 km/capita/year). This convergence in 1975 in countries

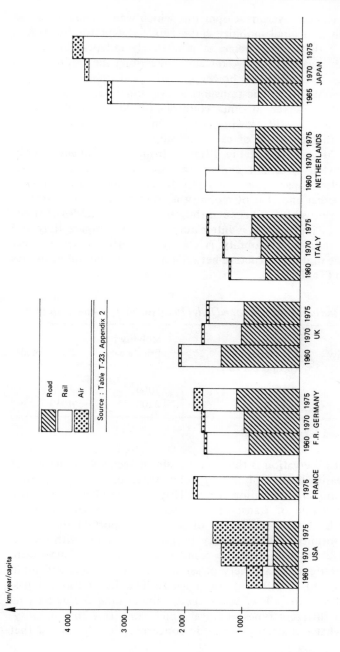

Fig. 3.10. Passenger mobility by public modes 1960—1975

with different car ownership levels developments, which were generally geared towards an increase in individual mobility since 1960 (except for the U.K.), would seem to indicate that public transport is relatively independent of the private car. Indeed, this recalls the above remarks concerning the particularities of the private car. The case of Japan, however, might lead one to tread with caution: individual mobility by public transport is two and a half times higher, there, than the mobility observed in other countries (4000 km/capita/year as against 1600 in 1975) and is still growing despite the rapid spread of private cars; it is true to say that the level of car ownership is slightly lower in that country[6] but in 1975 it was not notably different from the European level in the mid-60's. That obviously cannot explain this significant difference. The question remains whether Japan is an exception as far as the relationship between the spread of the car and that of mobility is concerned or if it bears witness to the substitution possibilities between the car and public modes of transport in a whole series of journeys. It is interesting, here, to compare Italy and Japan, where overall individual mobility is clearly similar although the car ownership levels and the mobility structure between individual and public modes are extremely different (Table 3.12).

Table 3.12. *Car ownership and mobility in Japan and Italy (1975)* (mobility in km/year/capita)

	Overall mobility	Car ownership (people per car)	Mobility by Private car	Public modes
Italy	6620	3.58	5000	1620
Japan	6250	6.49	2200	4050

Source: Tables T.4, T.15 and T.24 in Appendix 2.

Another important observation is that, once again, it seems as if the size of the country has no bearing upon mobility by public transport. However, this is not so in the case of modal distribution (Fig. 3.10); thus the plane, which is a more or less marginal mode of transport in small or medium-size countries, accounts for two-thirds of the total traffic of public transport in the U.S.A.[5]

This apparent uniformity in the mobility by public transport with the exception of Japan, in fact conceals far more complex realities. As we have seen, the different modes ensure quite a variety of services, both in frequency and in distance, which correspond to different travel needs. The distribution of passenger traffic by public modes allows one to better understand the underlying realities, especially the different types of travel which constitute this mobility. Thus, Fig. 3.10 and what has already been said concerning supply suggest that

---

[5] Additional indicators concerning air transport supply can be found in Table T.22, Appendix 2.

[6] See Appendix 2, Table T.4.

every increase in the mobility by public modes of transport has corresponded to an increase in long-distance road or rail travel in all countries. In addition, one may observe everywhere a decrease in the mobility of urban or short-distance travel in favour of long-distance trips. This trend towards the specialization of public transport in long-distance trips, may be explained by the increase in the professional trips — for which the car is not always suitable (business, congresses, etc.) — and of the undeniable advantages of the car for short and urban trips, where flexibility of time and routes is often crucial[7]. Consequential to this trend is, of course, the decrease in the frequency of public transport trips and a lengthening of distances; this, in turn, results in an increase of the average speed of these modes of transport and a reduction of the time spent by passengers in travelling. The evolution in the distribution of public transport traffic according to trip purposes, well illustrates this trend as is shown by Fig. 3.11;

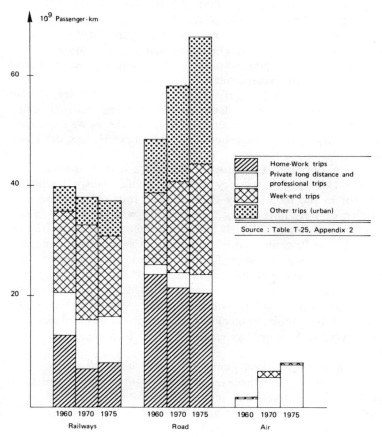

Fig. 3.11. Passenger traffic by public modes and trips purposes (Federal Republic of Germany, 1960—1975)

---

[7]   A phenomenon which was indeed evidenced in the analysis of the various car uses (see above).

the analysis, mode by mode, of the evolution of this distribution[8], shows that this trend also exists for each particular mode.

Let us now consider the mobility ensured by road transport, for it is useful to emphasize the differences between the various countries. We mentioned above that the supply of long-distance road transport was quite similar from one country to the next (22 vehicle-km/year/capita); these differences, therefore, occur for the most part in urban transport. Indeed, if one analyses the mobility by public transport (expressed in the number of trips per year and per inhabitant) in a group of different-size towns, situated in different countries, one notices most disparate situations (Fig. 3.12)[9]:

– in those large conurbations for which figures are available, this mobility may vary between 40 trips/year/capita (San Francisco, U.S.A.) to 260 trips (Rome, Italy) (i.e. a six-fold increase between the two);

– in large European towns (more than 500 000 inhabitants) the difference ranges from 80 (Marseilles, France) to 360 (Zürich);

– in smaller towns (less than 100 000 inhabitants) the gap is still wider since one may observe towns like St. Nazaire (France) where the mobility by public transport falls to 10 trips/year/capita, whereas in Heidelberg (Federal Republic of Germany) it reaches 300 trips/year/capita.

One must bear in mind that the differences may be even greater, in that the above figures only constitute a restricted sample of towns and that, moreover, we have no such information concerning Japan, where, as we have seen, public transport mobility is most important. One may, nevertheless, draw two significant conclusions:

it is not so much the size of the towns (beyond a certain threshold, of course) as the general development policy of urban public transport which is a determinant factor in the mobility by these modes: thus countries such as Switzerland, Sweden or Italy have a very high mobility rate, whatever the size of the town, whereas everywhere in the U.S.A. this mobility is small. In France, with the exception of the Paris area, which stands out as an exception, one may observe significant differences between like-size towns, with, generally, low mobility levels compared to those of other European countries;

the second conclusion, drawn directly from the first, is that in most towns, the possibility of expansion for urban public transport does exist; but certain precise recent examples (Grenoble, France) have shown that if this mobility may indeed increase rapidly, it does not systematically lead to a reduction of the mobility by car.

With respect to rail transport, three points deserve to be emphasized:

– most European countries (with the exception of France) show a great homogeneity both in the 1975 levels and in the post-1960 historical evolutions;

– in France, mobility by train is much more significant, mainly because of the greater development of the railway network, both on the urban (sub-urban railway network and underground in Paris) and inter-city level;

---

[8] See Appendix 2, Table T.25.

[9] See Appendix 2, Table T.26.

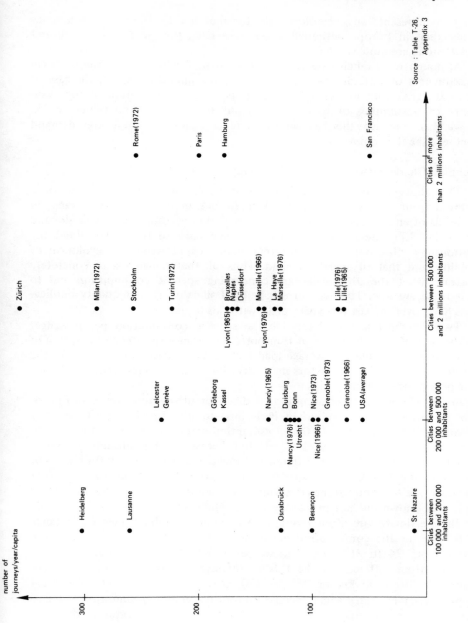

Fig. 3.12. Per capita mobility by public modes in large cities (1971)

— Japan represents an exception since the mobility by train is 3 to 5 times higher than in Europe, although as we have seen, the rail infrastructure and vehicle stock are quite similar.

Although the French case is interesting in so far as it shows the practical consequences of different view points as regards public transport, the case of Japan is even more interesting in that it provides an indication of the availability of possibilities of use of a given rail infrastructure and vehicle stock. As we shall now see, this has significant repercussions on the energy demand whether it be the volume or the structure.

Technical Characteristics and Specific Energy Consumption

The above-mentioned developments may, at times, have seemed quite removed from the basic energy problem. In fact, in view of the wide range in the levels of energy consumption per passenger-km according to the modes and uses (Fig. 3.7), these developments were necessary to fully understand the relationships observed in the different countries between the evolution of mobility and that of energy demand. Thus, all that remains is to concretely illustrate what the differences are concerning specific consumption and to what these are due. This section will be brief since many high-quality publications have, over the last few years, dealt with this topic[10].

Two principal factors determine the specific consumption per passenger and per km of a public mode of transport: the average specific consumption of the mode per km, and the average load factor. As we have already seen for the private car, both of these factors may vary, for a same mode, according to the type of trip urban or inter-city.

Buses. The specific consumption of diesel or urban buses varies in France from 35 litres/100 km (suburban Paris bus) to 49 litres/100 km (Marseilles network [59]); in the U.S.A. this consumption seems much higher the average is approximately 53 litres/100 km [59]. In other words, this consumption varies from 150 to 220 kJ/place-km offered in France and from 330–460 kJ/seat-km offered in the U.S.A.[11]. The specific consumption per passenger-km is often unknown due to imprecisions concerning the load factors (the traffic in vehicle-km is well known but not in passenger-km). There are estimates of load factors but these estimates are often very approximate and unreliable (see for instance [74]). The specific consumption per passenger-km of inter-city buses, varies in France from 24 to 36 litres of diesel per 100 km[12] or a bracket of 160 to 260 kJ/seat-km offered. In the U.S.A., this average consumption is approximately 39 litres/100 km or 250 to 330 kJ/seat-km offered. The Table T.7 (Appendix 2) indicates some average values of specific consumption per passenger-km of public road transport found in the relevant literature (urban and

---

[10]   See for instance references [18, 34, 5, 41, 46, 59].

[11]   The French and American figures are not directly comparable since, on one hand, it concerns place-km offered and on the other, seat-km offered.

[12]   Buses with approximately 50 seated places.

inter-city traffic together) and that of trolley buses which is approximately 2.
2.40 kWh/km or 90 kJ/place-km offered. The two principal factors which explain the differences in the specific consumption per place-km offered for a same
use are the size (proportional to the number of places or seats offered) and the
engine size: generally, the specific consumption per place-km offered decreases
when the number of seats increases.

Table 3.13. *Specific energy consumption of passenger trains* (France, 1978)

	MJ/place-km offered average	MJ/gross ton-km hauled diesel	electric
Trans Europe Express	46	42	34
Fast intercity trains	20–26	31–43	31–36
Turbo trains*	71	88–92	–
Local services	26*	46–56	44–50

Notes: 1 kWh = 9.3 MJ (electricity conversion losses included), * diesel traction.
Source: [59].

Trains. Again, in rail transport, we find differences in the specific consumption which are similar to those mentioned above. In addition to the afore-
mentioned causes (number of seats offered, type of use) two other causes may
be evoked: the train speeds, which may vary quite a lot according to routes and
services, and the traction modes. Table 3.13 allows us to identify the role of
these different factors and gives an almost exhaustive indication of the specific
consumption of trains; although of French origin [59], these figures also hold
true for most of the countries studied. This table indicates the respective influence of speed, service and mode of traction on specific consumption per
gross ton-km hauled, as well as the influence of carriage capacity and of the
type of use on specific consumption per seat-km offered. The major historical
phenomena have been the replacement of coal by diesel and by electricity in
traction energies and more generally the increasing electrification of networks.
On the energy level, this has resulted in a constant reduction of the specific
consumption of energy per gross ton-km hauled.

As regards urban rail transport (underground, tramway, and commuting
trains) which are generally electric the specific consumption, in general, varies
from 15 to 35 Wh/place-km offered. The number of carriages per train (i.e.
the number of places offered per train) is one of the determining elements
of this specific consumption, as shown by the Table 3.14 in the case of France.

Planes. Since the early fifties, aerial technology has considerably evolved as
regards the modes of propulsion, the size of the planes and the speeds reached.
Generally, the transition to turbo propulsion and later to jet propulsion has
resulted in an increase in specific consumption; similarly, the increase of speed,
for a given mode of propulsion, has also increased specific consumption. How-

Table 3.14. *Specific electricity consumption of electric public modes* (Wh/place-km offered, France, 1978)

	Electricity consumption	Average number of places offered per train	Location
Tramway	28	(100)	(Marseilles)
Underground	30–35	(350–380)	(Lyons-Marseilles)
	19*	(770)	(Paris)
Commuting trains	28	(more than 1000)	(Paris area)

* Average for the whole of the Paris underground; lowest consumption 15 wh.
Source: [59].

ever, the increase in the capacity of planes, which of course increases the overall consumption of planes, has always resulted in a reduction of the specific consumption per seat-km offered. Historically, the American example shows that the specific consumption of planes grew until the mid sixties and has been decreasing ever since[13]. Presently the specific energy consumption of conventional commercial planes range from 1.5 MJ/seat-km offered (Airbus, Boeing 747, DC 10) to 3 MJ (smaller planes as Caravelle or Fokker 28), with the exception of Concorde which requires approximately 6 MJ/seat-km[14].

To sum up, the main facts that have characterized the past growth in energy demand for passenger transport, are the following:
— Main factor explaining this growth, the mobility has increased everywhere in a considerable way during the last thirty years, mainly because of the spread of the private car.

— This phenomenon has been amplified — from an energy demand standpoint — because the private car is a mode of transport generally more energy intensive than the public modes it competes with, for equivalent services.
— Mainly used for urban and peri-urban trips, the private car has contributed to model the urban environment into a scattered and energy intensive urbanism, characterized by a lengthening of transport distances and a marginalization of walking, two wheels and public transport trips.
— If, on the whole, the mobility by public modes has remained stable, its characteristic have changed (decreasing importance of short distance and urban trips balanced by a development of intercity and long distance trips) and there has been a reduction of the networks and infrastructures balanced by an improvement in their utilization (and thus better energy efficiencies).

---

[13] The case of the U.S.A. is probably the only one which is truly indicative in view of the importance of traffic in that country.

[14] As a reference, a European car requires between 0.7 and 0.8/MJ/seat-km offered.

3. Freight Transport

All natural resources intended for processing, manufacturing, and finally consumption, at one time or another need to be transported; either in their original form (minerals, cereals, . . .) or in their semi-manufactured state (steel, flour, . . .) or as final products (car, bread, . . .); the number of transport stages and the length of each of these depend upon the complexity of the manufacturing process between the resource and the final user, the spatial concentration of this process and the distance separating the end user and the last stage of the process.

The mode of transport used at each stage will be chosen in terms of certain parameters linked to the goods to be transported (weight, volume, physical state, . . .), to the transport mode (price, delivery delays, . . .), to the distance and to the constraints and objectives of the company for which this transport is being made (availability or not of own fleet, production continuity constraints, etc.)

In macro-economic terms, the traffic of goods thus depends, as regards quantities, on the volume of production of goods and their structure according to different production sectors; as regards distances, this depends upon the size of the territory in which the production and consumption activities take place and the geographical organization of these activities. The modal structure of the traffic depends, on the one hand, on the distribution of traffic according to the nature of the goods and the distances which their transportation entails, and on the other hand, on the economic and technical characteristics of each transport mode. The energy demand for freight transport is thus determined by the choice of transport modes and the specific energy consumption of these modes (Fig. 3.13).

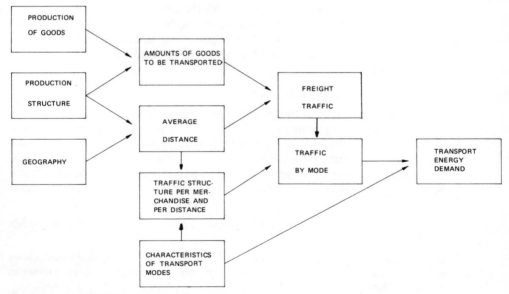

Fig. 3.13. Energy demand determinants for freight transport

In contrast to passenger transport, statistical data is, on the whole, available for goods transport, for both traffic (tons-km) and for the quantities of freight and distances covered. However, the distribution to the end user, principally carried out by small commercial vehicles (with a load capacity of less than 1 ton), is not statistically known and must be assessed on a rather approximate basis.

First of all, we shall try to pin point the significant features of the historical development of goods traffic, such as may be grasped through the statistics; then we shall analyze the economic and energy characteristics of the different transport modes ensuring this traffic.

3.1. Historical Trends

The volume of traffic and its modal distribution are, as we have seen, the determining factors of the energy demand of freight transport. Therefore, in view of the absence of statistics concerning this energy demand (the problem being the same as that for passenger transport) we shall conduct the historical analysis at the level of traffic. This is statistically observed within the different infrastructures: road, rail, waterway (internal traffic), port (maritime traffic), air, pipeline networks. They are estimated, as the case may be, in net tons-km transported, or in net tons loaded or unloaded[1].

We shall essentially consider road, rail and waterway transport. Pipelines in fact almost concern solely the transport of liquid (or gaseous) hydrocarbons; their energy consumption — quite negligible — is thus a consumption of the energy sector, and not truly a consumption of the transport sector[2]. Maritime transport consists, essentially, of international transport — with a significant proportion allocated to the transport of energy products and oil in particular. This kind of transport is linked to the volume and to the structure of inter-national trade, and can be evaluated through the goods loaded or unloaded; its future evolution will be strongly influenced by the future primary energy supply, i.e. the level of coal and oil imports (or exports). As to the air traffic of goods, it will remain negligible in terms of ton-km transported and will be discarded from this analysis.

Freight Traffic and Industrial Growth

The study of the overall freight traffic per capita, from 1950 to 1978, shows a relatively slow development in the U.S.A. (+ 25% in 28 years) more rapid and fairly homogeneous in Europe (a two-fold increase for all countries between 1955 and 1978), much more rapid still in Japan (four-fold between 1950 and 1978). The traffic levels per capita at the beginning of the period partly explain these growth differences (Fig. 3.14): very high in the U.S.A. (10 200 ton-km/

---

[1] Net means excluding the weight of the transport vehicle (in contrast to "gross" which includes it).

[2] Strictly speaking, all energy used in the transport of energy products should be considered as auto-consumed by the energy sector. Only problems of a statistical nature prevent us from proceeding in this way.

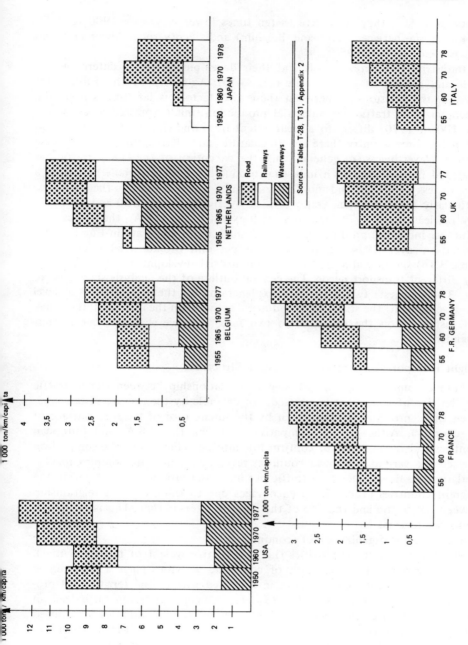

Fig. 3.14. Trends in the freight traffic per capita and distribution by mode 1950–1978

capita in 1950), they were five to ten times lower in Europe (900 to 2000 ton-km/capita between Italy and Belgium) and twenty times lower in Japan (400 ton-km/capita in 1950).

Industrial production levels and their development partly determine the levels and growth of goods traffic (Fig. 3.13). As shown by the Table 3.15, however, the relationship between these two factors is far from simple; the development of traffic per industrial production unit (expressed as an index, base 100 in 1970) differs to a great extent from one country to another, and within the same country there are irregularities and interruptions in the course of time. Nevertheless, in general (with the exception of the U.K.), traffic has developed more slowly than industrial production over the whole period, in a more or less significant and more or less regular way according to the countries. Particularly rapid in Japan (ratio divided by five between 1950 and 1978), in Italy (at least until 1974) and to a small extent in the U.S.A., the decrease of traffic per industrial production unit was much more moderate in Europe. The comparison over 1974 of traffic levels per unit of industrial value added (Table 3.16) shows that a similar level of industrial development can bring about very different transport needs. The general outline of the analysis shown above (Fig. 3.13) suggests two immediate explanations for these differences of level and development: the structure of industrial activity, on the one hand, the transport distances, on the other; these two factors, as we shall see, being interdependent.

Freight Transport, Distances and Industrial Structures

Simple common sense might suggest a relationship between freight traffic and the size of a country (expressed, for example by the average distance between the centre and the border, or by the square root of the total surface of the country). Although the comparison between the U.S.A. and European countries and Japan seems to confirm this intuition (Fig. 3.15), the comparison between the various European countries reveals a much more complex reality. Similarly, the development of traffic per industrial production unit within the different countries (Table 3.15) encourages one to think that the relationship between the traffic and the size of the country alters in time. This is essentially due to two factors:
- the geographic organization of economic activities
- the structure of these activities (i.e. the relative weight of these activities).

The geographical organization of economic activities plays a determining role when there is a concentration, in a limited part of the territory, of production and consumption activities (Sweden, Canada for instance); indeed, in this case, the traffic will depend upon the geographical dimension of this limited part of the territory, and not on its totality. However, this organization will only play a secondary role if the available space is really used in its entirety; in this case, the overall volume of traffic will be little affected; only its distribution amongst primary, secondary or final products may vary (and consequently its modal distribution). Thus, this may partly explain why small countries (such as Belgium and the Netherlands) where every square inch of available space is used,

Table 3.15. *Ratio freight traffic / industrial production* (indices, base 100 in 1970)

	1950	1955	1960	1970	1974	1975	1978
U.S.A.	157		120	100	94	95	87 (1977)
	(103)		(103)	(100)	(100)	(102)	(101)
Japan	333		122	100	77	82	69
			(50)	(100)	(80)	(90)	(79)
France		114	99	100	93	88	87
		64	(82)	(100)	(107)	(105)	(105)
F.R. Germany		114	117	100	99	94	95
		(49)	(95)	(100)	(108)	(112)	(122)
U.K.		90	94	100	96	106	102 (1977)
		(56)	(85)	(100)	(103)	(108)	(109)
Italy		164	128	100	88	89	113
		(148)	(119)	(100)	(88)	(97)	(124)
Belgium		138	101	100	87	90	98 (1977)
		(128)	(94)	(100)	(98)	(105)	(136)
Netherlands		113	117	100		86	84 (1977)
		(52)	(110)	(100)		(108)	(106)

Note: The figures in brackets relate to road transport only.
Source: Appendices.

Table 3.16. *Freight traffic per unit of industrial value added in 1974* (ton-km/$ 70)

Sweden	Japan	U.S.A.	France	F.R. Germany	U.K.	Italy	Netherlands	Belgium
5.4	2.1	9.8	3.7	2.6	2.2	2.3	4.4	2.3
(2.4)	(1.5)	(2.8)	(1.8)	(1.1)	(1.8)	(1.8)	(1.4)	(1.0)

Note: The figures in brackets refer to road transport.
Source: Appendix 2.

have a relatively more substantial traffic per production unit, with respect to their size (Fig. 3.15). In the case of the Netherlands however, a large amount of traffic per unit of value added (4.4 ton-km/US $ 70.00 as against 2.6 on average in Europe) is mainly due to its geographical location; i.e. to the fact that important quantities of goods bound for Federal Republic of Germany and Belgium transit along internal waterways (almost 40% of the traffic corresponds to transit).

The structure of production activities determines the traffic in two ways. First of all, the relationship between activity, expressed in economic terms (value added, for instance), and production, expressed in tons produced (thus requiring transportation), varies considerably according to the sector of the economy: the comparison between the steel industry and the computer industry

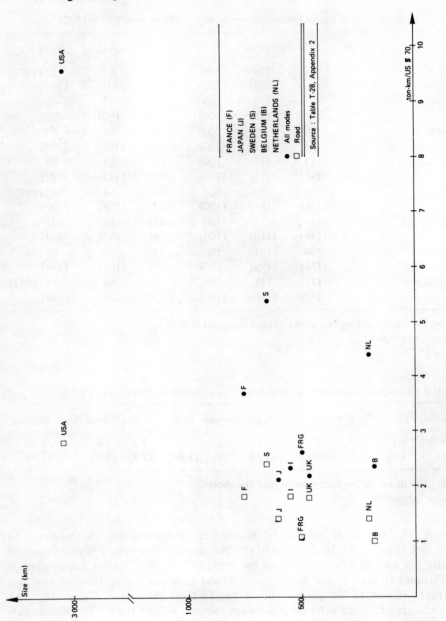

Fig. 3.15. Freight traffic and country size

provides a good idea of the size of these differences. Thus, the relationship of freight traffic to industrial production may be quite different according to the role played within the industry by intermediate industries which manufacture generally heavy materials with a low value added: the examples of Sweden, where the paper industry is highly developed, that of Belgium, where the steel industry is most important, and that of the Netherlands where the chemical industry has developed rapidly over the last few years, well illustrate this phenomenon. Moreover, if we relate freight traffic to the physical production of the principal intermediate industries (steel, aluminum, cement, ethylene and paper), one may observe for many countries a striking stability over time (the U.S.A., France, Federal Republic of Germany, Belgium, the Netherlands)[3]. This stability shows, better than anything else, that goods traffic, in a given country, is determined by the level of activity of certain key sectors, rather than by the general level of economic or industrial activity.

Nevertheless, and this is the second point, the traffic generated by the different key industries, for the same physical production, is very variable from one industry to another; construction materials − sand, gravel, cement − generally produced within the immediate vicinity of the consumption areas, are transported along very short distances (most of the time less than 50 km) and because of this cause little traffic. Intermediate goods (steel, aluminum, chemical products) however, generate a volume of traffic, which, to a large extent, is independent of their location; indeed, they are transported at different stages of manufacture, due to the geographical organization of the manufacturing industries. Thus, one may notice that the ratio previously used (overall traffic divided by the production of a group of key-industries) is all the lower when the proportion of construction materials is important; similarly, one may notice that the traffic excluding that of construction materials, divided by the production of the main intermediate industries, almost always remains constant in time for a country like France[4].

Traffic Structure and Modal Distribution

In addition to its twofold effect upon freight traffic, the production structure of goods also influences the distribution of this traffic among the various modes, through the physical or economic characteristics of the goods to be transported (iron ore or clothes for example) and their distance of transport. Indeed, road transport presents many undeniable advantages when the distances are short, or transport delays very limited (no loading and unloading during the transport); however, rail and waterways are much better suited to long-distance transport in the case of heavy goods or of cumbersome merchandise when there are no specific transport delays to be respected. This relation between the structure of industrial production and the modal structure is well

---

[3] See Appendix 2, Table T.28.

[4] See Appendix 2, Table T.29.

illustrated in a country such as the U.S.A., with its long-established tradition of road transport, where road traffic has increased at the same rate as industrial production over the last thirty years, at a time when the overall traffic was increasing significantly much more slowly (Table 3.14): on the one hand, the overall traffic was determined almost solely by the production of certain key sectors mentioned above (steel, aluminum, cement, . . .) whereas road traffic was directly determined by industrial activity as a whole. The similarity, in 1974, in the road traffic per unit of industrial value added, especially in countries with little or no waterways, reinforces this observation. Some countries, however, deserve greater attention: Japan, the U.K., and Italy where road transport in 1978 accounted for 80% or more of the traffic, or the Netherlands where it is accounted for less than a third. In the case of the latter, it is obviously the importance of the waterway network and of its transit traffic which explains the very high proportion of waterway traffic in the total (62% in 1978), and thus the small part played by road transport. In the other three countries, the absence of a waterway infrastructure, the slow development of the railway network (Italy) and the great reliance upon this infrastructure for passenger transport (Japan) all contribute to explain the importance of road transport.

Historically, the transport of goods by road, which was relatively unimportant at the beginning of the period in most countries (with the exception of the U.K. and Italy), has significantly increased everywhere, chiefly at the expense of rail transport (Fig. 3.14). In all countries, the increase of freight traffic seems to have relied almost entirely upon road transport; thus, in most countries, 80% or more of the traffic increase has been covered by road transport (except for the Netherlands where the figure is 60%). Two phenomena may explain this structural evolution. The first one, which we have already mentioned, is the alteration in the composition of the goods transported, brought about by changes in the structure of economic activities; this phenomenon, which has resulted everywhere in traffic increasing more slowly than industrial production, has led to a relatively slower development of the traffic of goods well suited to rail or waterways, in comparison to that of goods well suited to road transport. The second phenomenon is identical to that described previously for the private car: in a whole group of countries, the availability of plentiful and cheap hydrocarbons (Europe and Japan) greatly encouraged the development of road transport, more flexible and generally faster, by altering the conditions of competition between road transport and the other modes which are much less sensitive to changes in energy prices. The resulting substitutions appear clearly in the comparison between the development of the overall traffic and that of road traffic, both related to industrial production (Table 3.14). It is interesting to consider here the case of the U.S.A., for it shows that in a country where for many years hydrocarbons remained cheap, and where road transport is a long-established tradition, only the phenomenon of a structural type comes into play and not the substitution phenomenon; the relative unimportance of road transport in this particular country in relation to Europe or Japan, is not the result of some kind of belated development in the U.S.A., but of the much longer transport distances, which favour rail or waterway transport.

3.2. Technical Characteristics and Specific Energy Consumption

Freight traffic and its modal structure are, as we have seen, the most direct determinants of the freight transport energy demand; these two factors being related through the specific energy consumption of the modes. As shown in Fig. 3.16, the range of variations of these specific consumptions is quite vast (from 1 to 100 in land transport) and any modal substitutions or any changes in their conditions of use, may have most significant consequences on the total energy consumption. Thus, it is necessary to extend the historical analysis of freight traffic and modal distribution by a more detailed analysis of the supply conditions of the various modes (infrastructure and vehicles service) and of their technical characteristics.

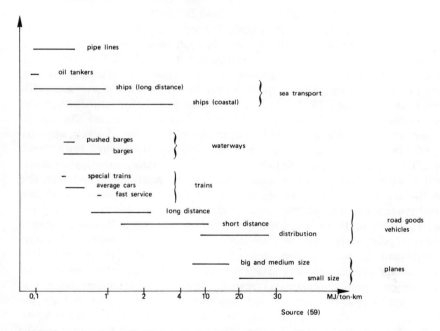

Fig. 3.16. Specific fuel consumption of freight transport modes (France as an example, 1978)

Road Transport

The infrastructure of road transport presents a physical — the road and motorway network — and commercial aspect. Little remains to be added on the road network; suffice it to underline once again, the disproportion between its possibilities and its real use. As regards the commercial aspect, it is worth mentioning the importance of companies whose principal activity is not transport but who cover their own transport needs: in 1976 in EEC countries three-quarters of the road transport vehicles and two-thirds of the loading capacity belonged to companies of this kind. Obviously it is most important to bear this in mind in the analysis of the conditions of use of road vehicles and the conditions of competition between these and other modes of transport; indeed, in one case, it is principally the operational costs, which are taken into account (wear and tear, diesel or petrol) whereas, on the other hand, all the fixed and proportionate costs are invoiced.

Goods transport vehicles can be classified according to the loading capacity and the kind of vehicle: vans with a loading capacity generally less than one ton, chiefly used for distribution to the end consumer; lorries regardless of their size, non-articulated vehicles with a loading capacity generally ranging from 5 to 20 tons; articulated vehicles with a tractor and a simple trailer, with a capacity generally greater than 25 tons; and finally, double trailers generally consisting of two trailers and one tractor, the loading capacity of which ranges between 20 and 40 tons. The number of vehicles (lorries, vans and tractors) per thousand inhabitants, ranged, in 1975, from 20 (Belgium) to 116 (U.S.A.)[1]; generally in Europe, it reached 20 to 30, France and the U.K. having higher levels (39 and 41 respectively). Historically, in most countries, the vehicle stock has developed more slowly than road traffic (excluding the U.S.A. and Italy); this phenomenon, which may be explained by an increase of the average loading capacity of road vehicles, appears quite clearly in the increase of average traffic per vehicle (at least until 1974, the last significant year before the disturbances brought about by the oil crisis and the general economic crisis). As regards traffic per vehicle, there is a relative homogeneity in the 1974/75 levels, approximately 40 000 ton-km/vehicle, the U.S.A. standing out with much lower levels (below 30 000) and Federal Republic of Germany with much higher levels (67 000 ton-km/vehicle)[2]. Once again, there is no relationship between the size of the country and the average traffic per vehicle, an absence which also appears between the size of the country and the average distance covered per vehicle. In addition there is a convergence of these average distances around 20 000 km/year; Italy and Sweden alone stand out with average distances of 37 000 and 33 000 km/year respectively (in 1978)[3]. The confrontation between average annual traffic and average annual distances (bearing in mind the above-mentioned observations) reveals significant differences from one country to another, in the average load transported; 1.1 ton-km/km in Italy, between 1 and 2 ton-km/km in France, in the U.S.A., in Japan, in the Netherlands, and in Sweden, approximately 3 ton-km/km in Belgium and Federal Republic of Germany. As we shall now see, these differences in the use of road transport vehicles (importance of transport without a load) and in their average sizes have major repercussions upon the energy consumption.

The specific consumption of a road vehicle, first of all, depends upon the vehicle itself (weight, number of wheels, type of engine, etc.) then on its load

---

[1]   See Appendix 2, Table T.32.

[2]   These estimates are not always comparable because in certain cases they may or may not include part of the distribution to consumers; thus the figures mentioned must be treated with caution.

[3]   Table T.32, Appendix 2 (see above comments on data uncertainties).

and finally upon the kind of trip. Generally, as the loading capacity increases, so does the specific consumption of a vehicle; but similarly the specific consumption per useful ton-km transported decreases (in the case of a fully loaded vehicle, of course). In addition, the specific consumption per useful ton-km transported depends upon the average load factor which includes the unavoidable empty running mileage. Thus, the specific consumption per useful ton-km at full load falls from 3.2 to 0.7 MJ/ton-km offered when we go from vehicles of 1 ton to 17 tons of load carrying capacity (with a consumption of 15 and 45 litres respectively) [59]. In France, in normal transport conditions, this leads to specific average consumption per ton-km transported ranging from 1.1 to 5.6 MJ/ton-km [59]. We shall also note that the transport conditions (own account or public haulage) which imply a different management of the transport modes especially as regards empty running, result in significant differences, in the average specific consumption; thus, the average specific consumption of public haulage transport (necessarily better managed) is 20 to 30% lower according to the size of vehicles [59].

The heterogeneity of the stock of goods vehicles and of their conditions of use renders very hypothetical (even meaningless) any attempt to measure an average specific consumption of goods road transport, per ton-km transported. As an indication, however, we have grouped the estimates which seemed to us the most homogeneous and which may be found in the publications of the different countries (Table 3.17). These estimates call for two comments:

Table 3.17. *Specific fuel consumption of goods road vehicles* (MJ/ton-km)

	1960	1975	Reference
U.S.A.		7.0 (1977)	[38]
Japan	5.9	5.3	[60]
France		4.4 (1978)	[59]
F.R.Germany	2.7	3.0	[63]
U.K.	3.2	3.2	[67]
Italy	2.7	3.7	[23]
Netherlands		3.6	[73]

— generally, they are based upon estimates of goods road traffic and of the breakdown of fuel consumption (petrol and diesel), which are not simultaneously measured and do not necessarily refer to identical realities; in particular, the traffic of vehicles with a load carrying capacity of less than one ton does not normally appear on the total traffic, although the energy consumption of these vehicles is included;
— the fact that the traffic of small transport vehicles is not taken into account artificially increases the average level of the estimated specific consumption, and this in a different way according to the country and to the importance of this traffic.

Railways

Having previously briefly described the rail infrastructure, we shall concentrate on what directly concerns the vehicles. Expressed by the number of goods wagons per inhabitant, the stock of rail vehicles has three principal characteristics:
– it is generally much more developed than the stock of passenger vehicles: 20 times greater in Europe, and 200 times more so in the U.S.A.; because of this, it is quite independent of the conditions of supply of passenger rail transport;
– excluding those countries in which the rail infrastructure is little developed (Italy, the Netherlands), the number of vehicles (goods wagons) is very similar from one country to the next, including the U.S.A.; the technical characteristics of these vehicles, however, may vary considerably: a 1 to 3.5 ratio in 1975 of the average capacities (in tons) of the wagons, between the U.K. (22 tons/wagon) and the U.S.A. (73 tons/wagon)[4];
– historically, the vehicles per inhabitant decreases everywhere, as the average capacity of the wagons increased; thus the number of vehicles was halved between 1950 and 1977 in the U.S.A., whereas the unit capacity increased by 50% over the same period.

The service ensured by these vehicles (expressed in ton-km per wagon) varies considerably from one country to the next; in 1975, for instance, an average British wagon could transport 114 million ton-km, whereas a French wagon could transport 280 and an American wagon 900. These differences may partly be explained by the average unit capacities of wagons, and partly by the distances covered. However though this second factor may explain the particularly low level in the U.K., it explains very little as regards the other countries; indeed, one may notice a quite significant uniformity in the annual average distances covered by the wagons (approximately 19 000 km)[5]. One may note once again the apparent absence of any relationship between the size of the country and the average distances covered. By dividing the real traffic of the wagons (ton-km transported) by the theoretical supply capacities (unitary capacity × distances covered) one notices that the average load factor of wagons varies considerably between Europe and the U.S.A. (between 30 and 40% in Europe, excluding the U.K., 60% in the U.S.A.)[5]: thus, may be explained the differences remaining in the average traffic per wagon. This, as we shall see, is not devoid of consequences upon the specific consumption of rail transport.

The analysis of the specific consumption of trains and the specific consumption per gross ton-km hauled having been developed above, on a general level, we shall only consider here the particularities of good trains. The specific consumption per net ton-km transported depends, for a given mode of traction and a given speed, upon the ratio between the net ton-km transported and the gross ton-km tracted. This specific consumption will thus be determined for a given

---

[4] See Appendix 2, Tables T.20 and T.34.

[5] See Appendix 2, Table T.33.

Table 3.18. *Specific energy consumption of goods trains (France, 1978)*

Type of service	MJ/TKO	MJ/TK	(Load factor)
Mail	0.305	0.85	(36%)
Special trains*	0.125	0.26	(48%)
Ordinary	0.17	0.40	(42%)
Average	0.18	0.44	(42%)

* Trains transporting only one kind of merchandise, allowing for door-to-door delivery.
TKO: Ton-km offered.
TK: Ton-km transported.
Source: [59].

wagon by the ratio between the load transported and the weight of the wagon and by the average load factor of the wagon. Table 3.18 shows in France, the influence of the speed and type of service (upon which depend the load factor and the kind of wagon) upon the specific consumption per ton-km offered, on the one hand, and the ton-km effectively transported, on the other.

Historically, the trend everywhere has been towards an improvement of the relationship between the net ton-km transported and the gross ton-km tracted, which has led to a decrease in the specific consumption per ton-km transported, partly offset by an increase in speed. In addition, the differences ascertained from one country to the next in the average load carrying capacity and the load factor of wagons lead to significant differences in the specific consumption per ton-km transported[6]: thus, in 1975 the average specific consumption of diesel trains ranged from 0.42 MJ/ton-km (U.S.A.) to 1.40 MJ/ton-km (Italy); and in the same year the specific consumption of electric trains varied from 0.067 kWh/ton-km (France) to 0.106 (Netherlands).

Waterways

Geography and history have shaped waterway infrastructures in very different ways from one country to the next, in terms of both the length and the carrying capacity of the waterways; thus, France, which has the longest waterway network in Europe (6900 km in use in 1976) is in third position as regards waterways with a large carrying capacity of vessels (more than 1000 tons of carrying capacity) with 1800 km, behind Federal Republic of Germany (3100 km) and the Netherlands (2300 km)[7]. Certain countries such as Italy or the U.K. have almost no waterway infrastructure. Other countries such as the U.S.A., Sweden or Japan resort more especially to lakes or estuaries to ensure internal navigation; the consequent absence of any possible significant comparison and the fact that maritime and river traffic are not always distinguishable on the statistical level, prevent one from including these three countries

---

[6]   See Appendix 2, Table T.35.

[7]   See Appendix 2, Table T.36.

in the study of waterway transport. Thus, we shall restrict this analysis to the three countries mentioned at the beginning and to which we shall add Belgium.

The total waterway fleet (towed barges, self-propelled barges) show that the use of the waterway infrastructure may considerably vary from one country to the next[8]; the fleet of vessels per km of waterways, quite similar in France and Federal Republic of Germany, is three times lower than in Belgium and four times lower than in the Netherlands; with respect to the population, the ratio increases approximately from 1 to 15. Expressed in tons of transport capacity per km of waterways, the relationship between France, Belgium and the Netherlands remains the same, whereas Federal Republic of Germany moves up to an intermediary level (1000 tons per km, on average, in Federal Republic of Germany, as against 400 in France, and 1500 in Belgium and in the Netherlands).

The service ensured by the fleet is also liable to vary quite significantly probably partly due to the size of the country (especially for the Netherlands and Belgium), partly to the unit capacity of the vessels, and partly to the rate of use of these vessels. Thus, one may note that Federal Republic of Germany experiences a very high level of traffic per vessel (10 million ton-km per year); five times higher, on average, than in France, seven times higher than in the Netherlands and nine times higher than in Belgium[8]. The unit capacity of the German vessels, which is generally double that of the other countries, does indeed partly explain these differences, but principally it is the conditions of use of these vessels which explain these differences.

The specific fuel consumption (in diesel or fuel oil) of waterway vessels depends upon three factors: the type of vessel (self-propelled, towed or pushed barges); the unit capacity; the average rate of use (product of the percentage of loaded traffic by the average load factor). A study [59] reveals that in France,

Table 3.19. *Specific fuel consumption for waterway transport according to the type of vessels (France, 1978)* (MJ/ton-km)

Type of vessel	Average capacity (tons)	MJ/ton-km offered	MJ/ton-km (range)
Pushed barges (convoy)			
Seine river	1300	0.13	0.36 (0.29–0.40)
Rhine	2000	0.23	0.34 (0.32–0.50)
Barges			
on river	750	0.21	0.54 (0.47–0.59)
on canal	360	0.27	0.68 (0.58–0.92)

Note: Estimates obtained from a survey.
Source: [59].

---

[8] See Appendix 2, Table T.36.

in 1978, the specific consumption per ton-km offered, varied from 0.12 to 0.27 MJ per ton-km offered; on average, in terms of the net ton-km transported, they ranged from 0.27 to 0.68 MJ/ton-km. Table 3.19, drawn from this study, shows the combined influence of the three parameters identified above upon this specific consumption; these figures are easily applicable to all the countries studied.

According to the goods transported (agricultural products, heavy goods, manufactured products), the kind of vessel and the conditions of use change, leading to variations in the specific consumption. This may be deduced from an American study [31], which shows that in the U.S.A. the specific consumption of waterway transport varies from 0.11 to 0.23 MJ/ton-km according to whether primary products (agricultural, rubber) or manufactured goods (instruments, for example) are transported. Table 3.19 indicates the average specific consumption of waterway transport obtained either directly in the relevant literature or calculated on the basis of the total consumption of energy and traffic.

4. Long-Term Prospects

The above analysis has allowed for the identification of the main historical trends underlying the development of the energy demand of the transport sector; this also made it possible to emphasize the relation between the development of society in general and the development of the direct and indirect determining factors of this demand to be emphasized and to determine its degrees of freedom. Before attempting, on the basis of this analysis, to outline the long-term prospects, it is necessary to study the effects of the 1973/74 oil crisis upon the transport sector and attempt to distinguish the purely short-term from the more fundamental effects which may well account for breaks with past trends. In view of the short time lapse which at present (1980) separates us from this crisis and which is insufficient for any exhaustive analysis, the following remarks should be treated with caution.

4.1. Impacts of the 1973/74 Oil Crisis

The oil crisis and the subsequent economic crisis which has lasted until now, have affected the transport sector in two ways: firstly, by the significant increase of fuel prices[1]; secondly, by the slow growth of economic activity and thus of incomes between 1974 and 1980.

In concrete terms, this has resulted, with respect to both energy demand and traffic, in a rather sudden and general fall in 1974/75, after the 1973/74 peak, followed by a slow and regular recovery until 1978 (Fig. 3.17). It is almost impossible to distinguish the relative influence of the two above-mentioned phenomena (prices, economic activity) upon this development. However, it

---

[1]   See Appendix 2, Table T.37.

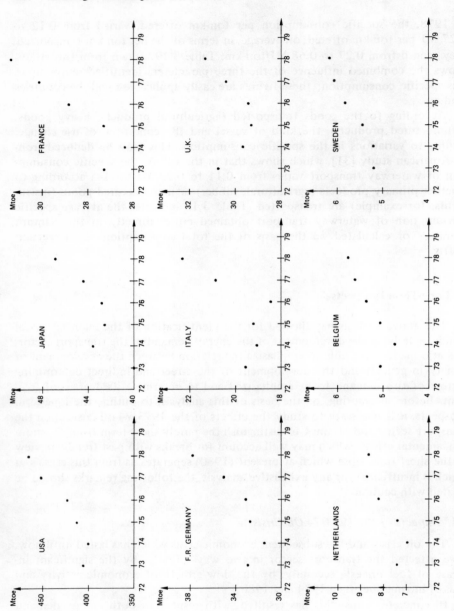

Fig. 3.17. Transport energy consumption 1972–1978

does seem that in the case of households (private passenger traffic), the price effect was all-important, judging from the respective impacts on the different modes (Fig. 3.18). The effect was absorbed in public transport which is relatively insensitive to the variations of energy prices. It was very substantial, however, in the case of the car which bore the brunt of the increases. In terms of goods transport, however, the economic recession has proved to be the dominant phenomenon since there were few noticeable variations in traffic per industrial production unit in 1974, in contrast to the dominant trend in the previous period (Table 3.15). In certain countries, the recession has even engendered an increase of traffic per industrial production unit (Italy, Belgium, Japan), thus revealing a certain inertia of freight traffic in relation to industrial activity (probably linked to the structure of this activity). The influence of economic growth, which is purely mechanical (the less one produces, the less one has to transport), does not indicate any real change in the relationship transport/growth. The price-effect, however, which is much more difficult to appreciate, may conceal alterations, even breaks, in the behavioural trends liable to bring about long-term alterations in the relationships of transport to the economy and to society. We shall thus, first of all, attempt to analyze further the observed price effect. Secondly, we shall look at the energy saving measures, adopted as a reaction against the rise in the price of imported energy, to see how these are liable to introduce long-term changes in the development of the transport sector, both on the economic and technical level.

The Price-Effect

Fuel prices may have several effects upon the transport sector; some of which may be immediate, others medium-term, and others more long-term.

In the short-term, any increase in the price of energy results in a rise of the cost of transport for the user. According to his financial limitations, to his relative preferences between different consumer goods and services, and to the constraints linked to his work and to his home, the user will react to this increase by more or less reducing his movements and eventually by resorting to a different mode of transport in the case of certain trips. This is indeed what we observe in 1975. Theoretically, if incomes increase faster than fuel prices, this effect should in time disappear; here again, the 1975–78 period, during which fuel prices in real terms fell, does confirm this theory. Therefore, nothing allows us at present to assert that what followed 1973/74 is something other than a short-term price effect, liable of course to recur under similar conditions[2]. This reality however could well conceal greater and more long-lasting behavioural changes.

On the one hand, the users' sudden realization of the total cost of the car may bring about, for some people, a long-lasting behavioural change mainly consisting in a change in their preference system. The week-end outing, for

---

[2]   The absence of detailed statistics for 1979 and 1980 does not yet allow us to appreciate the impact of the recent oil price increases implemented over the last two years.

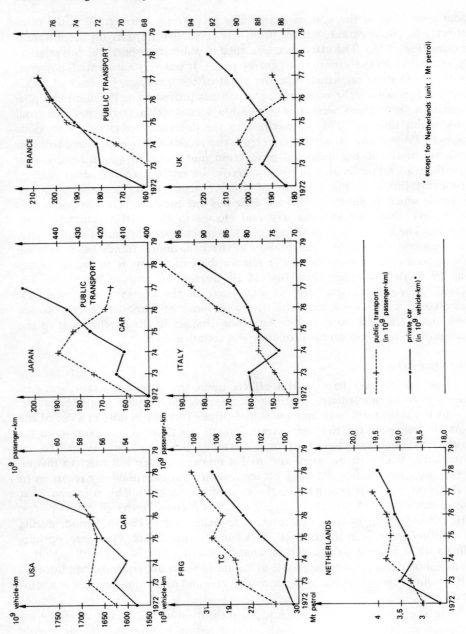

Fig. 3.18. Passenger traffic 1972–1978

instance, which is really a leisure among many others, may partly make way for other leisure activities. Similarly, the acknowledgement of the cost and constraints of the private car could lead some people to include these factors in the choice of the location of their main dwelling, etc.

On the other hand, resorting to public transport, even if at first this appears as a temporary measure, may engender a dynamic process which may be summarized in the following way: an increase in the use of public transport leads to an increase in its profitability and encourages its development, which, by means of an increase in frequency and a growth of the network, leads to an improvement of the service, rendering it necessarily more appealing, which, in turn, attracts more passengers, etc. The most important effect of such a process could be not so much the alteration of the modal distribution, but rather the fact that some people would lastingly give up multiple car ownership. The study of car sales over the last few years, even if it does show a decline, does not however suffice to confirm such an analysis, especially as the income effect did play a significant role in that case.

Once again, it is still too early to draw any reliable conclusions from these eventual behavioural changes, but they do obviously constitute very important factors of uncertainty for future prospects.

In the medium term, price increases will probably generate (or would have naturally generated, apart from energy conservation policies) a whole series of technical developments. This will operate both at the level of the transport vehicles themselves and of their management and will tend to reduce specific consumption per passenger-km or per ton-km transported. In the analysis of energy conservation policies, we shall indicate the most important developments to be expected in this field. These developments, especially important in the case of the less energy efficient modes, should progressively reduce, or even eliminate totally the short-term price effects.

In the longer term, in view of the more or less important changes (depending on the technical development of the different modes) in the conditions of competition among the modes, we should witness substitutions of one mode for another wherever such substitutions are possible. The appraisal of these substitutions should not present any difficulties for freight transport, at least not immediately; it is, however, much more difficult as regards passenger transport, since such a substitution could depend mainly on eventual long-lasting behavioural changes and especially on the development of public transport networks, which is a political variable. Their infrastructures in most countries are far from being saturated and even the available equipment may allow for significant progress in their rate and conditions of use; thus, from this point of view, no major general constraint upon substitutions seems to exist, even if in certain particular cases this constraint does truly exist (railways in general in Japan; certain particularly crowded rail routes in some countries; underground; . . .). But, as we shall show further on, other probably more important factors than the relative prices of transport modes will determine the long-term development of public transport.

Energy Conservation Policies

Some of the measures adopted in the 1973/74 period to fight against oil price increases were short-term, and others will have a long-term effect upon the energy demand of the transport sector, whatever happens.

Short-term measures mainly consist in incentives or regulations aiming at a better use — from the energy standpoint — of equipment:
— speed limitations (regulations or incentives) for all kinds of vehicles;
— incentives for more energy saving driving and vehicle management;
— incentives for more frequent controls of cars, etc.

The long-term regulations or incentives are usually of a technical kind: they all consist in achieving both a gradual reduction of the specific consumption of modes of transport and an improvement of their conditions of use. It could be tedious to give a complete list of all these measures, especially as they have been the object of numerous publications over the last few years[3]. However, it is on road transport, and especially on the private car, that the expected effects weigh most heavily. Given the importance of these modes in the energy demand of the transport sector, it is far from useless to spend a little time considering this point. The objectives of reduction of the specific consumption of private cars significantly vary from one country to the next, especially because of different initial levels (1974). In the U.S.A., for instance, the 1975 "Energy Policy and Conservation Act" stipulates a reduction from 18 mpg in 1978 (13 litres/100 km) to 27.5 mpg (8.6 litres/100 km) in the average specific consumption of cars brought into the market in 1985, in other words, a reduction of one-third in 7 years [62]! In France, the objective is also very ambitious in view of the initial levels: a 10% reduction from 1978/79 to 1985, and a 15% reduction over the whole period 1974/1985; these reductions should, according to the car manufacturers, continue after 1985 at an average rate of 10% every five years [65].

These very important reductions in the specific consumption of cars (the consumption of new cars produced in the year 2000 should average around 4 to 5 litres/100 km) should be achieved in two ways:
— a reduction in the weight of cars, by resorting to lighter materials (aluminum and plastic) and by reducing the size of the different models: thus, an average reduction in weight of 10 to 15% may be expected in the case of European vehicles [65]. It is probable that much more important reductions may be envisaged in the U.S.A., in view of the actual size and average weights of cars;
— significant engine improvements, aiming, in general, at regulating the richness of the air/petrol mixtures, the cylinder capacity and the compression rate according to the different engine uses.

4.2. Long-Term Prospects

The relationship between the development of society and that of the transport sector, will, in the long-term, be dominated by urban development and by the growth of the consumption of some intermediate goods.

---

[3] Most important references: [46, 65, 66, 75].

Urban Development and Passenger Transport

In industrialized countries where the great majority of the population lives in or around towns, the layout of the land — the distribution of towns, according to their size and economic activity — and urbanization plans will be the fundamental determinants of the development of both the passenger traffic and the different modes, and thus of the modal distribution of this traffic. In the long-term, the question that remains to be answered is not if and how the mobility needs and the behaviour of the population will change, but how and for what reasons the urban pattern will change. It is necessary to stress the fundamental importance of the relationship between the place of residence and the place of work in the urban configuration and its development. This is because the volume and structure of the economic activities determine the population of the cities and the geographical distribution of activities in these cities (especially evident between the primary sector, linked to the location of the resource, the secondary sector scattered around the cities and the tertiary sector located in the heart of the cities); and also because the location of housing in relation to working places will really shape the towns and determine both its geographic configuration and its density. The development prospects of the industrialized OECD countries suggest the following remarks.

The sectors of activity which are expected to develop the most over the next few decades are mainly industries with a high technological content (aeronautics, computers, etc.) and the services. In both cases, the location should in the main be independent of the location of natural resources and intermediate industries; in addition, none of these sectors necessarily require a high concentration of manpower. This economic development should not therefore, a priori, have any influence upon the land use. However, the search for economies of scale and a cutting-down on transport costs (upstream for the necessary intermediate goods, and/or downstream for the transport of products) may favour a spatial structuring similar to that experienced over the last three decades, in which case, the great urban and economic concentrations would predominate. In addition, the increase in the price of hydrocarbons and the fact that this price is to keep on increasing may encourage a trend to "shorten" distances, and bring about a substitution movement towards modes which consume less energy, such as rail or waterway transport. This, of course, only applies to products whose transport cost (upstream and downstream) is by no means negligible in relation to their price or value. The consequence may be a concentration of activities because of the need to be near the infrastructures. As can be seen, the geographical distribution of economic activities and the subsequent land use, are subjected to contradictory influences, only a small part of which we have tried to render explicit, in that it is linked to our energy problem. Here obviously lies the first great uncertainty and a first possible reason for a change in the historical energy demand of the transport sector in comparison with the past.

The development of town structures constitutes the second main question. The general trend which one may observe almost everywhere is that of an increasing separation in the towns between the place of residence and the place of work. This, linked to the significant development of the tertiary activities, has led to a sort of withdrawal from town centres in favour of the suburbs for the choice of places of residence, leaving the centre to be gradually taken over by the tertiary activities. The American business towns (Chicago, Los Angeles, etc.) are typical examples of such a development at its extreme: the spread of the private car and the freedom of mobility which it provides, has of course played a central role in this development. It remains to be seen:

— whether this development may occur everywhere, following the American example, or if obstacles of a geographical (available space), historical (age of towns) or human kind (behaviour of the city-dweller) may slow it down or even hinder it, in countries with different realities;

— whether a change in the conditions of use of the car (cost, traffic or parking difficulties) is liable to engender behavioural changes, expecially in terms of a more rational choice (in view of daily trips) of the place of residence;

— whether other, presently minor, phenomena, linked to the integration of housing within the economic and social environment, are not liable to develop a movement in opposition to that observed in the past (security problems, housing and land costs, greater integration within the urban environment), and how far they would be able to do so.

The answer to these questions, for several reasons, governs the prospects which it is possible to sketch concerning passenger transport. The first reason, simple and mechanical, depends upon the direct relationship between a town's density and the average length of trips within the town (the lower the density, the longer the trips). A second reason, with greater repercussions, originates in the circular relationship which exists between the urbanization layout, the development of public transport and multiple car ownership; in short, the spread of housing in the outskirts of towns encourages multiple car ownership, which as we have seen, results in a significant increase in car traffic and which hinders the development of public transport while, at the same time, reducing its efficiency (pursuit of the traditional "vicious circle"). The third reason, somewhat similar to the second, is that the preference given to public transport over the road network (either by means of special bus lanes or by independent underground or overground networks) and its development, if it alters behaviours and introduce some kind of "rationality" in the choice of housing places, may lead to a concentration of the dwellings and a slowing down of multiple car ownership, even a regression in certain cases (the above comparison between the U.S.A., France and the U.K. illustrates this point most clearly).

As may be ascertained from all the above considerations, the development of multiple car ownership on the one hand, of public transport networks on the other, are all-important in any long-term considerations.

The general opinion is that the purchase of the first car will remain everywhere an intangible and primordial factor and that car ownership will reach a saturation level by the end of the century, between 80 and 85% of households according to the countries. However, as we have seen, the spread of multiple car ownership is becoming gradually more uncertain. This issue is very important since any second car sold is, on average, used as much as first cars, thereby causing an increase in traffic corresponding to its own specific needs. Besides those factors which are liable to encourage multiple car ownership (urban organization and public transport infrastructure) there are other factors which may, in the future, play a most important role: the relative development of fuel prices and incomes, as well as decohabitation, or in other words the reduction in the size of households. The influence of the relative evolution of incomes and fuel prices upon multiple car ownership, mentioned above in relation to the crisis, will of course differ according to the development of car technology and the specific fuel consumption of cars. A rise in incomes which is faster than that of the operational costs of the car will obviously favour multiple car ownership, whereas the contrary may not necessarily be true: part of multiple car owner-ship is indeed determined by housing constraints and because of this should in the main be insensitive to price changes.

The other major problem which is central to long-term prospects of pas-senger transport is that of the development of the public transport network. At the urban level, we can only recall the differences, sometimes quite im-portant, which exist in the mobility ensured by public transport, among coun-tries with similar development levels and urban structures: there are thus signifi-cant expansion possibilities, but which will remain subordinated to national and local political motivations, expressed in investment terms (infrastructures, transport vehicles) and subsidies. The links we mentioned between multiple car ownership and the development of urban public transport reveal the issue of such a policy. With respect to intercity transport, the substitution possibili-ties between modes mainly exist with private trips other than week-end outings. The comparison between rail traffic in Japan and in other industrialized coun-tries has raised fundamental questions concerning this problem. It seems as if the possibilities of increasing passenger rail traffic are relatively important, although not necessarily on the principal routes. Because of this, it is not im-possible that certain substitutions occur in favour of rail traffic, or air traffic, especially with the prospects of reduction of household sizes. But these sub-stitutions should be attributed to a search for comfort and security rather than to a change in the conditions of competition among modes; besides, the prospects of a reduction in the specific consumption of cars will lessen this change. In this respect, any coherent policy aiming to develop the railroad service, both in quality and in quantity, while maintaining significant price differences with the car, should easily bring about such substitutions. As regards air transport, long-term forecasts are generally high, for both internal and international traffic; the growth of professional exchanges and the decrease in the cost (in real terms) of aerial transport encourage such an optimistic outlook. However, the spread of high speed trains will probably increase the distance limit from which planes can compete with trains and on certain routes may encroach upon the aerial traffic market or at least slow its development.

The development of teleconference and telecommunications should logically slow the development of certain kinds of professional traffic. However, it re-mains to be seen whether this primary effect will not be offset by a faster in-crease of communication needs which would be the direct result of the develop-ment of telecommunications.

Industrial Structure and Freight Transport

We shall only briefly consider the future prospects of freight transport. Industrial growth will be characterized, as we shall see in the next chapter, by a slow growth rate of the main intermediate industries which are traffic generators (mainly ferrous and non-ferrous metals, ans basic chemical industries). In addition, the construction sector is not expected to have any notable increase which means a slow growth of building materials production and transport. One may thus quite safely expect a continuation of the historical trends concerning the relationship between goods traffic and industrial production, and at best, a slow increase of this traffic.

With respect to its modal structure, the following observations may be made:
— the low activity level of intermediate industries and their location near the production or import centres of primary resources should contribute to altering the structure of goods traffic at the expense of rail and waterway transport;
— if the phenomenon of industrial concentration around these intermediate industries continues, it should reinforce the preceding phenomenon; however the American example, where the respective roles of railway and waterway transport has apparently been stabilized for several years, would seem to suggest that a limit is very quickly reached on this level; a limit which most industralized countries are at present approaching;
— on the other hand, the possible substitution among modes which may be brought about by changes in the relative fuel prices are quite uncertain. A detailed analysis of traffic, per good and per length of trip, could indeed allow one to situate the actual substitution possibilities; but no doubt these possibilities will be greatly modified by the technical innovations taking place especially in railway transport (containers, fast door-to-door service, etc.).

IV. Energy Demand in the Industrial Sector

1. Historical Survey

1.1. Overall Energy Use: 1950–1977

The study of energy consumption in the industrial sector from 1950 to 1977 allows one to isolate three groups of countries. Those with a rapid consumption growth, Japan, Italy and the Netherlands, where industrial energy consumption has respectively undergone a ten-fold, seven-fold and six-fold increase; then the U.S.A., France, Belgium, Federal Republic of Germany, and Sweden, with a rather similar growth rate but much slower than that of the three leading countries (a 2.5 increase approximately); finally the U.K., with a very slow development (of approximately 1%).

In the fifties, Japan and Italy's level of per capita energy consumption in the industrial sector was much lower than that of other countries; this may be attributed to their low level of development (Table 4.1); at the other extreme we find Belgium, the U.K. and the U.S.A. The early seventies were marked by the convergence of the consumption levels of Japan, France, Federal Republic of Germany, the Netherlands and the U.K. (between 40 and 50 GJ/capita). Since 1960, per capita consumption in the U.S.A. has grown rather slowly so that Sweden and Belgium have caught up with them; at the beginning of the seventies, these two countries had a per capita consumption reaching 70 GJ/per capita, significantly higher than that of other European countries.

The different growth rates of industrial production and the relative levels of production in the various countries obviously furnish the more immediate explanations for these developments and the differences in industrial energy consumption. Thus by reducing the consumption per inhabitant to a same level of industrial value added for 1974[1], one may notice a clear tightening of the situations, although significant difference do remain (Table 4.1): Belgium, Japan and the Netherlands catch up with the U.S.A. and Sweden; Federal Republic of Germany and France, however, remain in the background.

The historical development of energy consumption per production unit well illustrates the link between this consumption and industrial production (Table 4.2); but it also reveals a very great diversity within this relationship.

---

[1] 1974 is a good reference year since it is the last significant year before the disturbing effects brought about by the increase in oil prices and the economic recession.

Table 4.1. *Per capita energy consumption in industry* (GJ/capita)

	1950	1955	1960	1965	1970	1974*	1975	1977	1978	1979
U.S.A.			63	71	82	78/78	70	74	81	84
Japan	7	10	16	23	43	46/51	46	51	51	53
France	19	23	27	32	41	39/45	38	40	41	47
F.R. Germany	23	34	37	40	47	52/56	47	48	49	52
Italy	6	9	14	21	30	33/39	35	35	34	35
U.K.	40	44	43	45	47	45/45	40	42	42	43
Belgium	30	38	39	45	61	69/77	62	66	68	69
Netherlands	14	15	21	26	38	47/65	55	63	73	82
Sweden			48	55	69	72/79	78	68	69	71

* The first figure excludes non energy uses of oil in the chemical industry; they are included
in the second figure and for the years 1975 to 1979.

Source: Appendix 3, Table I.1.

In fact, the important differences among countries and the changes in trends
in certain countries even suggest the absence of any systematic relationship
between industrial growth and the development of energy consumption.

In four countries, the U.S.A., Japan, Federal Republic of Germany, and
the U.K., consumption increased at a slower rate, over the whole of the period
under study, than did industrial production. The growth differential was particularly important in Japan and Germany; from 1950 to 1960, Japanese industrial production increased about twice as fast as its energy consumption;
in the period stretching from 1955 to 1970, energy consumption in Japan and
Germany underwent an increase which was, on average, 1.5 times slower than
the industrial production. In France, in the Netherlands, in Belgium and in
Sweden, however, one may notice a fairly close relationship between energy
consumption and the volume of industrial production. In the Netherlands,

Table 4.2. *Energy consumption per production unit in industry* (in indices, base 100 in 1970)

	1950	1955	1960	1965	1970	1974*	1975	1977	1978
U.S.A.			112	101	100	83/83	82	75	79
Japan	222	156	122	104	100	93/102	103	102	97
France		110	100	100	100	81/92	84	81	83
Italy	88	88	88	100	100	94/111	112	101	99
F.R. Germany	175	154	121	111	100	103/112	99	89	91
U.K.	131	127	115	104	100	92/92	86	85	82
Netherlands	104	84	96	97	100	103/142	129	138	159
Belgium	100	105	100	90	100	96/106	95	94	95
Sweden			116	97	100	91/100	100	90	95

* See Table 4.1.

Source: Appendix 3, Tables I.2, I.3.

this relationship recently changed and from 1974 to 1977 energy consumption grew much faster, whereas the same period in France was characterized by the inverse phenomenon. In Italy one may note two periods — 1950 to 1960 and 1965 to 1977 — during which time energy consumption and the volume of production in the industrial sector grew at exactly the same rate; a change occurred however between 1960 and 1965 when consumption increased much more rapidly.

This diversity in the relationship between industrial production and energy consumption is due to two principal factors: the structure of industry, especially the importance of industries with a high energy consumption per production unit ("energy intensive industries") and technology, whether on the level of production processes, or on that of the installations using energy.

Firstly we shall define, quantitatively — on the basis of historical analysis — as well as qualitatively, the role of these two factors and try to bring out future prospects; then we shall consider in detail two energy intensive industries (steel and cement) which play a determining role in overall industrial energy consumption. This monographic analysis will look both to the past and to the future; it will consider the growth of these industries (development of their market, and production) and their energy needs (development of the specific energy consumption per process).

The analysis scheme is the same as that of the other sectors (Fig. 4.1). Every industry transforms a raw material or an intermediate product into a product delivered to other industries or to the final consumers; one way or another, these transformations require energy (useful energy) in a thermal, mechanical, chemical or electrical form, which is obtained from the use of final energy products (fuel oil, electricity, gas, . . .) by means of appropriate installations (boiler, furnace, engine, . . .). Needless to say, the useful energy required is proportional to the quantities to be transformed (that is to say to the level of production), but it is also dependent on the production processes used (the amount of heat needed to manufacture a ton of steel is necessarily different if the raw material is scrap iron or iron ore). The consumption of the final energy product is proportional to the useful energy needs and depends upon the efficiency of the installations, which in itself is partly linked to the production technology.

Fig. 4.1. illustrates the relationship, analyzed above, between energy consumption and industrial production. The useful energy needs per unit produced vary quite significantly according to the different industrial sectors (steel, textiles, building materials for example). Thus can we easily understand how, as regards the whole of industrial sector, the energy required is partly determined by the structure of industrial activities, in other words by the relative importance of these different activities ("structural effect"). On the whole, technology plays a double role: on the one hand it is involved in the determination of useful energy needs, through the relative importance of the various production processes; on the other hand it influences the final demand through the energy efficiency of industrial thermal and mechanical installations (boilers, furnaces, engines, . . .).

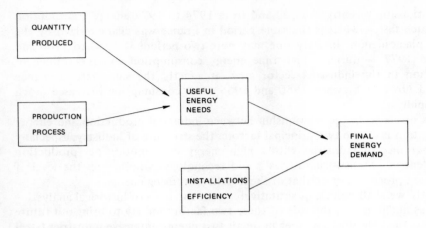

Fig. 4.1. Energy demand determinants in industry

Before defining the role of these main structural and technological determinants in the historical development of energy consumption, we shall undertake a brief analysis of the major energy uses in industry.

1.2. Energy Uses in the Industrial Sector

The energy used in industry is required, on the one hand, in production processes and, on the other hand, for various general purposes in industrial plants (heating, lighting). Within the industrial uses of energy, one usually distinguishes the thermal uses corresponding to (useful) heating needs, the mechanical uses and the specific electricity uses. In addition, thermal uses may be broken down according to required temperature levels, or, which is more or less the same, according to the main installations (kilns, boilers, dryers, etc.)[1].

Approximately three quarters of the process energy correspond to thermal uses, the rest being mainly used to provide mechanical energy (Table 4.3). Most of this mechanical energy is obtained from electricity, from 70 to 75% depending on the countries. The study of the distribution of thermal uses according to temperature levels (Table 4.4) indicates significant differences between, on the one hand, France and the U.K. where low temperature uses account for approximately 20% of the total and Italy and Germany, on the other hand, where these same uses do not exceed 10%. These differences may come from different factors, the respective role of which is difficult to estimate: unreliability of the estimates which seem more exhaustive in the case of France,

---

[1]   We shall illustrate this section with the example of four countries France [1, 15, 16], the U.K. [10, 11, 14], Italy [12], and Germany [13]; electricity will be measured everywhere according to its calorific value.

Table 4.3. *Distribution of energy uses in industry*

	U.K. (1976)		F.R. Germany (1973)	Italy (1975)	France (1978)
	all industries	steel excluded			
Production processes	83%	77%			81%
Thermal uses	85%	80%		85%	85%
(Low temperature: < 120°C)	(22%)	(36%)	(7%)	(9%)**	(21%)
(Middle temperature: 120–250°C)	(24%)*	(28%)*	(13%)***	(16%)	(39%)
(High temperature: > 400°C)	(54%)	(36%)	(80%)	(75%)	(40%)
Mechanical uses (of which	15%	20%		15%	15%
electricity)	(75%)	(75%)			(70%)
Heating, lighting, . . .	17%	23%			19%
(All low tempera- ture uses)	(31%)	(43%)			(24%)
References	[11]		[13]	[12]	[1]

* Includes some uses under 120°C.
** Including space heating.
*** < 200°C.

where there has been a follow-up since 1961[2], and of the U.K.; differences in temperature thresholds; and different share of the chemical and steel industries (the determining influence of the steel industry, for instance, is well illustrated in the case of the U.K.).

The high temperature energy uses correspond to direct energy uses in the kilns and to a lesser extent in other installations (for example drying ovens). Medium and low temperature uses almost only concern steam uses. In addition one may note that in some industries, steam is used to meet low temperature energy needs (steam excesses, simplification of energy networks, . . .), so that some low temperature uses may, erroneously, have been classified in the medium temperature category. Thus three kinds of installations account for most of the energy used in the industrial sector; boilers, kilns and electric engines; therefore the analysis will mainly concentrate on these installations.

The distribution of thermal uses per temperature level greatly varies from one group of industries to another. Thus textile, food, chemical, pulp and paper industries are characterized by significant low temperature energy needs as shown in Table 4.4, mainly met by steam. In spite of the differences and un-

---

[2] The French estimates, done by the CEREN, are obtained by surveys of the major industrial firms.

Table 4.4. *Low temperature thermal energy needs in some industries according to temperature level* (% of all thermal energy needs)

			U.K.		France		Italy
Food industries	Heating	< 100°C	14 49* } 63		5 56 } 61		} 70
	Process	100–150°C	} 33**		23		} 30+
	Heat	150–200°C			16+++		
		> 200°C	4		–		
Chemical industries	Heating	< 100°C	11 44* } 55		5 5 } 10		3
	Process	100–150°C	} 33**		29		} 40+
	Heat	150–200°C			38+++		
		> 200°C	11		27++		57
Textile industries	Heating	< 100°C	34 31* } 65		19 53 } 72		} 40
	Process	100–150°C	} 34**		26		} 60+++
	Heat	150–200°C			} 2		
		> 200°C	1				
Paper industries	Heating Process	< 100°C	13 29* } 42		5 3 } 8		–
	Heat	100–150°C	} 58**		60		} 100+
		150–200°C			32+++		
References			[14]		[15]		[12]

* < 120°C, ** 120–200°C.
+ 100–250°C, ++ 250°C, +++ 150–250°C.

certainties associated to the estimates given in this table, one may set out the following characteristics[3] :
– in the textile industry, most of the thermal needs (60–70%) are below 100–120°C, and there is almost no need for temperatures higher than

---

[3] The figures given in this paragraph aim at giving an approximative order of magnitude, from the basis of the various afore mentioned studies.

150–200°C; 85% of the heat in the U.K. and 95% in France is obtained from steam;
– in the food industry, 60% of the uses are below 100–120°C and almost all the energy is required at less than 200°C; approximately 80% of thermal needs are met by steam (France 79%; U.K. 85%);
– in the paper industry, the majority of uses occur within a bracket of 120–150°C, and there is no energy need over 250°C; steam is the only energy form and accounts for 100% of these needs;
– in the chemical industry, great differences exist among the countries; these may probably be explained by differences in the nature of the chemical products manufactured, since the required temperature levels vary enormously between the basic chemical industry (petrochemicals for example), in which high temperature uses are dominant, and the other chemical productions. According to an ENI study [12], 67% of the thermal energy needs of the basic chemical industry require more than 200°C and the rest between 100–200°C; in the remaining part of the chemical industry high temperatures are almost negligible, and approximately 80% of thermal needs vary between 100–250°C and the rest requires less than 100°C; 68% of thermal energy is provided by steam in the U.K. as against 80% in France.

In the other intermediate goods industries, high temperature uses prevail (essentially in kilns) (construction materials, glass, steel, non ferrous metals). Engineering industries are characterized by large space heating requirements (30% in Italy, 39% in france, and 50% in the U.K.),the other uses being mainly related to thermal treatment kilns (20% in the U.K., 53% in France, 70% in Italy); the a priori surprising differences between countries may be explained by the heterogeneity of these industries and the relative share of their various subsectors which encompass the primary stages of metal processing (casting production), the manufacture of equipment goods (motorcar and electrical industries, for instance), and the electronics. Similarly, different sectoral definitions may also explain certain differences in the energy uses of these industries.

1.3. Energy Consumption and Structural Changes

Depending upon the country, from 60 to 80% of the industrial energy consumption may be attributed to industries producing intermediate goods (production of metals, chemicals, building materials, paper and pulp). These industries consume, on average, two or three times more energy per unit of value added[4] than the other industries (such as textile or food industries or the production of electrical household or industrial appliances). Therefore, any change in the contribution of these intermediate goods industries to the overall industrial value added will affect the average energy consumption per unit of value added, and thus the relationship between industrial growth and the in-

---

[4] We shall use value added as an indication of industrial production; industrial growth being measured by the increase of the volume of value added (at constant prices).

crease of the sector's energy consumption[5]. For instance, a reduction of the share of the steel industry, balanced by a development of light industries, such as the computer or electronics industries, will result in a reduction of the energy consumption per unit of industrial value added. Therefore, a slower growth rate of the value added of intermediate goods industries than that of the overall value added of industry leads to a reduction in the elasticity of the energy consumption in relation to the industrial value added and inversely.

In an attempt to understand the influence of this "structural effect" in the past, we have examined, in the countries under study, the development of the share of intermediate industries in the industrial value added. Unfortunately the statistics available did not allow us to go further back than 1960 (and in some cases 1965). It emerges from all these statistics, that in the period from 1960 to 1974, the share of intermediate industries, on the whole, remained quite even, with the exception of the Netherlands; this would tend to indicate that the structural effect, at least at such an aggregate level, has been of little influence since 1960. In the Netherlands, intermediate industries developed most rapidly from 1965 to 1974, due to a massive development of the chemical industry (which in terms of the share in the industrial value added went from 16% in 1965 to 29% in 1974); this explains why, in this country, industrial energy consumption has increased much faster than industrial production over the last ten years.

Another phenomenon, similar to the structural effect, may also come into play: the "product effect". We shall refer to a product effect when a change in the energy consumption of a sector per unit of value added is brought about by a change in the distribution among products with different energy intensities[6]. This effect may presently be seen in chemical industries where there is a movement away from the production of basic chemical products, which are heavy energy consumers and have low value added (ethylene, benzene, . . .), towards more elaborate products (plastics, pharmaceutical products, cosmetics, . . .) requiring little energy and with a high value added. Similarly in engineering industries there is a move away from the transformation of metals and smelting towards products with a high value added and a low energy intensity (electronics, computers, . . .). These two examples concern a product effect resulting in a reduction of the energy consumption per unit of value added. The case of food industries over the last few years illustrates an inverse situation since there was a trend towards the development of more elaborate products, which in this case implies products with a higher energy intensity (deep frozen foods, ready to cook meals, . . .).

Unfortunately, the available statistical data do not allow for the quantitative evaluation, in the countries under study, of the role of the structural and prod-

---

[5] The relationship industrial growth/increase of energy consumption may be expressed by means of an elasticity coefficient; we should then speak of the elasticity of energy consumption to the industrial value added.

[6] By "energy intensity" is meant the amount of energy required per unit of value added.

Table 4.5. Distribution of per capita energy consumption according to industrial sectors in 1974 and 1977 (GJ/capita)

	1974					1977				
	Total	(Steel)	(Chemicals)	(Petrochemicals)	(Others)	Total	(Steel)	(Chemicals)	(Petrochemicals)	(Others)
U.S.A.	78.3	(11.6)	(1.7)	(9.6)	(55.4)	74	(11.8)	(3.9)	(10.8)	(47.5)
Japan	51.1	(19.3)	(4.9)	(8.6)	(18.3)	51	(15)	(5.9)	(8.3)	(21.8)
France	44.9	(12)	(7.1)	(4.3)	(21.5)	40	(9.3)	(7.3)	(4)	(19.4)
F.R.Germany	56.4	(19)	(10.5)	(5.6)	(21.3)	48	(13.4)	(7.9)	(5.7)	(21)
Italy	38.9	(7)	(5.7)	(9.8)	(16.4)	35	(6.1)	(5.1)	(8.5)	(15.3)
Belgium	76.7	(31.7)	(12.6)	(7.5)	(24.9)	66	(21.6)	(13.3)	(5.1)	(26.0)
Netherlands	64.8	(8.9)	(18.7)	(19.6)	(17.6)	63	(7.9)	(18.3)	(18.9)	(17.9)
U.K.	45	(8.9)	(6.6)	(5.2)	(24.3)	42	(7.9)	(7)	(4.7)	(22.4)
Sweden	78.6	(12.8)	(6.3)	(5.6)	(53.9)*	68	(10.6)	(4.7)	(4.0)	(48.7)

* Out of which 20 GJ/capita in 1972 for the pulp and paper industry (against 8 in the U.S.A. and less than 2 in Japan and Italy) [8].

Note: Non energy uses of gas and oil in the chemical industry are included in this consumption; thus the total consumption differs from the values given in Table 4.1 for 1974.

uct effects in the historical development of the relationship between energy consumption and industrial production (absence of long series both for the values added and for the energy consumption on a sufficiently detailed level). In France, a study undertaken by the CEREN indicates that from 1966 to 1977, the structural effect led to a 6% reduction of the fuel consumption but to a 2.8% increase of electricity consumption.

However, it is possible to quantitatively assess this structural effect for a given years − 1974 or 1977[7] for instance − by restricting (for statistical reasons) the energy intensive sectors to three sectors only: the steel, chemical and petrochemical industries. In 1974, these three industries represented 60 to 70% of the industrial consumption in Japan, Federal Republic of Germany, Italy, Belgium and the Netherlands; approximately 50% in France and the U.K. and approximately 30% in the U.S.A. and Sweden. By examining the distribution of industrial energy consumption according to the steel industry, the chemical and the petrochemical industry and the rest of industry (Table 4.5), one notices first of all that the consumption per inhabitant for industries other than the three mentioned above are very similar for Japan and all European countries, with the exception of Sweden (between 16 and 26 GJ/capita). The aforementioned over-consumption in Belgium is explained, almost entirely, by the importance of steel production in this country; with a per capita production in 1974 more than 1500 kg of steel, Belgium is well ahead of other countries (less than 1000 kg in Japan and 900 kg in Germany). One may also note the importance of the chemical and petro-chemical industries in the per capita consumption of the Netherlands. The very high level in the U.S.A. and Sweden, however, does not come from any exaggerated importance of the chemical and petro-chemical industries in industrial energy consumption; in this respect, we may note that the U.S.A. and Sweden have a fairly similar consumption structure (the chemical, petrochemical and steel industries have the same relative weight).

The special situation of the U.S.A. and Sweden may partly be explained by higher levels of industrial activity per inhabitant. In order to be rid of this effect, it is necessary to express the energy consumption per inhabitant in terms of a same level of industrial value added. Two ratios have been worked out (Table 4.6): the first takes into account the whole of the industrial sector, whereas the second excludes the steel, chemical and petro-chemical industries in order to identify the structural effect of the energy intensive industries. Three groups of countries stand out. In the lead, once again, we find the U.S.A. and Sweden, followed by all the other countries, grouped relatively close together, with the exception of Federal Republic of Germany characterized by a smaller consumption. As for Sweden, part of the over-consumption may be attributed to the importance of the paper industry, since the latter accounts

---

[7] Contrary to the method used up till now to measure energy consumption, the non-energy uses of oil and gas in the chemical industry are included in the 1974 and 1977 data. In the Netherlands, this consumption represents approximately 35% of the total as against approximately 15% for the other European countries.

Table 4.6. *Per capita industrial energy consumption expressed in terms of a same level of industrial activity** (1974)

	Industry as a whole	Industry without the steel, chemical and petrochemical industries
U.S.A.	78	55 (47)**
Japan	78	32 (26)**
France	57	35
F.R. Germany	51	23
Italy	69	34
U.K.	73	40
Belgium	84	30
Netherlands	76	31
Sweden	88	63 (43)**

* The indicator of industrial activity used is the value added in constant price (expressed in dollar 1970 on the basis of 1970 exchange rates); the energy consumption is divided by an index of industrial activity, taking the U.S.A. as a reference (index = 100 for the U.S.A.).

** The figures between brackets exclude the paper industry.

for approximately 30% of industrial consumption (as against 8% in the U.S.A., 5% in Japan, Italy and Federal Republic of Germany). Thus, by excluding the paper industry from the consumption per capita and per unit of value added, one may notice a likening of the situations in Sweden and in other countries (represented by Japan), the U.S.A. remaining by far in the lead.

Having eliminated the influence of the structural effects, at least as regards the energy intensive sectors, what are the origins of the remaining differences between the U.S.A., Sweden and Germany, and the other countries.

As will be shown by the analysis of the steel and cement industries, most of the energy over-consumption in the U.S.A. may be attributed to technological differences; in fact this aspect has given use to numerous studies[8]. These differences have, it would seem, two principal causes: on the one hand energy prices which, historically, have been much lower in the U.S.A. than in Europe and in Japan (on average 2 to 3 times lower[9]), on the other hand an outdated production apparatus, with an inferior performance capacity (lesser penetration of new processes or of modern equipment).

As for Sweden, the influence of the climate on the energy consumption is quite certain, but is obviously difficult to evaluate. As regards the heating of industrial premises, one may, all things being equal, assess the needs as being

---

[8] We have in mind the studies of Darmstadter [4] (comparison between the U.S.A., Europe and Japan), Schipper [5] (comparison between Sweden and the U.S.A.), Brookhaven [6] (comparison U.S.A./Japan) and of the Stanford Research Institute [7] (comparison Federal Republic of Germany/U.S.A.).

[9] For both electricity and fuels (obviously by comparing the dominant fuels, gas in the U.S.A., fuel oil in Europe and Japan).

approximately 1.5 times higher than in other countries[10], which means that heating plays a much greater role in overall energy consumption than anywhere else; in the metal processing industries and the industries manufacturing machinery and equipment, heating represents in Sweden 60 to 70% of the consumption, as against 30 to 40% in France and the U.K.; for steel and non-ferrous metals, this proportion is approximately 20 to 30% as against less than 5% in the other countries. The climate may also have an influence as regards the other thermal uses (kilns, boilers) if the installations are not better insulated than in the other countries.

Germany's overall energy intensity does not strike us as being due to a better use of energy; at least, no such indication was given by the detailed studies of the technologies used in this country. In our opinion, the explanation lies in the existence of a higher proportion of highly sophisticated industries with a substantial value added and a small energy input; thus electrical and electronic industries which belong to this category represented in 1974, in Germany, 12% of the industrial value added, as against 8% in France and 6% in Italy. It could thus be due to a structural effect, which could only be made clearer by a more detailed analysis of the energy consumption per industrial product, which goes well beyond the framework of this study.

We shall now look more closely at the role of technology in the development of industrial energy consumption.

1.4. Technical Trends and Energy Consumption

Technical trends in the industrial sector influences energy consumption in two different ways. On the one hand, the specific energy consumption may be improved through the growth of the size of the installations, the concentration of production units, the substitution of one form of energy for another (especially the shift from coal to hydrocarbons), the substitution between processes in energy intensive industries and the progress in the use of energy in these processes; on the other hand the specific electricity consumption may increase through the development of mechanization and of automatization.

Moreover, low oil prices probably encouraged, until 1973, the development of energy intensive techniques and of low efficiency (in terms of energy) installations, especially in light industries where energy expenditure represents a negligeable part of overall production costs. However, although the oil crisis did reveal how much energy was being "wasted" and the poor energy optimization of industrial processes and installations, it is nevertheless difficult to ascertain if there was, in the past, beyond the phenomena mentioned, a progress or a deterioration in the specific energy consumption of light industries (in other words an increase or decrease of "waste")[1].

---

[10] Estimate based on degree-days (3700 for Sweden as against approximately 2500 for the other countries).

[1] We know for example that in France, the theoretical efficiency (at full capacity) of boilers and industrial ovens have improved, greatly due to the norms required for new installations. But we still don't know how the real efficiencies have improved; these depend upon their use, their maintenance, . . .

Statistically, it is difficult to estimate the impact of the different influences mentioned above, upon the development of specific energy consumption, outside the structural and product effect. On the whole, it seems that technical changes have, in most countries, led to a reduction of specific fuel consumption and to an increase of specific electricity consumption principally due to mechanization. The CEREN study [2] of French industry estimates that technical progress may explain a 12.6% reduction of the specific consumption of fuel from 1966 to 1977 and a 7.6% increase of specific electricity consumption; if all energy forms are considered together, the decrease in the specific consumption was 6.3%. It is appropriate to note that from 1973 to 1977 following the oil crisis this decrease slowed down somewhat in comparison with the 1966—73 period. Unable to quantify separately each of these influences, we shall, nevertheless, consider their major features.

Effect of Size and Concentration

In the past, the search for economies of scale in the new production units resulted in a continual increase of the average size of installations. This phenomenon certainly engendered a reduction in the specific energy consumption, but to an extent which is difficult to estimate. Indeed, any increase in the size whether it be for the motors or for thermal installations, results in the improvement (however slight) of the energy efficiency; in the case of ovens or boilers this improvement essentially comes from the reduction of radiation losses (reduction of the ratio volume to be heated). A typical example of this is the Japanese steel industry which obtains extraordinary energy efficiency in its blast-furnaces, partly due to the gigantic size of its installations.

The 1960's and 1970's were characterized, for these very same reasons of scale economy, by a marked concentration of industrial complexes and the development of what we may call integrated plants; integrated plants of pulp and paper, chemical and petrochemical complexes, integrated steel factories, . . . This concentration has often given use to energy savings due to a better production organization: on site rolling of liquid steel; transformation of liquid pulps into paper, thus saving on the drying, . . .

Substitutions Between Energy Forms

Coal having a lower efficiency than hydrocarbons, the substitution coal/hydrocarbons which occurred over the last twenty years has thus led to a reduction of energy intensities; in other words the energy consumption of the industrial sector has grown at a slower pace than if coal had remained the dominant source of energy. The decline in the use of coal, since 1960, has been most noticeable in all those countries which, at this particular time, depended on this source of energy: Japan, France, Federal Republic of Germany, the U.K., and Belgium. From a proportion of 60 to 77%, according to the countries, the use of coal in industry fell to an actual 30%[2]. In the 1950's, the U.S.A., the

---

[2] See Appendix 3.

Netherlands and Italy had already greatly replaced coal by natural gas, so that the energy supply of industry in 1960 was much less dependant upon coal than in other countries (27%, 21% and 44% for the U.S.A., Italy and the Netherlands respectively); since then, the use of coal in those three countries has fallen to below 15%. The share of electricity in the industrial energy supply has shown a slight increase, except for Italy (where it has remained stable at 15—16%) and Japan (around 19—20%). Belgium stands out with coal still playing an important role (38% in 1974) and a lesser use of electricity (12% as against 14 to 20% for the other countries in 1974).

Due to the difficulty of correctly measuring the energy efficiency of industrial installations, it is no easy matter to quantitatively ascertain the role of substitutions in the development of energy intensities in industry[3]. Their effect varies in each country and the greater the substitution coal/hydrocarbons the more important this effect is; thus in the 1960's the effect in the U.S.A. and Italy was slight; moderate in Belgium and more important in all the other countries (lowering of 30 points of the coal share in the energy balance sheet from 1960 to 1970). From a study by the IEJE[4] for France, it appears that the average end-use efficiency of fuels (useful energy/final energy ratio) increases from 58% in 1961 to 66% in 1971, which means that the substitution coal/hydrocarbons brought about an 8% reduction of specific fuel consumption from 1961 to 1971; in other words, final energy consumption increased at a slower rate than useful energy over this period.

Substitution Between Processes in the Energy Intensive Industries

The substitutions between production processes may engender significant changes of the specific energy consumption in energy intensive industries, if the energy needs per process are very different. These substitutions may also greatly affect the whole of industry's energy consumption, because of the importance of these industries in this consumption. This effect, obviously, is only significant over a rather long period of time, because of the delays necessary for the new processes to capture an important share of the market. The rate of penetration of the new processes largely depends upon the development rate of new production capacities; it is thus linked to the industrial growth, and to the capacity utilization rates. In addition, it is often linked to the size of the industrial sector. In small countries, such as Belgium or the Netherlands, for example, the distribution of production among processes may rapidly and erratically change with the opening or closure of a factory. As an example of

---

[3] Without attempting to give accurate figures, one may nevertheless make one or two remarks. In the case of use in boilers, the efficiency of coal is only slightly less than that of hydrocarbons (approximately 5 points lower); for direct uses such as ovens, coal has a definitely lower efficiency than hydrocarbons — approximately 20 points in relation to oil and 25—30 points in relation to gas.

[4] The study considered the period 1961—71 and excluded from the industrial sector, steel, construction and energy industries.

process substitution one may mention the transition from the wet to the dry process in the cement industry and the substitution of the oxygen process for the other processes (open-hearth, mainly) in steel making, or the substitution of oil for coal in the chemical sector. In the second part of this chapter, we shall come back on some of these substitutions and emphasize the differences among countries.

Energy Efficiency Improvements in Processes

The improvement of energy efficiency and the reduction of energy losses has always been a major preoccupation of industrialists in certain energy intensive industries (steel, cement, aluminum, for example). Indeed, energy costs in these industries represented, even before the oil crisis, a significant proportion of production costs[5] and for the companies in these sectors the reduction of energy losses plays an imported role in their competitiveness. Thus in the aluminum industry, the electricity consumption of electrolysis has regularly decreased in such a way that, in France, it has gone from 30 kWh/kg in 1940 to an actual 14 kWh/kg and in the U.S.A. from 26.5 kWh to 17.5 kWh/kg for the same period. The other characteristic example is that of blast furnaces where the coke rate − specific consumption of coke per ton of pig-iron − has also regularly decreased, going in Japan, the leading country in this field, from 716 kg/t in 1955 to 479 kg/t in 1977, and in France from 1019 kg/t to 585 kg/t over the same period.

Development of Mechanization

The substitution energy/labour has given rise to numerous econometric studies. Nevertheless none of these studies allow for a satisfactory identification of the influence of mechanization on the development of the consumption of energy and electricity. Statistically, one may notice for most of the countries a quite clear increase of the specific consumption of electricity in mechanical industries without the possibility of dissociating the mechanization effect from the influence of other factors (improvement of working conditions, reduction of pollution, . . .). Thus the specific consumption of electricity per unit of value added in these industries has grown by 36% in the U.K. and by 26% in France between 1960 and 1976.

2. The Future Prospects

The historical analysis has highlighted two major factors which explain trends in the long-term energy demand evolution: the rate and nature of industrial growth (in other words, the share of the various sectors in this growth as well as the relative importance of different products within these sectors), and technological development.

---

[5] About 20% for cement and aluminum and slightly less for steel before the oil crisis (average figures among various countries).

We shall successively consider these two problems by looking, first of all, at the technological possibilities and the conditions of technological change in industry, especially in the context of expensive energy; we shall then consider some quite general ideas concerning the major trends of industrial growth which one may perceive at present.

2.1. Long-Term Technological Changes

The technological changes which are liable to alter industrial energy needs in the future may be classified as follows:
− the improvement of the specific consumption of energy consuming installations (kilns, boilers, motors): especially the improvement of their efficiency and of their utilization;
− substitutions among energy forms, generally to replace oil products, or even gas, by coal, electricity and even solar energy;
− changes in the manufacturing processes, especially the development of production processes of basic materials from waste products (linked to the recycling of materials);
− lastly, changes in the energy management of industrial sites (co-generation, use of waste heat and other waste products).

Each of these aspects has given rise to numerous publications, especially since the oil crisis. Our goal, here, is to attempt to sum up their major conclusions, in order to better determine the possibilities of changes in each of these field. For a greater understanding of the mechanisms governing these technical changes and to avoid tedious repetitions, we shall, first of all, analyze the industrialists' attitude towards the existing technological possibilities of saving energy, of replacing one form of energy by another or of changing the production processes.

The Industrialists' Behaviour and Technical Choices

Any identification of the possibilities of substitution among energy forms or of changes of installation or processes remains abstract if it does not take into account the industrialists' attitude towards these changes, especially within the context of high energy prices[1].

Firstly, the industrialists' behaviour will depend upon the importance which they attribute to the "energy" production factor. Although in the energy intensive industries, energy represents a significant input, liable to increase production costs, the same cannot be said of most of the engineering, food or textiles industries where energy expenditure usually represents less than 5% of production costs. This is why industrialists, in the energy intensive industries, are constantly seeking, and this well before the oil crisis, to minimize their energy expenditure and generally have specialized departments at their disposal

---

[1]   To avoid lengthening the presentation, we shall speak of techniques of energy conservation in reference to these changes since their implementation results from the intention of reducing energy expenditure.

within their company to do this. In other industries, however, energy uses are, on the whole, unknown — this is perhaps changing — and waste may be significant without industrialists worrying about it. The pressure of price increases will thus be differently perceived in these two kinds of industry: in the first case, the specialized departments will know when it becomes economically viable to make such or such investment whereas in the second case, the problem will be neglected because it will often be of little importance. However, the present situation might lead most industrialists to pay greater attention, than they would normally, to the possibilities of energy conservation, and this for two reasons. First of all, the long-lasting nature of the oil crisis and the risk of oil imports restrictions have a psychological impact on industrialists; in addition, most industrialized countries have introduced energy conservation policies, which aim in particular at making industrialists more aware of energy issues: investment subsidies in the form of loans at reduced rates, tax deductions or subsidies, advisory service for small and medium-size firms, . . .

Let us now examine, within this context, the factors which come into play in the appraisal of the cost effectiveness and the timing of energy conservation investments. The cost effectiveness criteria of energy conservation investments are generally different according to whether they concern investments on existing installations (efficiency improvements, energy substitutions) or productive investments for the renewal or creation of production capacity, which may result in the introduction of new processes.

As for productive investment, the extra cost linked to the most energy efficient process — or what we have labelled until now "energy conservation investments" — will be perceived in its entirety along with overall investment and the same cost effectiveness criteria will be applied. The decision on whether to develop or not a new process will depend on the appreciation of the cost effectiveness of this process in relation to the others; the industrialists behavior will depend on the likehood of changes in the cost of the major production factors (for instance energy) and on the risks involved in this new process (the firm's level of know-how with the new processes).

Investments in existing installations resemble much more the other defensive investments which industrialists repeatedly have to face (renewal of machinery, improvement of productivity, reduction of pollution, improvement of working conditions, . . .) and for which they expect very short payback times (generally two to three years, five years at most). The choice between all these defensive investments will obviously depend upon their respective cost effectiveness, which the government may influence by means of subsidies or lower interest loans, but it will also depend upon the existing regulations (such as quota limits on the consumption of certain energy forms, pollution standards, regulations pertaining to working conditions, . . .), as well as upon the institutional or social constraints. The size of the defensive investments and a fortiori of energy conservation investments, will depend on the one hand on the financial possibilities (self-financing, conditions of access to the financial market, . . .) and on the other hand, on the choice between defensive and offensive investments (growth of the production capacity, diversification within other sectors, . . .). At a time of slow economic growth and in the case of industrial sectors experiencing a crisis, the financial constraint will be an important element to take into account in the appreciation of energy conservation possibilities.

Changes in the respective advantages of the various competing processes and in the volume of cost effective investments will mainly depend on the evolution of the relative price of energy in relation to capital; in other words on the drift of energy prices in relation to that of average interest rates applicable to this kind of investment.

Let us now examine in greater detail the different kinds of technical changes, which may be envisaged in the industrial sector and liable to significantly affect its energy demand.

Improvement of Efficiency and Management of Industrial Installations

We shall concentrate on three kinds of installations (boilers, kilns and motors) since as we have already seen, they account for most of the energy used in industry. It is worth distinguishing here the case of present installations from that of new installations liable to come onto the market at a later date.

No significant change in the specific electricity consumption of existing motors is to be expected; the only possible actions are limited to the improvement of their condition of use (for instance the introduction of a regulation to reduce the time of idle running). In the case of existing·thermal installations (kilns and boilers), however, improvements in their efficiency may result from the improvement of the seals on the doors, the insulation of the sides and of the piping (steam distribution), . . . In the kilns, the pre-heating of the incoming combustion air and even of the raw materials entering the kilns, using the waste heat from the exhaust gases or from the products, is possible, whenever it is not already done. All these technical improvements require investments, which may greatly vary in importance from one industry to another and from one factory to another, according to the age and characteristics of the existing installations and the amount of recoverable heat. The same applies to the level of energy conservation achievable. The management of thermal installations may also be improved, especially with kilns, by making the production rates more regular (reduction of temperature increases and idle running times); this presupposes an increase in mechanization but could also have an impact on working conditions (in the case of night or week-end interruptions). Similarly, the reorganization of certain energy installations, especially in steam production with several pressure and temperature levels, can bring about significant energy savings (for instance, a better adequation between the required temperature levels and the energy form used, especially in the food and textile industries).

Substantial improvements may also be made in the heating of the premises, especially in mechanical or textile industries where this use is important: improvement of the insulation, temperature regulation, . . . Any progress made in this particular area will also improve working conditions (reduction of draughts, of overheating, . . .). According to a British survey done in 2200 industrial premises, the average payback times for the improvement of the insulation of industrial premises would, on average, be of 4 to 5 years (a bracket of approximately 1.5 to 8 years) [17].

In order to evaluate the energy conservation which may be achieved with existing installations, we shall again refer to the British study. This has allowed for the evaluation of energy savings, in the short and medium term, for approximately 30 industrial sectors by taking into account only those changes which may be paid off in less than 3 years. The rate of energy saving varies within a range of 9 to 20%, with, nevertheless a strong concentration around 18—20% (more than 20 of the sectors studied).

The energy efficiency of new installations may, in most cases, be significantly improved in relation to that of existing installations. The amount of change will depend upon several factors:
— the attitude of the firms which manufacture these installations;
— the attitude of the users (increased cost acceptable for more efficient machinery): in certain cases the user cannot even choose the equipment himself, for instance in the case of the motors which are part of another installation;
— research-development efforts aiming at developing new products;
— government policy: the financing or subsidies allocated for research and innovation in the field of energy saving installations, regulations concerning the efficiency of the industrial installations (in France, for instance, there are minimum efficiency standards for boilers); the compulsory labelling of efficiency for electric motors, . . .

The long-term impact of the introduction of more efficient installations will, of course, depend on the flow of installations put onto the market every year and thus on the rate of industrial growth and of renewal of the installations. A slow economic growth rate as presently experienced by most industrialised countries obviously limits the introduction of energy saving measures through new installations.

As regards kilns using fossil fuels and especially gas, one may expect quite significant improvements, which is not the case for electric kilns which are already most efficient; moreover, the development of highly efficient gas kilns could slow down the expected substitution of electricity for fossil fuels. The efficiency of foundry gas kilns (reverberatory kilns for non-ferrous metals) may thus increase from 35 to 45% with pre-heating and even to 65% with heat recovery systems; in most gas kilns the efficiency may be increased from 35% to 50—60% by means of different innovations [18].

In the case of boilers, the efficiency gains seem more limited as the present efficiency of new boilers is already quite high, approximately 80—85% in the most current boilers (nominal efficiency).

Contrary to what is often accepted, electric motors do not always prove very efficient, especially if the real efficiencies which are a function of the conditions of use are taken into account rather than the nominal efficiencies. The latter may fall to 50% for small motors and will average around 85% for 10 kW motors, with a maximum of approximately 90% for large motors. In order to get a better idea of the meaning of these figures, one may note that approximately 50% of the electricity used in the U.S.A. by electric motors is used by motors with an average size of 10 kW^2. Efficiency gains (of approximately 5 points) are possible, especially for small motors; one may note that according to a survey of the American electric motor market, the efficiency of electric motors of less than 10 kW has deteriorated in the last decade. Although the possibilities of improving the motors themselves are minimal, energy savings could be achieved by better adapting the motor sizes to their conditions of use, since their real efficiency decreases with their load factor; thus, with no load a motor still uses the equivalent of 40% of its nominal consumption (at full load) (60% when it is working at only half its capacity). Murgatroyd and Wilkins [23] went into this question in detail in the U.K. in the chemical and engineering industries. Their rather surprising conclusions indicate that the load factors are generally quite low, around 40% (25–70% bracket), and that on average 65% of the electricity is lost (55 to 70% bracket). Some progress may be made in this particular field by the introduction of regulation and motors with variable speeds.

Energy Form Substitutions

Oil and gas acquired, until 1973, an increasing share of the industrial market. In the wake of the upheaval in relative prices since 1973, these two energy forms could well give way to coal, electricity and even solar energy. The rate of penetration of these energy forms cannot be analysed purely in terms of relative prices. Indeed, each energy form has its own characteristics (efficiency, flexibility of use, . . .) both on the technical and strategic levels (risk of supply shortages, uncertainties concerning the price evolution, . . .). In addition, the substitution possibilities will depend upon the time horizon considered; if, in the long-term, any substitution may be considered, the same cannot be said of the short and medium term where the transfer from one energy form to another entails adaptations and/or changes of the installations, which can only occur whenever these installations become obsolete. Finally, the strategy of energy utilities (e.g. electricity utilities) may also be a determining factor in the spread of new energy forms as substitute for hydrocarbons: one may mention for instance the technological and commercial efforts of electricity utilities to open new industrial markets.

The present use of coal in industry is, with a few exceptions, concentrated in the steel and, to a lesser extent, the cement industries. The future penetration of coal could, first of all, concern the steam market where coal proves quite efficient, although slightly less than hydrocarbons (a difference of approximately 5 points). At present relative prices, coal is already in a competitive position in most countries. Nevertheless no significant return to coal has so far been noted; several factors may explain this: uncertainty as to the future prices of coal in relation to the investments to be made, lack of storage areas, labour and pollution problems, . . . The use of coal in kilns does not seem very promising in the medium term, except for cement factories, in view of the inefficiency of coal in relation to hydrocarbons and of the competition of electricity. In

---

[2] See References [1] for France and [19] for the U.S.A.

the long-term, the use of coal in kilns will especially depend on the evolution of relative prices of electricity/coal/hydrocarbons; and despite the drawbacks in the use of coal, which we previously underlined, it is quite certain that significant and long-lasting price differentials could encourage industrialists to return to coal for these particular uses. Finally, the last field within which coal could develop is that of carbo-chemicals, but we shall consider this aspect a little further on since it concerns a change of process rather than a substitution of one energy form for another.

Electricity is especially used in industry for what is currently known as captive (or specific) electricity uses: lighting, motors, electrolyses and a few well-defined thermal uses (scrap iron smelting, high-quality glass fusion, . . .). Several new markets could become open to electricity: kilns, dryers, large motors at present steam-powered, the heating of industrial premises and lastly steam production. On the whole, the transfer to electricity pre-supposes changes in installations and sometimes in processes. If it does take place, the development of electricity will thus be a slow process, depending upon the rate of renewal of the installations and the creation of few factories (for example, a kiln is thought to last ten years). The development of relative production costs from hydrocarbons or electricity will be the determining factor for the penetration of electricity, but the speed of this penetration will also depend upon the industrialists' attitude. On the one hand, even if electricity appears more competitive, industrialists will be unwilling to give up installations or processes which they have been satisfactorily using for a long time (know-how and habit) to adopt new techniques. Electricity may, on the other hand, seem attractive – even though more expensive – because of its security appeal, both in terms of prices and supply, its flexibility and its cleanliness. As regards kilns, it is difficult to concretely determine the real competition threshold – i.e. independently of the industries' own decision criteria – of electricity in relation to hydrocarbons, and experts disagree on this point according to whether they favour the electric, oil or gas sector. Indeed, in addition to the relative prices of hydrocarbons to electricity, other factors come into play at this stage: relative efficiency, investment costs, . . .   The relative efficiency varying quite significantly from one kind of kiln to another, this competition threshold will greatly depend on the type of kiln and thus on the industrial sectors concerned; it must be recalled here the innovation expected with respect to fuel kilns, which should significantly improve the relative efficiency of hydrocarbons in relation to electricity. Thus, electricity might be first introduced for small kilns (especially mechanical and eventually ceramic industries), and in the longer term for large kilns (glass or chemicals).

The development of heat pumps could allow electricity to be used for drying. But, on this market, it will be in competition with steam, especially when free – since obtained from an internal recovery process, as in the paper industry – and, in the medium term, with solar energy in certain countries. The substitution of electricity for steam in motors or compressors (mainly in the chemical industry) generally implies a reorganization of the steam networks in factories and depends upon the possibility of reducing steam production or of alternative uses which may be made of this steam.

The electric heating of industrial premises, quite scarce nowadays, represents a development outlet for electricity, but which, in our view, will be restricted to industrial sectors without possibilities of waste heat recovery, and to well-insulated and well-sealed premises.

The production of steam from electricity does not represent an immediate market for electricity, so little competitive is electricity at present.

Solar energy may be used, on a purely technical level, for the heating of premises, for drying and other thermal uses requiring a low ($< 100°C$) or medium temperature (100 to 200–250°C). The production of temperatures higher than 100°C entails the use of slightly more sophisticated systems (with concentration) than the traditional flat collectors which can only provide low temperatures. If we refer to Table 4.4, we may appreciate the order of magnitude of the potential market for solar energy, globally and per sector. The installations will be paid off more rapidly if the solar energy is directly used in processes (all-year round use) rather than for heating (seasonal use). At present, solar energy is not competitive according to the industrialists' criteria for cost effectiveness; in this respect a study carried out by the Solar Energy Research Institute [20], shows that the pay-back time is approximately ten years in the U.S.A. The future competitivity of solar energy will depend on the development of installation costs in relation to the drift in competing energy prices; it will also depend upon possible government subsidies, upon the areas concerned (well exposed, such as the south·of the U.S.A. and of Europe, and upon the manufacturing processes (storage limitations, manufacturing continuity, . . .).

Changes in the Energy Management of Industrial Sites

The energy supply of industrial sites and the energy management on these sites are determined by numerous factors: the characteristics of the supply in the energy sector, the nature and proportion between the different thermal needs, . . . The period of decreasing oil prices prior to 1973 and the development of the inter-connection of electric networks have led to the situation which presently faces industrialists and which may be characterized as follows:
– low level of industrial electricity production (co-generation),
– negligible use of thermal wastes and other industrial waste products, because their recovery, at a time of cheap energy, was rarely cost effective,
– heat distribution systems (steam/hot water) which are simplified and ill-adapted to the needs and temperature levels of the various industrial processes (for instance, as previously mentioned, low temperature needs supplied by steam).

The present and expected energy price levels and the long-lasting nature of the crisis, can only encourage industrialists to revise energy supply schemes, especially concerning heat, and eventually electricity, and to take into account the possibility of recovering thermal wastes and waste products with an energy value (wood, agricultural wastes, . . .) – for internal use or external sales – and the possibility of combined heat and power production.

Recovery of Thermal Waste. Due to the layout of heat distribution systems, to the nature of the processes and to the unsatisfactory efficiency of industrial thermal installations (kilns and boilers), more or less significant amounts of heat are wasted either in fumes or exhaust gases, or in waste waters; the temperature levels and the volumes of thermal wastes vary according to the industrial sectors; in the pulp and paper industries 70% of the wastes are at less than 150°C (50% at less than 65°C) whereas in the chemical industry, 50% are at more than 150°C[3]. According to a CEREN study of French industry (including the energy sector), thermal wastes at more than 50°C (including the energy sector) could in 1975 be roughly classified according to their temperature levels in the following manner: 10% between 50 and 80°C, 55% between 80 and 120°C, 3% between 120 and 200°C, 25% between 200 and 500°C and lastly 7% above 500°C: most of these wastes come from fumes and exhaust gases (65% approximately); the total potential represented by these wastes is of approximately 5 Mtoe (209 PJ)[4]. In order to appreciate the potential uses of this energy source, several remarks need to be made:

— the improvement of the efficiency of installation, as previously mentioned, will result in a proportionate reduction of thermal wastes; the CEREN study indicates that the potential will decrease in time (approximately 4 Mtoe or 167 PJ by the year 2000);

— the production costs of recovered heat is dependent upon the investments which are needed (exchangers);

— the possibilities of use are often limited inside the factories, except perhaps to heat industrial premises in certain industries with significant heating requirements, and thus the thermal waste must be used outside (factories of another industrial site, neighbouring residential or tertiary buildings), which thereby increases their cost.

It would be unwise to provide recovery rate figures because it is necessary to know all the afore-mentioned factors and this is only possible if each case is treated separately. One may nevertheless refer to the CEREN study in which a systematic geographical comparison of the energy needs under 100°C and the production of thermal wastes was undertaken, for all French towns of more than 100 000 inhabitants and for all large industrial sites situated near a town of more than 25 000 inhabitants. It emerges from this study that the thermal potential which exists near such markets is of 3.2 Mtoe (134 PJ) and that 2.3 Mtoe (96 PJ) could effectively be used (1.8 of which in industry) taking into account modulation losses and cases where the supply is greater than the potential uses. One must nevertheless consider these results with caution as they do not include the possible valorization of thermal wastes under 50°C, which do, however, represent the majority of thermal wastes (especially of the conventional or nuclear thermal power plants). The valorization of such

---

[3]   See Reference [22].

[4]   The potential was in fact estimated at 9 Mtoe (377 PJ), but if one takes into account the heat which may effectively be valorized to produce hot water at 90 or 30°C, one reaches 4.9 and 5.4 Mtoe respectively (205 and 266 PJ).

wastes indeed requires more sophisticated technical installations (use of heat pumps for instance) but the potential involved is considerably more important.

Recovery of Waste Products. The main industries concerned are the wood, pulp and paper and food industries (and the refining industry). Although difficult to estimate, there are important recovery possibilities for agriculture or food waste products by direct combustion (waste products with a low humidity content) and more especially by fermentation (high humidity content): straw, vinasses, slaughter-house wastes, sugar-beet pulp, dairy wastes[5], . . . At present the recovery of all these waste products may be considered to be non-existent. An improvement of the fermentation route and continuing fuel price increases could make this recovery most appealing. In addition, one must note that these waste products constitute a pollution which it will become increasingly necessary to reduce or even eliminate; hence their energy valorization will become even more cost effective.

In the wood and paper (and pulp) industries, all waste is already to a large extent being recycled (bark, sawdust, black liquor,. . .). Thus, it is thought that in France, 60% of the wood industry waste products are already used within the industry (especially in saw mills) either as an energy form, or to manufacture chip-boards; there remains on approximate potential of 1 Mtoe (42 PJ). In the paper industry, the recovery ratio of waste products varies with each country, with the sophistication of the installations and the type of production: thus, the waste products contribute to satisfy 50% in Sweden (1973) and 45% in the U.S.A. (1976) of the overall demand for fuel and electricity, as against 1% in the U.K. The recovery is most significant in chemical pulp factories, where the residues (black liquor) can be burnt in special boilers. In Sweden, in 1973, 75 to 80% of the steam used in non-integrated Kraft pulp (or sulphate chemical pulp) factories came from internal recovery (40% for unbleached sulphate pulp and 60% for bleached sulphate pulp) [24]. In mechanical pulp factories and non-integrated paper factories, the recovery possibilities are on the contrary quite small. In the most modern chemical pulp units, a full recovery of waste products results in an energy self-sufficiency: there are even steam surpluses which may be used, if there exists an associated paper factory. The increase in energy prices, linked to the renewal of production units should eventually lead to the pre-dominance of this kind of "self-sufficient" factories.

Industrial Cogeneration. The combined production of heat and electricity on industrial sites (cogeneration) may, from a collective point of view, seem most attractive (an efficiency of 30–35% in the production of electricity alone and 70% in the case of cogeneration). For an industrialist, the appeal of cogeneration may well vary from one country to another, from one industrial sector to another, even from one industrial site to another, according to the range of goods manufactured. Four sectors are especially concerned by co-

---

[5] Thermal potential estimated at 0.5 Mt (21 PJ) of dry matter for dairy wastes and 0.4 Mt (17 PJ) for vinasses in France [21].

generation due to combined needs of steam and electricity: the pulp and paper, chemical, food and textile industries (and refining)[6]. Cogeneration has developed differently in the various countries (Table 4.7) depending on the characteristics of the electric network (reliability), the pricing policies (price of the electricity purchased from the network, selling price of self-produced electricity). The development of cogeneration will greatly vary from one country to the other according to the success of nuclear energy. In those countries where this energy is widely and successfully developing, one may expect a reduction in cogeneration (nuclear energy theoretically allowing for a disconnection of electricity prices from other fuel prices), except perhaps in the paper industry where the valorization of waste products and cogeneration will develop simultaneously. In other countries, however, the uncertainties concerning the electricity supply (in particular linked to the opposition to nuclear energy) and the governmental encouragement policies could, on the contrary, stimulate the development of cogeneration (Denmark, the U.S.A., for instance).

Table 4.7. *Industrial cogeneration (1977)* (% of the electricity consumed which is self-produced)

	Paper	Chemicals	Textile	Food
F.R. Germany	60	42	25	21
France	35	15	10	13
Italy	49	75	32	15
U.K.	38	47	7	7
E.E.C.	45	41	18	14

Source: Eurostat [26].

Process Substitution

The share of the various processes in present production capacities is the result of the choices made by industrialists in the past, and thus of the economic conditions which prevailed; thus, in the U.S.A. and in the U.K., the very energy intensive wet process is mostly used in the manufacture of cement, whereas in France the dry process dominates. The energy crisis has altered competition conditions among the various processes, favouring the most energy efficient, as well as those requiring energy forms least affected by the crisis. We shall make here a few general remarks, on the rates of process substitution and the possible future process changes, concentrating more especially on recycling processes, which are generally less energy intensive and the appeal of which can only grow. We shall later analyze in more details the cement and steel industries (§ 3 and 4), sectors which are both energy intensive and the most sensitive to price increases, in order to determine the possible consequences of the crisis upon the development of the different competing processes.

---

[6]   This sector, part of the energy sector, is not included in this study.

The development of a new process in an industrial sector may occur during the expansion of its production capacity or during the renewal of its installations; the rate of process substitution will thus be linked to the growth rate of the sector and the obsolescence of existing installations. In a period of economic recession, as that experienced by industrialized countries since 1974–75 and especially by energy intensive sectors (steel, cement and chemical industries, . . .), the development possibilities of new processes through the creation of new units are, of course, very limited. Process substitution within existing installations is indeed linked to the age of the installation but also to the changes occurring in the economic environment of companies, in so far as the competition with other companies, and/or changes in the relative costs of production factors, or the discovery of new processes may favour and accelerate the replacement of an existing process. The rapid development of oxygen steelworks during these last two decades can mostly be explained by the conversion of existing steel works to the oxygen process; this conversion aiming more especially to resist national and international competition.

Let us briefly look at the process changes which are liable to occur in the future in the main energy intensive industries. Three major steel production processes will be competing against each other: the blast furnace process (with oxygen steel works), the direct reduction process (with electric furnace); the recycling of scrap iron in electric furnaces. Because of the lack of gas and iron ore and because of the know-how acquired in the traditional route (blast furnace), the direct reduction process (based on gas) has little chance of being developed and the competition will only concern the traditional and electric processes. These two processes being entirely different in their conception, the conversion from one process to another is not possible and the growth of the electric process will only come about through the creation of new factories, which will probably limit its development potential, moreover this development will in addition depend upon the availability of raw materials (scrap, reduced ore), the prospects of long-term electricity supply, and the kind of steel products to be manufactured (flat or long products). The raw materials of electric steel works can be either scrap iron, the availability of which depends upon the internal losses of steel mills (in reduction with the development of continuous rolling) and the recycling rate of ferrous waste products on the internal market (bound to governmental policy), or pre-reduced ores (metal sponges) which are likely to be imported from countries producing iron ore. The development of the electric process engenders a substitution of electricity for other fuels (especially coke) and a significant reduction of energy needs (primary divided by approximately 3.5).

In the cement industry a progressive conversion to the dry process is expected in factories using the wet process, which has been condemned by the energy crisis due to its high fuel consumption (40% more). This conversion could occur quite rapidly in certain countries where the government provides subsidies (for instance in France). Another significant change in the energy field might come from the substitution between pure cements and blended cements (i.e. containing additives); this represents more a change in the nature of the products manufactured than a real process change. The government could also play an important role in establishing standards concerning the composition of cements (as in France for example).

With respect to the production of aluminum, the dominant process (Bayer-Heroult) may, in the long run, be partly replaced by a new less electricity intensive process (ALCOA) (11 kWh/kg instead of 15), and to a lesser extent by a greater production from waste products, if there exist sufficient input materials; in this last case, the energy demand for the aluminum production would be significantly reduced since recycling requires much less energy than the production from bauxite or shale (primary energy consumption approximately 20 times lower).

In the manufacture of glass, two technical changes in the present process (fuel kilns) may be expected: on the one hand, the development of electric fusion kilns, although certain problems need to be solved for large kilns, and on the other hand, the adaptation of the present process, by introducing electric resistances in the fusion process (mixed fuel/electricity fusion), and/or by increasing the use of glass debris as raw material. This last technique would lead to slight energy savings by reducing the fusion temperature level and the consumption of calcium carbonate which is energy intensive if it has to be manufactured.

In the chemical industry, it is difficult to deal with process substitution in view of the wide range of products manufactured and therefore of possible processes. If we consider energy intensive products alone (ammonia, ethylene, for instance) the change which is liable to have the greatest impact upon energy is the substitution of coal for hydrocarbons as raw material. Technically, it is quite possible to replace present petrochemical processes (naphta or gas → ethylene or ammonia) by process based on coal (coal → ethanol → ethylene or coal → ammonia). The transfer to carbochemicals pre-supposes that the petrochemical processes, under the control of the oil industry, should be abandoned and that a large sector of the chemical industry should be reconverted; industrialists will accept this technological and financial risk only gradually and if the coal process proves much more profitable than the petrochemical process. Thus the development of the carbochemical industry does not in the medium term seem possible and is only likely to occur in the long-term should coal prices be much lower than those of hydrocarbons.

In the paper industry, the manufacture of paper from waste papers could significantly increase by means of vigorous recovery policies, more based on economic or environmental motivations rather than on energy saving. The energy impact of the increase in recycling greatly depends on the nature of the waste paper (whether or not they need processing) and the kind of pulp for which recycling pulp may be substituted; thus, the energy saving is not obvious in the case of chemical pulp because of the large utilization of waste as previously outlined.

2.2. Long-Term Industrial Growth

We shall not attempt to define what the industrial growth of industrialized countries will be over the next twenty years; we shall rather attempt to recall the major trends which characterized the industrial growth of these countries in the last two decades and roughly outline possible long-term scenarios, relying on several prospective studies (especially that of the group "Interfutures")[1].

Major Past Trends

A few key sectors have played an active role in the development of industrialized countries over the last twenty years: chemicals, oil, the electric and electronic equipment and finally cars and telecommunication. On the whole, industries with a high capital and technological input, such as equipment and durable consumer goods industries, have experienced a rapid growth. Similarly, the declining sectors or those with a slow growth rate were generally the same in all countries: coal and current consumer goods (textiles, clothings and food industries). Another characteristics feature of industrial development, also to be found in all countries, is an increasing integration within the international market, through a significant increase both in the exports of the more active sectors and in the imports of the declining sectors. In addition, the increase of commercial exchanges was accompanied by the emergence of new exporting countries, mainly linked to the transfer, by multinational firms, of production units to zones with low labour costs (industries with a high labour intensity such as textile or electronic industries) or to zones near energy and raw material sources (steel, aluminum). Countries, in South East Asia especially, thus established production units competing with industrialized countries on their own markets; the U.S.A. and Japan were more affected than Europe by this competition. In addition, the increased role of trade reinforced the competition between industrialized countries for the control of the key sectors (data processing, communications, . . .).

The economic crisis presently experienced by industrialized countries emphasizes these trends by reinforcing the role of certain countries in international trade (Japan, East European countries and a few Third World countries) and by forcing industrialized countries to adapt their industrial structures. In the intermediate goods industries (steel and chemical industries), the existence of excess capacities on the worldwide level has increased the competition from newly exporting countries and Japan in relation to the U.S.A. and Europe. In the labour intensive industries, competition from Third World countries has continued to grow: as a consequence, the U.S.A., Japan, and Federal Republic of Germany have withdrawn from these sectors and are quite open to imports. In the case of Japan and Germany, this withdrawal has been offset by a specialization strategy in the sector of equipment goods and of durable consumer goods.

---

[1] This part of the analysis greatly relies on the following studies: [27, 18, 29].

Long-Term Prospects

Two kinds of factors will play a determining role in the long-term industrial growth of industrialized countries:
— the individual's value system and life style which determine both the development of internal markets and the nature of the growth;
— the nature of international relations, between industrialized countries on the one hand, between industrialized and Third World countries on the other hand (north/south relations) and finally between East European and all other countries.

Since the late sixties, new values have been emerging in industrialized countries, questioning the kind of "material" growth experienced by these countries until now and aspiring to a new type of growth. Although most of the population of these countries remains attached to traditional values, one may not, nevertheless, exclude in the long-term a trend reversal (for instance, with the accession of individuals more open to these aspirations to leading positions, or as a possible reaction to a long-lasting economic crisis, . . .). One may thus identify two kinds of possible long-term developments in this field: on the one hand, the predominance of traditional values and the continuation of the present development pattern ("the consumer society"); on the other hand, the gradual establishment of a new growth pattern, more "qualitative" and less "quantitative". In the first case, the growth of a national market for durable consumer goods will continue, with a gradual saturation of the most current equipment[2] (household equipment and motorcars) and the spread of new equipment (such as audio-visual . . .). In the context of a change of values, the consumer goods market would certainly undergo a deep change (goods more durable, goods sold in kit form, . . .).

With respect to relations between countries, the "Interfutures" [29] study emphasizes two kinds of development which to our mind give a correct idea of the range of possibilities:
— the change over to a more collegial management of common interests, leading to greater economic stability and the return of a sustained growth rate;
— conflicts between countries regarding certain markets and a partial return to protectionism.

North-South relations could develop in several ways according to the degree of cohesion among Third World countries and their ability to impose a change in the international division of labour, on the one hand, and the kind of development experienced by these countries, especially the main ones such as Brazil, Mexico, India, Indonesia, . . . (endogenous development or development open to industrialized countries), on the other hand.

The combination of the preceding assumptions results in the two following alternatives:
— a development of North-South relations either world-wide, or regionally

---

[2]   We refer the reader to the preceding chapters concerning the foreseeable saturation levels for the car and the main household appliances.

(U.S.A./South America, East Asia/Japan) in the event of hypothetical conflicts between industrialized countries;
— North-South confrontation, due to the establishment of endogenous development strategies by Third World countries, rendering them relatively independent of industrialized countries; this confrontation being accompanied by an intensification of trades between industrialized countries on the one hand, and between Third World countries on the other.

The first alternative does correspond to a continuation of recent trends. It could lead to an increased integration of countries in the international economic system together with an increase of their specialization; industrialized countries specializing in sectors requiring a highly qualified manpower (aeronautics, nuclear energy, industrial electronics, . . .) and an advanced technology (data processing and communications) as well as in the manufacture of more elaborate intermediary products (special steel) and food products.

The economic relations of the USSR and of East European countries with Western industrialized countries will reflect East/West relations; they should continue to develop except if important tensions arise (trade in equipment goods and food products from the West towards the East, and of intermediary goods and raw materials from the East towards the West). Their relations with Third World countries will reflect North-South relations in general.

From the basis of these different considerations and assumptions of development, four scenarios of industrial development may be outlined for industrialized countries:

(1) A significant industrial growth, allowing for a rapid adaptation (and thus a great transformation) of industrial structures in favour of an increasing share of equipment and durable consumer goods industries (within a context of the survival of predominant values, and the absence of conflict between industrialized countries and in North-South relations).

(2) A crisis situation and the revival of a semi-protectionism, leading to a more balanced growth between the sectors and thus to a relative stability of industrial structures (conflict between industrialized countries).

(3) The establishment of a new kind of growth pattern, slower but more balanced; the consequences upon industrial structures being little different from those of scenario (2).

(4) Tension in North-South relations and the setting up of endogenous strategies in major Third World countries: slow industrial growth rate and little transformation of industrial structures in industrialized countries.

Two main trends appear from these different scenarios, and may be taken as characteristic of future development of industrial structures in the countries under study (trends which can obviously be more or less emphasized according to the scenarios).
— On the one hand, the growth (in the event of a growth) of intermediary goods industries will be slower than in the past and than that of other sectors.
— On the other hand, equipment goods industries will constitute the dynamic sector of industrial growth; their development will be faster than that of other sectors.

3. The Steel Industry

3.1. Steel Production: Past Trends and Future Prospects

Steel is the basic product which sparked off the industrial development of most countries, Japan perhaps more than any other. Since 1950, steel production has grown at quite different rates according to the country: low growth (approximately 2% per year) for the U.S.A. and U.K., higher for France, Federal Republic of Germany, and Belgium (6%) and very high for the Netherlands and Italy (10%); Japan experienced an explosive growth rate of its steel production since in 1974 it produced more than 100 millions tons, 25 times more than in 1950. In order to understand the reasons for the differences in the production rates, it is necessary to consider the development of the two factors which determine this production: consumption on the one hand and foreign trade on the other.

Per capita steel consumption is often used as an indicator of a country's level of development. Although the industrialization process of less developed countries is accompanied by an increase in their need for steel, this need does not, however, increase indefinitely with the economic or industrial growth. In the course of the development process, the gap between steel consumption and industrial growth tends to diminish. For example, per capita steel consumption increased very little in the U.S.A. and the U.K. between 1950 and 1974 because in 1950 these countries had already reached an advanced stage of development. In Italy however, which at this time was little developed, per capita consumption underwent a six-fold increase in the same period. Due to these different developments, the per capita consumption levels have tended to become more similar: thus, in 1974, these ranged in Europe from 400 to 600 kg/per capita and in the U.S.A. where the level was noticeably higher, it averaged at about 700 kg/per capita (in 1950, the range was of 70 to 300 for Europe and in the U.S.A. the level was of 680).

We have, until now, only spoken of the demand for steel products (rolled steel). However, what is crucial on the energy level is the demand for crude steel, which develops at a different rate than that for rolled steel. Historically, because of technical progress and changes in the structure of the demand for products (flat products, long products) we have witnessed a reduction of losses at the transformation stage of crude steel into rolled steel: thus in France, approximately 1.45 tons of crude steel were needeed in 1950 to produce one ton of rolled steel, 1.3 tons in 1970 and 1.2 tons in 1978. Since 1970, these improvements have especially been made possible by the development of a new rolling process — continuous casting — which induces a reduction of material losses. This process is developing very rapidly since its use has increased from 9% in 1973 to 16% in 1976 for the total world production (in the case of Japan, the increase was of 22 to 36% over the same period). One may expect that by the end of the century, most of the rolling will be done in this way, thus reducing rolling losses to 5—10%[1]. This means that the consumption of crude steel will grow at a slower rate than the users' need for rolled steel.

---

[1] Japan plans to increase the proportion of continuous casting from 42% in 1977 to 60% in 1985 and 65% in 1990.

The other factor which influences the level of steel production is foreign trade: the production has increased faster than the actual needs in certain countries such as France, Federal Republic of Germany or the U.K. and of course Japan, which, at present, exports approximately half its production. Other countries such as Italy and the U.S.A. have had to resort to importing steel to satisfy the national demand over these last twenty-five years.

The prospects of steel production will naturally depend upon the consumption and import or export prospects. The aim of this study is not to make forecasts about the steel industry, but to emphasize the main trends which may be perceived for the next twenty years.

With respect to the consumption level, several phenomena may explain a slow increase, in the countries concerned, for the three main uses of steel: industrial equipment (machine-tools, turbines, . . .), durable consumer goods (cars), construction and civil engineering (construction steel). As seen previously, equipment goods industries should undergo a significant growth by the end of the country, but this will especially apply to light equipment goods — computers, microprocessors — with nevertheless some exceptions — energy or aeronautics sector. On the whole, this means that the elasticity of the demand for steel used for equipment goods in relation to industrial growth should decrease. As for durable consumer goods, they will reach a saturation level, at least on the national market, which will progressively restrict the production to replacement needs and thus reduce the need for steel in this sector. The most striking case is obviously that of the car industry since it accounts for 10 to 20% of the steel consumption of producing countries; an increase in the export of these equipment goods to the Third World could however compensate for this trend. In addition, steel will continue to be rivalled by other materials (plastics or aluminum) in the manufacture of many consumer goods. The use of steel in the building sector will decrease due to the reduction in the construction of new dwellings and the completion of major civil engineering projects (motorways for example).

The lack of detailed quantitative information concerning the use of steel in industrialized countries unfortunately does not allow one to further evaluate the prospects of steel consumption and especially to quantify them.

The development of steel trade is a crucial aspect of a major debate, which we have already mentioned above: that of the new international division of labour. What should we think of the repeatedly-mentioned idea of a relocation of steel production in the Third World? The increase in the difference in energy costs between energy producing countries and most industrialized countries can only reinforce the advantage those countries have in this particular field. However, other factors are detrimental to Third World countries: much higher investment costs, lack of highly qualified labour and transport infrastructure, . . . It is, on the whole, quite difficult to ascertain the level at which differences in the energy costs will place certain Third World countries in a strong position. The experience of the last ten years does encourage one to tread with caution when speaking of delocalization: indeed, many steelworks projects have either never seen the light of day or have been drastically revised (high costs, technical difficulties, existence of an excess capacity, . . .). Some countries have nevertheless experienced a great expansion of their steel production (for instance, Mexico, Brazil, Korea) but this has especially been aimed at satisfying domestic needs; one cannot be sure that these countries, except for a few exceptions (Korea perhaps) can produce a surplus which may be exported to industrialized countries. In view of the delays and necessary time span, it does not seem possible for significant quantities of steel to be exported from the Third World to industrialized countries in the coming decade. In return, industrialized countries which export steel must expect their exports to be reduced due to the construction of steel plants in semi-industrialized countries which are heavy steel consumers and to the competition from Eastern European countries and possibly certain Third World countries.

This analysis thus supports the generally accepted notion, that for socioeconomic and strategic reasons, industrialized OECD countries will, on the whole, try to adapt their steel production to their domestic demand (with the exception may be of Japan). This adjustment, however, will probably hide the growing disequilibrium in the case of certain products, due to a redistribution and specialization of steel production on an international level: prereduced ores and common steel products in Third World countries, special and very sophisticated steel in industrialized countries. Nevertheless, one cannot completely exclude the possibility that in the 90's, new large-capacity units of steel production will appear in certain less developed countries which would be liable to threaten steel production in industrialized countries.

3.2. Energy in Steel Production[1]

The steel industry is by far the most energy intensive industry. In 1974, depending on the country, it accounted for 20 to 45% of all the energy used in industry; more than 40% in Belgium and in Japan, 35% in Federal Republic of Germany, and 30% in France. In Belgium and Japan, the importance of the steel industry in the overall energy balance has been increasing ever since 1950, whereas in France and Federal Republic of Germany it has fluctuated between 30 and 35%.

The average energy consumption per ton of steel has regularly decreased in all countries (Table 4.8). The most spectacular reductions have occurred in Japan and the Netherlands since in 1974 they were using approximately 50% less energy than in 1950 (but it is true that at this time their consumption level was much higher than in other countries). In 1974, the differences among these consumptions were much smaller (within a bracket of 18 to 23 GJ/t). But, the respective levels of each of these countries do not allow for a true appraisal of the energy efficiencies achieved since they include different processes and practices. Thus, we shall now closely examine the processes used and the ways in which energy is used within the processes.

---

[1]   We shall refer throughout this paragraph to the study [30].

Steel production may rely upon a great diversity of processes in which the amount of energy required and the energy forms used are very different. Thus the substitution of one process for another entails a change in useful energy needs and substitutions among energy forms. Steel production is roughly carried out in two stages: firstly the conversion from iron oxydes into iron, either as pig-iron in a blast furnace, or as pre-reduced ores with the so-called direct reduction process; the next stage consists in transforming the iron into steel, an operation which may either be done in an electric furnace (as in the case of scrap iron and pre-reduced ores) or in a steelworks. Any consideration of the steel industry and its energy consumption cannot in fact stop at the level of crude steel but must include the various rolling stages up to the production of semi-products: long products (reinforcing steel bars, rails) or flat products (steel plate).

Table 4.8. *Average energy consumption per ton of steel* (GJ/t)

	1950	1955	1960	1965	1970	1974
U.S.A.			24	21	19	18
Japan	33	25	20	19	19	18
France	26	26	25	24	24	23
F.R. Germany	26	25	23	20	21	21
Italy	23	15	16	18	17	17
U.K.			27	26	24	22
Belgium	21	21	20	19	20	19
Netherlands	38	28	25	24	21	21

Sources: Appendix 3, Tables I.6 and I.9.

Blast Furnace

The main energy form used in a blast furnace is coke. Because of the importance of coke prices in the production cost of pig iron, the ever-present worry of steel producers has always been to reduce the coke rate — in other words, the consumption of coke per ton of pig iron. Thus, the coke rate has constantly decreased in all countries, as shown in Table 4.9. This fell by 40 or 45% in most European countries (France, Federal Republic of Germany, Belgium, the Netherlands), but only by 30% in Japan and 20% in the U.S.A. between 1960 and 1976. The low reduction in Japan may be explained by the fact that in 1960, Japanese blast furnaces were much more efficient than in other countries and that ever since, the other countries have tended to catch up with Japan. Although the range of coke rates was quite important in 1960 (615 to 970 kg/t pig iron), this has since been reduced: thus, in 1976 the range went from 427 (Japan) to 600 (the U.S.A. and U.K.). The U.K. and the U.S.A. have fallen behind other countries, probably because of the slow growth rate of the steel industry in these countries (slower renewal rate of installations). This important decrease in the coke rate has two major causes: growing use of agglomerated ore, and the development of injection techniques which consist in injecting fuel-oil (and/or tar) or gas into the blast furnace, in order to replace coke which cheaper[2] fuel and to improve the blast furnace operation. Table 4.9 indicates the order of magnitude of the injection rates observed in certain countries. Having rapidly developed after 1965, the injection rate has remained stable since 1973 at approximately 50 to 60 kg of fuel-oil per ton of pig iron, replacing a similar quantity of coke.

Table 4.9. *Average fuel rate per ton of pig iron in the blast furnaces*

(kg of coke + oil/t pig iron) (figures between brackets: coke rate only in kg coke/t pig iron)

	1950	1955	1960	1965	1970	1973	1975	1976	1978
France	994	1019	970	793	667	617	598	585	562
	(994)	(1019)	(970)	(781)	(626)	(557)	(532)	(520)	(492)
Japan			716	615	538	512	493	483	479
			(716)	(615)	(505)	(469)	(434)	(440)	(427)
F.R. Germany			834			566		544	
			(834)	(672)	(559)	(494)	(497)	(482)	
Italy			680						
			(680)	(633)	(524)	(518)	(479)	(472)	
Netherlands			787						
			(787)	(559)	(484)	(475)	(467)		
Belgium			852						
			(852)	(658)	(586)	(557)	(545)		
U.K.						628		631	
						(577)		(606)	
U.S.A.			(770)	(650)	(636)	(594)	(612)	(598)	(595)

Sources: France [31]; U.K. and Japan: [32]; F.R. Germany, Italy, Netherlands, and Belgium: [57] for the coke rate and [32] for the total consumption; U.S. A.: [56].

The great reduction in the coke consumption analyzed above in fact conceals the replacement of coke by other energy forms, with respect to both the agglomeration and the blast furnace (injection). The relevant indicator of the progress achieved in the energy use is not the coke rate but the specific net consumption of fuel per ton of pig iron for the agglomeration and the blast furnace — after the substraction of the amount of blast furnace gases produced, which anyway tend to decrease with the injection. Thus, in the case of France, the only country for which we have statistical data over a long period of time, this specific net consumption went from 20 GJ/per ton of cast iron in 1950 to 19 GJ/per ton in 1970 and 17 GJ/per ton in 1978. The process achieved is thus

[2] At least until 1973.

much lower than the above-mentioned coke consumption decreases. This saturation of the progress in energy savings may certainly be traced in all the other countries; it is due to the fact that the blast furnace has reached a very high level of energy efficiency, approximately 80 to 90% (real losses are approximately of 55% but due to the recovery of most of the blast furnace gas, one may quote such a high efficiency).

Direct Reduction

We shall only briefly consider this process as it is still little developed and almost inexistent in the countries under study. Two major processes have been commercially developed which represent about 3/4 of the direct reduction capacity — MIDREX and HYL. These two processes use gas in the reduction of iron ore. Gas consumption is higher in the HYL process, which also has other disadvantages (high labour costs, lower iron content of the pre-reduced products). Thus, it would seem that the MIDREX process is the most promising. Although only recently developed, its specific consumption has already fallen considerably: 11 GJ/per ton of pre-reduced products (or 13 GJ/per ton of iron) as against 15 GJ/per ton a few years ago. The gas consumption of the HYL process is approximately 20% higher than that of the MIDREX process.

Steel Making

The transformation of pig-iron into steel may be done with three main processes: the open-hearth process — which uses a variable mixture of pig- and scrap-iron, depending on the availability of these two materials —, the THOMAS process, and lastly the oxygen process. This last process has developed rapidly; although almost non-existent in 1960, it is now the main steel-making process[3]. If we extrapolate these trends — and little can be seen to stop this development — it may quite reasonably be expected that by 1985 the oxygen process alone will be used in the transformation of pig-iron into steel. The oxygen process only requires a small amount of energy: approximately 50 kWh/per ton of electricity[4] (i.e. about 0.2 GJ/per ton) and no thermal energy since the reaction is exothermal. The heat thus produced is used to melt scrap-iron so that the converter is fed with a variable mixture of pig-iron and scraps (20 to 30% is scrap-iron, in other words 220 to 300 kg of scrap per ton of liquid steel). The composition depends upon the amount of scrap-iron available within the factory and the quality and price of the scrap-iron available on the market. Certain countries such as France use little scrap-iron, as opposed to countries like Japan. The consequence is a higher energy consumption per ton of steel since more pig-iron must be produced in one case than in another. The development of scrap-iron consumption will be, as we shall see later, an important factor liable to reduce energy consumption in the steel industry.

---

[3]   See Appendix 3, Table I.10.

[4]   Including the electricity necessary for the production of oxygen.

The electric steel making process was originally developed to recycle scraps by melting them in an electric furnace. The share of the electric process has regularly increased in all countries: from 8 to 20% in the U.S.A. between 1960 and 1975, from 9 to 14% in France, and from 7 to 26% in the U.K. In most countries, 15 to 20% of the steel is on average produced in electric furnaces. Italy stands out as an exception for, since 1965, more than 40% of the steel production is done in small electric steel furnaces[5]. Electricity consumption varies very little from one country to another: on average 600 kWh/per ton (i.e. 2 GJ/per ton)[6]. To this must be added the carbon consumption for electrodes (on average 10 kg/per ton). More recently the development of direct reduction has led to the use of similar furnaces for the smelting of pre-reduced ores — in this case, the electricity consumption is slightly higher depending on the quality of the pre-reduced ores. As with oxygen converters, the furnace load consists of a mixture of scrap-iron and pre-reduced ores (approximately 30% to 70%).

Rolling

Rolling includes all operations for transforming steel into intermediate products. Depending on the degree of transformation of the products and the share of rolling done by continuous casting — which leads to a saving of approximately 150 kg of material per ton of rolled steel — material losses at this particular stage are more or less high. The losses are then recycled as scrap-iron either in electric furnaces or in oxygen converters. The material yield varies from 65 to 85% according to the country, the highest yields being registered in France and Japan. In addition to material savings — and thus to upstream energy savings — continuous casting avoids the use of ingot reheating furnaces — "pit furnaces" — thus allowing for a direct saving at this stage (a bracket of 0.8 to 2 GJ/per ton)[7]. Most other thermal needs appear in the reheating furnaces at the various rolling stages. In 1975, the thermal energy used for rolling varied between 4 to 5 GJ/per ton of crude steel[8] in the case of most countries under study, with the exception of the U.K. and the U.S.A., where it was higher (6 and 7 GJ respectively). These differences may be due to a different delimitation of the sector. These thermal energy needs underwent very few changes between 1960 and 1975, often even showing a slight tendency to decrease. However, the differences in the electricity consumption are smaller (a range of 190 to 290 kWh or 0.7 to 1 GJ) with, this time, a slight tendency to increase.

3.3. *Present and Future Changes in Production Processes*

Process Substitution

The hegemony of the blast furnace for the first stage of steel production is not likely to be questioned in the countries under study and the development

---

[5] See Appendix 3, Table I.10.

[6] See Appendix 3, Table I.12.

[7] See References [30, 34, 37].

[8] See Appendix 3, Table I.13.

of the reduction process should remain quite marginal; access to national or imported coke from zones which are considered reliable (such as Australia) being better guaranteed than access to gas. In addition, these countries have developed a high level of know-how in the technology and operation of the blast furnace and this will make then hesitate to take the risk of introducing a new technology. Lastly, the present capacities of blast furnaces may well prove sufficient in view of the low development prospects of steel production, and of the probable reduction in the pig iron needs per ton of steel (a problem which we shall consider later); thus the market open to the direct reduction process should prove too small to allow for the implementation of major projects. As a consequence, the oxygen process which is the logical prolongation of the blast furnace process will continue to play a dominant role in the production of crude steel.

The electric process may continue to develop in countries where cheap electricity and sufficient electric capacity are available, but its production will be tied to the available quantities of raw materials — scrap-iron — as well as to the growth of the steel production capacity. Limitations in the availability of scrap iron may be offset by importing pre-reduced ores, should an international market for these products develop and their cost prove sufficiently appealing.

With respect to rolling, the spread of continuous casting should continue. Since at present not all products may be obtained by this process, its development is likely to reach a certain limit[1].

Energy Savings in the Processes and Installations

As previously mentioned, little progress may be expected with respect to the blast furnace. One can simply wonder if the fuel or gas injection will be maintained, increased[2] or reduced. The answer to this question is far from simple and depends mainly on the future changes in the relative price of fuel-oil, gas and coke. According to French steel industrialists, the injection of fuel-oil is cost effective up to an oil/coke price ratio of 1.5. In the medium term one may nevertheless expect present injection rates to continue, on the one hand to amortize the heavy investments made in the injection techniques, and on the other hand because oil (or gas) presents advantages which renders it still attractive at present prices. In the longer term, injection will only continue if large quantities of by-products (heavy fuel, tars, . . .), for which no other valorization exists, are available in the refineries, which will undeniably be geared towards an increased production of motor fuels. The average specific consumption of blast furnaces will gradually move towards that of the presently most efficient installations[3]; by the year 2000 we may expect a fuel rate (coke and

---

[1] Some people mention 70% as the maximum limit for the continuous casting, but one may rely upon technical progress and quality changes of the products to increase this limit.

[2] Injections of more than 100 kg are possible; IRSID in France has even reached 190 kg of fuel — although on an experimental basis [30].

[3] We are referring here to the following studies [37, 38, 39, 40].

fuel-oil) of approximately 470 kg in European countries and slightly less in Japan (420—430 kg)[4].

Two changes could take place in the oxygen process: the systematic recovery of all the steel-works gases — a technique being developed in Japan, but little implemented in other countries — and a pre-heating of scrap-iron or pre-reduced products with which the converters are fed. Oxygen converters produce approximately 0.6 GJ of gas per ton of steel (60 to 80 m^3) which until now was not recovered for economic reasons: the general increase in energy prices now renders cost effective its recovery, which is envisaged in most countries. In Japan, this technique is well under way since the recovery rate has risen from an average of 16 m^3 in 1970 to 58 m^3 per ton of steel in 1977; by 1985 the Japanese expect to recover the totality (80 m^3 per ton of steel) [32]. The aim of pre-heating scrap-iron is to increase the amount of scrap-iron which may be melted at the same time as pig-iron in an oxygen converter. From 20 to 30% in present conditions, this ratio could increase to 40%, reducing in the same way the pig-iron needs and the related energy consumption. Pre-heating entails an extra consumption of 0.31 GJ/per ton of steel.

The average electricity consumption of electric furnaces, previously mentioned to be 600 kWh/per ton, should improve, judging from the efficiency of the large furnaces presently in use (500 to 540 kWh) [30, 35, 37]. In electric furnaces, the main innovation could also be the pre-heating of raw materials — scrap-iron or pre-reduced products — to reduce the electricity consumption and improve the overall primary energy balance. Such a technique is only likely to develop in countries where the relative price fuel/electricity will allow it (one kWh of electricity being replaced by approximately 1.5 kWh of gas or of fuel-oil [35]). In the case of a modern furnace using 525 kWh, the electricity consumption could thus fall to 360 kWh with an average additional gas consumption of 0.9 GJ/per ton. With the use of pre-reduced products, the gas consumption could be further reduced if the pre-reduced products can be used while still hot, i.e. if they are produced nearby.

There are two kinds of changes which are liable to occur in the rolling process apart from the development of continuous casting, mentioned earlier. Firstly, an improvement in the efficiency of re-heating furnaces, which generally have quite low efficiencies; secondly, a replacement for the furnaces of fossil fuels by electricity, in countries where cheap electric energy is available.

The main restriction imposed upon the development of the electric process will be the availability of scrap iron (in quality and in quantity): the development of continuous casting and the probable increase of the use of scrap-iron in oxygen converters will reduce the quantities which may be used in electric furnaces. In the absence of a recycling policy aiming to significantly increase the recovery of scrap-iron or of the imports of pre-reduced ores, one may expect a share of 75 to 80% for the oxygen process and 20—25% for the electric process.

---

[4] The Japanese expect to reduce this figure of 470 in 1977 to 440 by 1985 and 430 by 1990 [32].

4. The Cement Industry

4.1. Cement Production: Past Trends and Future Prospects

In almost all countries, cement is the basic product which is a close second to steel for energy consumption. As in the case of steel, the growth of cement consumption is very closely linked to economic growth during the economic and industrial take-off period; thereafter, its consumption tends to increase much more slowly. Thus, the cement consumption per inhabitant grew quite slowly at the rate of 1 to 2% per year from 1950 to 1970 in countries such as the U.S.A. and the U.K., which were already heavily industrialized in 1950[1]. However, countries such as Japan and Italy, and to a smaller extent other European countries, have experienced a very rapid growth of their consumption: 5 to 6% in France and in Germany, and over 10% in Japan and Italy. Due to these opposing developments, the differences in per capita consumption levels have been reduced, within a range of 300 to 600 kg/per inhabitant in 1970 (as against 50 to 250 in 1950). Since 1970 per capita consumption levels have remained almost unchanged in most countries and have even decreased in certain countries (Federal Republic of Germany, the U.K.).

Cement is a heavy product and of low value added; consequently it cannot be transported over long distances because transport costs quickly increase its price. Indeed, with the exception of border exchanges and exports to Third World countries without cement production units, production and consumption do not generally differ[2]. Thus, we shall speak indifferently of production or consumption because their development rates will always be quite similar.

In order to better understand the past development of cement consumption, as well as the differences existing between countries, it is useful to recall the uses of this product. On the whole, we may identify three main markets: the building of new dwellings; the construction of industrial, agricultural and tertiary buildings, as well as the maintenance of dwellings and buildings; finally, civil engineering (dams, roads, bridges, . . .). In France, for example, the building of dwellings has accounted for 35% of the consumption since 1973, which corresponds to an average use of approximately 20 tons per dwelling. The share of civil engineering rose from 20% in 1973 to 28% in 1978, to the detriment of the construction of other buildings and of maintenance which, from 45% of the market in 1973, fell to 37% in 1978. Because of its main uses, the development of cement consumption — and thus of its production — is closely related to the growth of the construction sector; in France, for instance, the growth rate of cement consumption has in the past been about one point lower than that of the construction sector. For a same development level, differences in the consumption of cement among countries may come from differences in the

---

[1] Source of data: [49].

[2] In the case of small countries such as the Netherlands, international trade may play a significant role; indeed, the Netherlands import approximately half their total cement consumption from neighbouring countries.

techniques of construction (choice of building materials) and in the growth of the housing stock. The stagnation of consumption since 1970 reflects the slowing down of the activity of the construction sector in most industrialized countries, partly related to the slowing down of population growth and thus of the need for dwellings, as well as the reduction of major civil engineering projects. By raising cement production costs, the 1973–74 oil crisis, as well as the economic crisis that industrialized countries have been experiencing since 1975, have certainly contributed to further reducing cement consumption.

Can we therefore indicate any long-term prospects? Even if oil price undergoes only minor increases and even if industrial economies quickly emerge from the present economic crisis, no significant recovery of cement production seems likly to occur in these countries. Indeed, two of the principal reasons for the slowing down of production which we mentioned above are irreversible: the need for new dwellings will go on decreasing as well as all major civil engineering works. In addition, within the construction sector, cement may have to compete against other materials such as wood or aluminum, both because of the users' preference and because of a change in the relative prices of these raw materials (rising burden of energy costs). Thus, in any case, cement production should grow much more slowly than the economy over the next twenty years.

4.2. *Energy in Cement Production*

Cement is obtained by mixing a product baked in a kiln, therefore with a high energy content — clinker —, with various other additive products. The quality of the cement depends on the proportion of additives; it varies from pure cement (5% of gypsum and approximately 95% of clinker) — or pure Portland cements — to cements sometimes containing up to 40% of additives. Some countries such as the U.S.A. and the U.K. only produce pure cements, while others such as France or the Netherlands produce cements containing a large proportion of additives (Table 4.10). These differences obviously have significant consequences upon the energy needs per ton of cement, since in one case the cement will almost only consist of clinker — we shall speak of its energy content further on — and in the other case, it will contain important quantities of materials without any energy value, such as ash or blast-furnace slag.

Clinker is obtained by baking raw materials in a long rotating kiln (90 to 200 m long). The kilns account for almost all the fuel used in cement production. On the whole, one may identify three major cement — or clinker — production processes according to the crushing method of the raw materials sent to the furnace: the dry process, the wet process and the semi-humid or semi-dry process, halfway between the two. The quantities of fuels necessary to produce the clinker are much greater in the case of the wet process because of the need to evaporate the water contained in raw materials.

Table 4.11 compares the specific energy consumption of the different cement manufacturing processes in various countries. American consumption levels are systematically higher than European levels, which on the whole are fairly similar (3 to 4 GJ per ton of clinker for the dry process, and 5 to 6.7

Table 4.10. Cement production by processes

	France 1964	1970	1975	1978	U.S.A. 1974	F.R. Germany 1974	Italy 1974	U.K. 1974	Netherlands 1974
Clinker production (%)									
Wet process	60	35	23	16	59	5	13	69	67
Dry process	40	65	77	84	41	66	40	15	33
Semi-dry process						26	46	16	
Others						3	1		
Proportion of blended cement (%)		47*	58	58	3	24	46	2	55
(% of additives)		(15)*	(25)	(25)					(47)
(ratio clinker/cement)		(0.81)*		(0.76)	(0.95)	(0.84)	(0.84)	(0.94)	
References		[49]			[45, 47]	[45]	[45]	[45]	[45, 51]

* 1973.

Table 4.11. *Specific energy consumption by production process in cement production*

	France	F.R.Germany	Italy	U.K.	Netherlands	U.S.A.
Thermals energy (GJ/t clinker)	5.9–6.3	5–5.9	6.2	6.5–6.7	6.2	7.1
Wet process						
Electricity (kWh/t cement)	92		94	93		136
Thermal energy	3.8	3.1–3.8	4.1	3.5–3.7	3.8	5.7
Dry process						
Electricity	87		107	119		154
Thermal energy		3.3–4.6	4.2	3.8	5.4	
Semi-dry process						
Electricity			104	109		
Thermals energy	4.7	4.1	4.4	5.8	5.4	6.6
Average						
Electricity	97		103	100		145
References	[30]	[45]	[45]	[45, 48]	[45]	[45]

GJ per ton for the wet process). Several factors may explain this difference between Europe and the U.S.A.[3]: the age of American installations (on average they are more than 20 years old), the smaller size of the furnaces (more widespread market) and finally the low price of energy[4].

The use of the different processes considerably varies from one country to another: the U.S.A., the U.K., and the Netherlands still have significant wet process production capacities (from 60 to 70% in 1974) whereas other countries have abandoned it in favour of the dry process (or semi-dry) (see Table 4.10). The major reason for the conversion from the wet to the dry process is related to energy since it aims at reducing energy costs. Already high prior to the oil crisis, these costs have since undergone a significant increase (at present more than 30% of the selling price in France and the U.K.). From 60% in 1964, the proportion of the wet process fell to 16% in 1978 in France through the closing down of wet process plants and the conversion from the wet to the dry process plants. The slow conversion from the wet to the dry process in the U.S.A., the U.K., and the Netherlands may be mainly explained by the slow development of their cement production in the sixties and seventies, which limited the possibilities for change-overs and for the building of new factories, and little encouraged industrialists to undertake costly conversion programmes; in addition, the low

---

[3] See for instance references [45] and [47].

[4] The NATO study [45] emphasizes significant differences for modern like-size kilns between Europe and the U.S.A.; for instance, in the case of the dry process and for kilns of 1000 to 2000 t/j the typical European consumption is 3.4 GJ per ton of cement and the American consumption is 5.4 per ton.

cost of gas in the Netherlands and in the U.S.A. probably further reduced the appeal of the dry process as against the wet process.

In view of these differences in the production processes and energy efficiencies, one could observe in 1973–74 the following disparity in the average consumption of thermal energy per ton of clinker: between 4.1 and 4.7 GJ per ton for Italy, Federal Republic of Germany, France, and Japan — the most energy efficient countries —, 5.4 for the Netherlands, 5.8 for the U.K., and lastly 6.6 for the U.S.A. — i.e. 60% more than for the high-efficiency countries. Now, if we take into account the cement composition (clinker/additives proportion), we obtain even greater differences between the countries: 3.4 GJ per ton of cement in the most energy efficient countries as against 6.3 GJ per ton in the U.S.A. — i.e. twice as much as in France or Germany. The specific electricity consumption is also much higher in the U.S.A. than in Europe (low efficiency grinding mills, environment control): 145 kWh per ton as against 90–100 kWh per ton; Japan being halfway between the two with 120 kWh. Most of the electricity consumption (approximately 60%) is due to the crushing of raw materials and of cement; this proportion has tended to increase in the past due to mechanization, the installation of pollution control equipment and the development of dry crushing.

4.3. Present and Future Changes in Production Processes

France and Japan have made significant progress in the specific energy consumption for clinker production, by means of a combination of the different technical changes which we shall discuss below. In Japan fuel consumption went from 4.5 GJ per ton of clinker in 1973 to 3.7 GJ per ton in 1977 (a 20% decrease); in France it decreased from 4.7 in 1973 to 4.1 in 1977. The goal of industrialists and of the administration in these two countries is to reach by 1985 an average of 3.1 GJ per ton in Japan and 3.3 in France (Table 4.12).

The adjunction of additives such as ash or blast furnace slag to clinker is an immediate and cheap way of saving energy in cement production. Since the 1974 oil crisis, changes in this field have occurred or are planned. Thus, in France, where the production of blended cement was quite widespread, the government authorized a derogation to the regulation concerning the proportion of admissible additives so that the average proportion of additives rose from 15 ± 5% to 25 ± 5%. New regulations should soon increase this to 35%. For a similar production structure, the mere fact of going from 15 to 35% of additives allows one to expect a fuel saving reaching about 12%. In the U.K. where this type of cement does not exist, it is planned [48] to replace approximately a quarter of the production of pure Portland cement with cements containing up to 20 to 35% additives. The Japanese are also considering introducing blended cements. On the purely technical level, it is possible to add approximately 40% of additives in cement; the use of such additives slightly reduces the short-term resistance of cements (necessity for a longer drying period) but does not affect their mechanical qualities. In addition to the technical limits, the grade of blended cements and their volume of production will depend upon

Table 4.12. *Change in the energy consumption for cement production*

	Fuel consumption (GJ/t of clinker)				Electricity consumption (kWh/t cement)		
	France	U.S.A.	Japan	U.K.	France	U.S.A.	Japan
1967		8		6.3			
1970		7.1 (1971)	4.7	6	92		118
1973	4.7	6.7	4.5	5.7	91	145	121
1974			4.2	5.6	97		126
1975			4	5.5			126
1976			3.8	5.3			126
1978	4.1		3.7		95		123
1973	4.0				97		
1985	3.8*		3.1*				
2000	3.4*						

* Projections.

Sources: France [1, 49, 52]; U.S.A. [47]; U.K. [48]; Japan [50].

the cost and the available quantities of additives (heavy products the cost of which is largely dependent upon transport distances). This availability may in the future vary from one country to another according to the coal consumption since ash represents an important source of additives; part of this ash may come from the cement plants themselves in so far as they use coal (see below).

The substitution of the dry process for the wet process may seem inevitable in all countries and as previously mentioned is already quite widespread in some countries. The only question mark is the rate at which this will occur. The investments required to substitute one process for another are very substantial; thus, in view of the poor development prospects of this industry, industrialists will not willingly transform their installations without government subsidies. Some plants which at present use the wet process cannot be converted to the dry process because their raw materials have too high a humidity content; consequently, the introduction of the dry process may not be complete (it may be limited, for example to 90% of the production).

The energy efficiency of the dry process is of approximately 50 to 55% in modern kilns: about 20% of the energy goes out with the exhaust gases (gas at approximately 300°C) and 5% of the losses are due to radiation and convection; the other losses occur at the time of the cooling of the clinker, which leaves the kiln at over 1400°C (the clinker is cooled by air to about 100°C and cooling losses may thus partly be found in the cooling air and partly in the clinker on its exit from the furnace); a fraction of this air is re-used for the pre-heating of the combustion air in the burners, the drying of raw materials and eventually their pre-heating. The techniques which may be envisaged to improve the energy consumption of the dry process are: additional recovery, the production of electricity from exhaust gases — a common practice in the past according to a

British study [48] —, the increased recovery of the heat of the exhaust gases to dry and preheat the raw materials (in France, only 2/3 of this heat is considered to be recovered). The efficiencies of the best actual kilns — 3 GJ per ton of clinker-give an indication of the possible gains per country. The Japanese have developed a new dry process, which they are expecting to use systematically in the future; this process is based on the use of an additional kiln for the pre-heating of raw materials. In addition to a slight reduction in the thermal energy need, this process presents two important advantages: a reduction (almost by half) in the size of the kiln and a reduction in the atmospheric pollution.

Present grinding mills have very low efficiencies (around 2%). Known techniques allow one to expect slightly better efficiencies (around 5%) the result of which would be to halve the electricity consumption involved in the crushing. In the long term (2000) we may thus expect the electricity consumption to fall from its present 100 kWh per ton of cement to 70 kWh per ton.

Cement production has the advantage of being able to use all sorts of fuels (shale, coal with a high sulphur content, oil coke, household litter, . . .) with a minor impact on the environment (in particular with respect to sulphur). In the past, the low cost of hydrocarbons led cement factories to greatly rely upon them at the expense of "bad fuels"; but the sombre outlook for the hydro-carbon market, as well as the vigorous governmental measures to minimize risks linked to the oil supply may well lead to the return to less noble energy forms; thus, in France, the proportion of coal which at present is approximately 3% should rise to 50—75% by 1985. In addition, the return to coal presents cement factories with the advantages of providing the additives needed for the manufacture of cement without posing the problem of the elimination of ashes.

V. Forecasting Methods and Models

An exhaustive knowledge of energy demand, of its determinants, of its dynamic aspects, which underlies any prospective analysis, is indeed necessary to decision making in the energy field, whether it concerns a choice between energy production units or the definition of an energy policy or of a research and development program; but it is insufficient in so far as the decision requires clear and rapid answers about the future.

Forecasting is the subsequent and inevitable step which consists in the transcription of this analysis into a methodological tool allowing one to draw from the past and from the present one or more quantified images of the future in terms of which the decisions may be made. According to the aspects outlined in the analysis — short, medium or long-range — economic or technical relations, the forecasting methods and tools will greatly differ.

Thus, the forecasting of energy demand has been the object over the last two decades, and especially since 1973, of a growing sophistication both as regards methods and evaluation tools. Energy demand forecasting was carried out mainly by the producers in the period of abundant and cheap energy, and thus was subordinated to a logic of production; demand forecasting nowadays concerns far more diversified social groups, often with dissimilar objectives and rationalities: the awareness, following 1973, of the reality and the acuteness of the energy problems, the emergence of new constraints and of new energy policy requirements thus led to an alteration of energy forecasting in spirit and in method.

Today we are witnessing a triple evolution as regards methods:
— An attempt to expand classical econometric methods.
— A development of new methods allowing one to better understand the principal factors determining energy demand and combining an economic and a technical analysis (process analysis).
— An extension of the macro-economic models of general equilibrium in order to further consider the energy sector and the principal sectors of energy consumption.

Each of these methodological evolutions corresponds to a different spirit and a different goal: improvement of the reliability of traditional forecasting, in the first case, greater flexibility of forecasting in the second, and lastly coherent integration of the energy evolution in a macro-economic framework. As we shall see further on, these different concerns are somewhat contradictory and explain the variety of methodological efforts.

Any forecasting method relies upon a vision of the mechanisms through which the factor, whose evolution one attempts to forecast, is driven by one or several explicative factors, and the formalization of this vision by means of a model. From whence the sometimes erroneous assimilation of model and method.

The usual terminology of "forecasting model of energy demand" in fact concerns a sub-group of forecasting models, within which relationships are formalized in a mathematical way: generally they refer to a most precise forecasting method, but do not consider it in its entirety. We shall here look at this sub-group of the mathematical models of energy forecasting. After having identified the main groups of models developed and used at present, we shall point out the nature of the questions they are expected to answer and their general conditions of application. We shall conclude by presenting in greater detail one particular approach (the MEDEE approach).

1. General Considerations on Energy Modelling

1.1. Classification of Energy Models

As we have already claimed, any model consists of a group of mathematical relations linking to each other a given set of variables, and allowing for the calculation of the value of one variable from the basis of one or several others. Some of these variables are considered to be "exogenous" to the model in so far as no mathematical relation allows for their calculation, but are, however, used in the calculation of other variables, the latter being considered "endogenous".

A forecasting model is generally said to be deductive if the variable which is to be forecast, does not, in turn, influence any other explicative variable (it does not enter into the calculation of any other explicative variable): otherwise it is called "deductive-inductive" or "of equilibrium".

The relationships of a forecasting model are causal relations or relations of equilibrium[1]. In the energy field, this causality or equilibrium may have a physical or economic origin, thus introducing a fundamental dichotomy between the models related to the economy and those related to physics.

Thus, four types of forecasting models may be identified:

Mode:	Type of phenomenon:	Economic	Physical
Deductive		deductive economic models	deductive physical models
Deductive-Inductive		economic equilibrium models	physical equilibrium models

---

[1] In theory, only a deductive model may be a forecasting model, in so far as forecasting implies the causal inference between two phenomena and the causality allows no feedback. In practice, we speak of forecasting model everytime a model allows for the description of the evolution in time of the variable concerned.

We shall not speak of the physical models. Suffice it to say that the deductive physical models are those usually concerned with energy analysis or energy accounting; the equilibrium models are, as yet, little developed and refer mainly to the problems of resources[2].

Over the last few years, the importance of economic models of energy forecasting has grown significantly and any attempt to analyze them all, however briefly, is beyond the scope of this study. We shall therefore try to classify them according to the nature of the relationships involved, and more especially according to their formalization mode.

Several factors may determine the relationships of a model and the choice of explicative variables.

– Either an attempt to transcribe into mathematical form an explicative phenomenon deriving from theoretical considerations (that is to say representing the mechanism such as theory perceives them): for example, a model of the structure of household consumption allocating the disposable income according to different kinds of goods and services and to changes in the relative price of products and in the overall income (L.E.S. type model)[3].

– Or the mathematical expression of a link of a statistical kind, without necessarily referring to a theoretical explanation of the causality (model relating the G.D.P. and the energy consumption at an aggregate level, for example).

– Or, finally, the breaking-down of the technical and economic mechanisms related to energy; for example, a model simulating the development of household energy demand, by relating this demand to various technico-economic factors such as the size of the home, energy uses, the price of energy, . . .

The final form of these relationships will depend upon the rigidity of the link between this form and the true significance of the relationships: thus some relationships will be completely determined by the phenomena which they express (for example the specific consumption of cars multiplied by the average mileage of one car and by the car population gives the petrol consumption); others, however, will have the mathematical formalization which provides the best results on the statistical level; and finally others will result from a compromise between simplicity and the accurate reproduction of phenomena or statistics.

The first class of model resembles the general equilibrium models and because of this, we shall refer to them as such in our study.

Models of the second kind, where the relationships are based on the statistical analysis, will be referred to as econometric models of statistical inference, and more simply econometric models.

Models of the third kind shall be labelled phenomenological models or technico-economic models because they attempt to describe the very essence of the phenomena by relying upon the technical and economic factors which explain the development of the energy demand. It is one of these models that we shall later develop further.

---

[2] An example of these models is Malcolm Schlesser's STER model ("System, Time, Energy and Resources").

[3] L.E.S.: Linear Expenditure System.

This classification is not without overlapping; nevertheless it does seem to us to give a correct interpretation of the different approaches to energy demand, underlying the usual models, that is to say, on the one hand the economic theory, on the other statistical relationships and finally the phenomenological analysis. A bibliography of these three kinds of models, which especially emphasizes models recently developed, is given at the end of the book.

1.2. Analysis and Evaluation of Models

In general, a model can only answer the question for which it was originally designed. However, having been analyzed, the original question fades, whereas the model remains and continues to be used, often in order to answer other questions. The problem is thus to know if it may really, and in a relevant manner, answer these new questions. Generally, one may claim that a model remains relevant in so far as it fulfills the following two conditions:
− the model's relationships remain reliable,
− these relationships remain sufficient to explain the whole of the phenomenon (exhaustivity), in our case the development of the energy demand.

The reliability of the relationships may be partly or totally jeopardized if one strays from the conditions of validity of the underlying theory (if indeed there is a theory) and/or from the conditions necessary.for the validity of the analysis or of the statistical calculations.

The exhaustive investigation of relationships is proved deficient when a new phenomenon begins to acquire significance whereas it had been set aside from the theoretical diagram or the phenomenological analysis, or could not be evaluated on the basis of the statistics (the instance of the price of energy or of certain structural alteration).

One may thus point to three principal causes likely to diminish or eliminate the relevance of a forecasting model:
− the preservation − and a fortiori expansion − of the time horizon of forecasting in a socio-economic environment, which is rapidly changing or subjected to sudden ruptures,
− the transposition of the model to different socio-economic systems,
− finally, the change in the spatial scale (for instance regionalization).

According to the kind of model and the use made of it compared to the model's original conditions of use, the forecasting will be more or less reliable. This is where the experience and common sense of the model builder come into play (in a most fundamental way) in order to appreciate the limits of the possible uses of the model and its relevance. Indeed, more or less advanced methods have been suggested to deal more systematically with the relevance of a model: validation in the past, confrontation with reality, consistency of the results according to variations of the input variables (sensitivity tests), comparison with other models.

Past validation is a method which probably only provides a most ambiguous indication of the relevance of a forecasting model, and, especially, its ability to forecast accurately: if it is an econometric model, its past validity, which is one of the components of statistical analysis, is necessarily guaranteed; if it is a phé-nomenological model, its reliability is necessarily ensured as soon as the exoge-nous variables are attributed their true values.

Similarly, the confrontation of a previous forecasting with reality is of little interest; a forecast may prove excellent without the model being so, simply because this particular forecast was made by a producer and supports his ob-jectives, which he has the means of attaining; inversely, the dissimilarity of a forecast with reality does not necessarily imply that the model is of bad quality; at the most, it confirms either an erroneous use or, more often, erroneous assumptions concerning certain exogeneous variables.

The relative stability of model results, in the case of variations of input variables, is more a guarantee of the reliability of the results in the event of a change in the model's conditions of use, than a guarantee of the relevance of the model itself (in its original conditions of application). Only when one is convinced that this stability is one of the components of the reality one wishes to describe will it be possible to draw conclusion concerning the relevance of the model.

The comparison with other models does not allow one to evaluate the model, but it may lead, through the analysis of the differences with other models, to the discovery of imperfections in the representation of the model. One may mention the efforts of the Energy Modelling Forum which has con-centrated on the analysis of energy models developed in the U.S.A.

In the wake of these observations, we shall now consider the three types of models mentioned above, looking more especially at their characteristics and limits. We shall of course bear in mind the analysis of energy demand, set out above, to see how the various kinds of models are able to account for it.

1.3. The Econometric Models

The principle of econometric models is simple; from the basis of a few conventional economic indicators, supposed to give a synthetic, total or partial, representation of the economy (G.D.P., national income, value added per sector, . . .) they allow for the calculation of the level of the energy demand, globally or per sector[1], or else per energy form. The relationships involved in these models are of a purely statistical kind: their shape and parameters are established on the basis of correlations between the energy demand and the economic indicators concerned. The quality of these relationships is directly linked to the quality of the statistical correlations, the latter being evaluated on the basis of some conventional statistical tests (R^2, Durbin-Watson, Student-Fisher, . . .). The constant search for the improvement of these relationships, on the statistical level, has led to a growing sophistication of the econometric

---

[1] We may thus distinguish: global models, sectorial models which analyze the energy demand at the level of the main sectors of the economy (residential, tertiary, industrial, agriculture, transport, etc.) and the analytical models which go further still into the disaggregation.

models both on the mathematical level, and on the level of phenomena taken into account (introduction of random variables for instance).

However, the fundamental characteristic of these models remains their complete subjection to the statistics, so closely bound are the input variables (economy or energy) and relationships to available statistics. Three consequences result from this:
— these models can only take into account explicative economic variables which, on the one hand, are statistically measured, and which, on the other hand, have had a statistically significant relationship with the energy demand (this excludes, a priori, any variable which has shown no or little development in the past);
— they can only reproduce in the future past evolutions; or, more precisely, past relationships between the economic variables and the energy demand;
— the disaggregation possibilities are directly dependent upon the accuracy of the statistical observations concerning the energy demand.

Until the 1973—74 crisis, these models were undeniably privileged by producers and governments, for three principal reasons.

In the first place, these models have always been considered by engineers and economists as having a strong "scientific" content; as mathematical translations of observed past phenomena, they resembled the physical models whose strictness they were meant to reproduce.

Secondly, they appeared as a synthetic but exhaustive representation of all the complex mechanisms linking the economy to energy demand: from this point of view, they were meant to be most coherent, which also reinforced their "scientific" content.

Finally, it is undeniable that, as long as these models were used for limited time horizons (5 to 10 years), within the context of a regular economic growth and stable energy prices, they provided reliable answers.

Following 1973/74, the radical alteration of the economic and energy context called for an important reconsideration of the reliability of these models, all the more so in that producers and governments alike were continually seeking to widen their forecasting horizons. In short, one may say that their subordination to the past and to the statistical framework prevent them from satisfactorily taking into account the rapid growth of energy prices and the significant variations in the development of economic structures. As revealed by the comparison between countries, the relationship between energy consumption and economic growth, globally or per sector, has proved very different according to the country, or has even undergone quite a large variation in the course of time within the same country; unexplainable solely in terms of energy prices or of economic structures, this heterogeneity provides a good indication of the range of possibilities for change in comparison with the past. In this respect, the comparison of studies pertaining to the measurement of the price elasticity of the energy demand is quite striking. R. Pindyck, for example, showed that the price elasticity estimates varied according to the studies from 0.28 to 1.1 for the residential sector, from 0.49 to 0.9 for industry and from 0.22 to 1.3 for motor fuels [6].

Over the last few years, various attempts have been made to overcome these

obstacles, and thus give a new credibility to these models. The first ones consist in the maximum disaggregation of these models according to the available statistics, this in order to find at a more disaggregate level the conditions of invariability which had disappeared at the more global level. These attempts unfortunately encounter two new obstacles:
— the reduction in the overall coherence of the model in the course of dis-aggregation (which, historically, has led to the fact that analytical econometric forecasts always provided results further removed from reality than global forecasts);
— the impossibility to appreciate the degree of "invariability" of a statistical relationship — however disaggregate — since it only relates to a past reality, and in no way explains this reality.

The other attempts aimed at introducing into the models relationships which do not rely upon statistical observation but which are based on technico-economic studies of the kind we developed above (for instance the energy con-sumption in relation to prices). Quite appealing at first sight, these attempts do, on second thought, present great problems of coherence: the statistical relation-ships of the model constitute a synthetic and coherent representation of a past complex reality, which includes, among others, those phenomena which one henceforth wants to model distinctly on a different basis, without having identified and isolated them from this past reality.

1.4. The Phenomenological (Technico-Economic) Models

Mostly developed to go beyond the limits of econometric models, too rigid and too closely bound to the past, the phenomenological models are based upon a mathematical identification and representation of the overall mechanisms which explain how energy demand is created and evolves. These models share the following characteristics:
— they are all very disaggregate models considering the energy demand at the level of end-uses;
— the energy demand is apprehended both in terms of useful energy and final energy, so as to isolate the influence of substitutions among energy forms which have different end-use efficiencies;
— the useful energy needs are linked, as often as possible, to physical indicators of activity or of needs (for instance number of cars, of homes, steel production, heating temperature), or else to economic indicators (value added, incomes, . . .).

As we shall see below in the description of the MEDEE models, the principal characteristic of these models stems from the importance attributed to technol-ogy in the creation and development of energy demand. In particular the role of prices in the development of energy consumption is mainly taken into account through technical choices (industrial processes, insulation of homes, etc.) and the substitution of one form of energy for another (as regards industrial installa-tions, heating appliances, etc.)[1].

---

[1] Some phenomenological models also attempt to take into account the influence of prices on the consumers' needs (heating temperature, mobility, . . .) and upon the economic activity (steel production, value added, etc.), which, in our opinion, conjures up great problems of coherence over a long period.

The limits of these models are essentially due to their high level of dis-aggregation; they are linked to:
— the availability of plentiful and varied information, both in the technical and economic field (although this information does not only consist of statistical series);
— the difficulty of ensuring a sufficient coherence between all assumptions on exogenous variables;
— the difficulty of also ensuring a sufficient coherence between all the exoge-nous assumptions and the evolutions evaluated by the model (feedback problem).

In spite of their limits, these models have known a rapid growth since the energy crisis, in so far as they may provide, over a relatively long time horizon, the initial elements to answer some fundamental questions pertaining to the role of prices, the structural development of the economy or to alternative energy policies. In addition, their exceptional simplicity and their transparence make them significant pedagogic tools, and thus particularly well-suited to any investigation of the energy future.

The present developments of these models are geared towards the search for a greater coherence, both between the exogenous assumptions and between these assumptions and the results. Thus, on the one hand we witness the de-velopment and the improvement of scenario design methods aiming at setting up plausible and coherent images of the future, in the économic, social and technological fields; on the other hand, we can observe the development of various methods for the control of coherence which, among other things, aim at ensuring the compatibility of energy development with the underlying eco-nomic assumptions. In so far as these models are deductive, it is obvious that these improvements will always be limited by the explicit non-integration, within these models, of the feedbacks (from the results calculated on the original assumptions): such an integration, apart from destroying the logic of the model, would also be in total contradiction with the search for a greater co-herence of the initial frameworks (since the results would be likely to modify the assumptions).

1.5. *Models of General Equilibrium*

Prior to the oil crisis, the general equilibrium models were essentially used for macro-economic projections, considering energy in monetary terms and in an aggregate way. Ever since the crisis, the oil price increases and their conse-quences on the commercial balance, economic growth and the inflation rate on the one hand, the vigorous energy policies implemented in answer to these increases, on the other hand (nuclear, energy conservation), have drawn the attention of economists to the growing interdependence between energy and the rest of the economy. This has led to the development of equilibrium models combining a macro-economic and a technical approach where energy, as regards both the supply and the demand, is considered in a disaggregate way. The modelling efforts may be grouped into two classes. On the one hand, models are derived and adapted from classical macro-sectorial[1] models (MSGE in Norway, mini DMS – energy in France, EPM in Sweden, Eta-Macro or Hudson Jorgenson in the U.S.A., . . .)[2], the more disaggregate energy modelling being done within the framework of satellite models of the central macro-sectorial model. On the other hand, we may find what is commonly called "model chains" made up of a group of models (macro-economic, energy demand and supply) which should operate simultaneously (models of the EEC, of IIASA, of BNL[3]); although these "models chains" resemble the equilibrium models, because of the feedback effect taken into account, their lack of homogeneity and of a theoretical reference framework (each model having its own underlying theory) removes them from the true equilibrium models of the first kind, which are our main concern.

The goal of these models is, first of all, to analyze the macro-economic consequences of the alternative energy policies (tax policy, for instance), together with other economic projections; in addition, they may be used to project into the future the level of the energy demand. In their more recent developments, they combine a classical macro-sectorial central model with technico-economic satellite models, which are capable of attaining a very high degree of detail (industrial processes, energy saving measures); these satellite models, in fact, represent a disaggregation of certain parts of the macro-economic model, and aim at evaluating the development of a certain number of the latter's technical coefficients, the development of which cannot be deduced from classical statistics.

The Swedish EPM model, which strikes us as one of the more interesting models of this type, contains satellite models for refineries, household space heating, and it is planned to add to it physical models for some energy intensive industries. Within this model, the choice between processes of production or of energy savings is endogeneous and results from a minimization of the costs.

The particularity of these models, which is also their weakness, is that they combine, within the framework of an overall economic equilibrium, a study of the energy demand in purely economic terms with a technical approach: the combination of the coherence of the economic theory and fidelity to concrete realities. This combination contains its own contradiction, since any economic theory pre-supposes the existence of preliminary conditions (market conditions, the behaviour of economic agents, etc.) which are often quite far removed from concrete realities: either one must preserve the coherence of the economic model, and in this case it is necessary to subject the satellite models to the conditions of validity of the theoretical model (in particular, anything

---

[1] We shall refer to macro-sectorial models in the case of multiple sector macro-economic models, that is to say rather disaggregate.

[2] See References.

[3] EEC: European Economic Community (Brussels, Belgium), IIASA: International Institute for Applied System Analysis (Laxenburg, Austria), BNL: Brookhaven National Laboratory (Brookhaven, U.S.A.).

pertaining to technological development), which removes them from the reality of the technicol-economic mechanisms linked to energy; or one reproduces as far as possible the real conditions of energy development, thus necessarily weakening the coherence of the economic model.

One of the most obvious consequences of this contradiction is the difficulty of taking into account the role of prices in a truly satisfactory fashion: on the one hand (the central macro-economic model) prices and volumes are simultaneously determined from the basis of a very rough but homogeneous representation of behaviours (KLEM[4] or LES functions for instance); on the other hand (the satellite models) the relative prices of energy and capital govern the technical choices, and thus the development of energy consumption, in a much more pragmatic and realistic manner, but which quite clearly may not be reduced to the representation of the central economic model. The price, theoretical measurement in the first case, real information in the second, does not have and cannot have, the same significance in the two models: any search for identity among these prices is, from this point of view, meaningless and can only lead to important distortions regarding the central macro-economic model.

2. The MEDEE Approach: An Example of a Phenomenological Method

We have chosen to present the MEDEE approach in greater detail for three reasons:
– few publications have been devoted so far to phenomenological methods, whereas there are numerous descriptions and analyses of econometric methods;
– the MEDEE approach, conceived and developed by the authors, is of course the approach they are best acquainted with;
– it renders explicit the relationship between the analysis and the forecast.

We shall first of all concentrate, in this presentation, on the general characteristics of this approach, which are quite similar to all phenomenological methods; then we shall turn to the specificities of the MEDEE models and of the associated scenarios.

2.1. General Characteristics

The MEDEE approach was designed in order to overcome some of the limits previously outlined for the traditional forecasting methods, and for this purpose it was based on the following main ideas.

Energy demand is induced by *socio-economic determinants* that is, by economic activities and by the satisfaction of social needs (e.g., mobility of persons, temperature in rooms, . . .). These determinants lead to a demand for *useful energy* (e.g., process heat, mechanical energy, . . .) whose intensity depends on the technologies used to satisfy the social needs or to perform the economic

---

[4]   KLEM functions: econometric functions relating production factors: capital (K), labour (L), energy (E), materials (M).

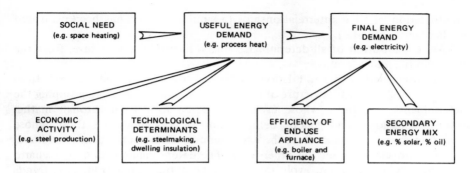

Fig. 5.1. General scheme for energy demand analysis in MEDEE

activities. The demand for energy commodities, or *final energy* (e.g., coal, electricity, gas), can be calculated from the level of useful energy demand and will depend upon the efficiency of the equipment (e.g., furnaces, boilers, engines) used to convert the final energy into useful energy. Thus the *final energy demand* of a society is directly related to its social, economic, and technological pattern of development (see Fig. 5.1 for the general scheme of energy demand analysis).

In order to explore the impact of structural changes in the socio-economic development on long-term energy demand, it is necessary to disaggregate the social, economic and technological system so as to be able to take these changes explicitly into account. These include changes in: social needs (e.g., saturation); the international division of labor (e.g., the eventual shift of heavy industries such as steel from industrialized countries to developing countries, resulting in lower costs for energy, raw materials, and labor); government policies (e.g., transportation and energy conservation policies); technology (e.g., substitution of current processes for less energy-intensive ones); energy prices (especially oil prices).

The various aspects of the development of society, which determine the long-term energy demand growth, must be described in an exhaustive, consistent and plausible way, that is to say within the framework of a methodically de-signed scenario, in which must be included studies of sociologists, economists, policy analysts, etc.

Finally, the approach must lead to an operational tool which could easily be applied to various countries and various scenario cases.

In respect to those main guidelines, the MEDEE approach involves the following steps.

1) Disaggregation of the total energy demand into relevant homogeneous end-use categories or modules (cooking and space heating for instance) whose selection depends upon the objectives pursued by the model-builder, on data availability and on the characteristics of the country (see Fig. 5.2 for the basic reference structure).

2) A systematic analysis of the social, economic, and technological factors determining the long-term energy demand evolution within each module, and

identification of their interrelationships (a similar analysis has been presented in chapters 2, 3, and 4).

3) Organization of all determinants into a hierarchical structure, from the macro to the micro level.

4) Construction of a simulation model and of an associated scenario structure by simplifying the structure of the socio-economic system and grouping the determinants into those whose evolution can be formalized through mathematical equations (endogenous determinants or variables) and those whose evolution cannot be quantified, the exogeneous determinants on the one hand, the scenario elements on the other hand. The determinants chosen as scenario elements are those whose evolution cannot be extrapolated from past trends and for which the range of future possibilities is fairly wide in the time horizon under consideration (e.g., thermal characteristics of homes, public transport supply, use of private cars); their evolution is specified in a scenario. The exogeneous determinants encompass those factors whose evolution is difficult to model (e.g., population growth, number of persons per household) but for which their long-term evolution can be adjusted suitably from past trends or from other studies (e.g., demographic studies).

2.2. The MEDEE Models

Two computerized models have been built so far: MEDEE 2 and MEDEE 3[1]. Firstly, they differ in their level of disaggregation, MEDEE 2 being more aggregate (the trip purposes, the age structure of the housing stock, the various services sectors as well as the energy intensive industries are not accounted for in a detailed way). Secondly, in MEDEE 2, the development of new energy forms and technologies (e.g., solar, heat pump, electricity) as replacements for fossil fuels is normative and defined within the framework of the scenario, while in MEDEE 3 this development is simulated on the basis of the energy prices, the energy policy, and the decision-maker's behaviour. Thirdly, there is associated with MEDEE 3 a systematic procedure for the scenario design, aiming at improving the scenario coherence. Finally, MEDEE 3 simulates the whole evolution of the socio-economic system (e.g. evolution of people's mobility, industrial activities) and calculates the energy demand for each module: MEDEE 2 is more an accounting framework than a real simulation model, which translates or quantifies a given scenario in terms of useful and final energy demand.

The main characteristics of the MEDEE 3 model are developed hereafter. As shown in Fig. 5.2, which shapes the structure of the model, MEDEE 3 is made up of three interrelated sub-models.

The sub-model of the urban system operates the following simulations and calculations:

— simulation of the evolution of the structure of the human settlement, and

---

[1] MEDEE 1 is a mathematical model which has never been computerized; it has only been used for the first MEDEE study on France [5].

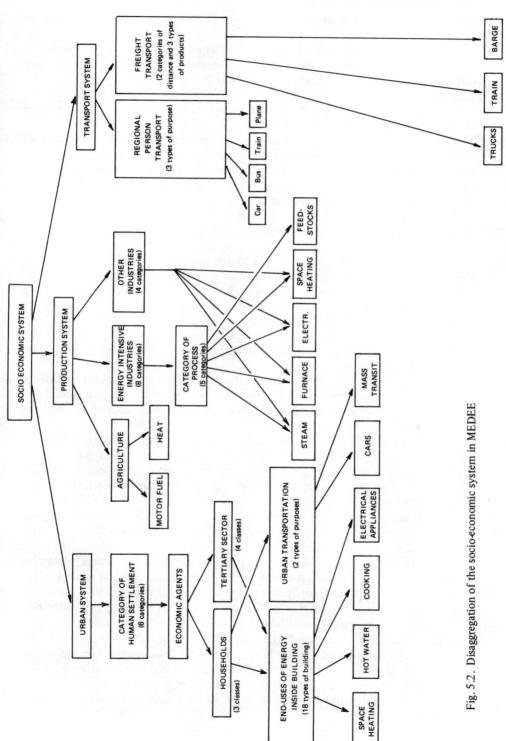

Fig. 5.2. Disaggregation of the socio-economic system in MEDEE

calculation of some indicators characterizing the evolution of the urban system as a whole;
— simulation of the evolution of district heating and of the average distance of urban trips; calculation of some indicators characterizing the evolution of urban settlement as a whole (population distribution within towns);
— simulation of the evolution of the housing stock, of its structure (apartment versus single family houses; by age; by class of household), and of its main characteristics (insulation and superficies);
— calculation of useful and final energy demand for space heating by class of dwelling, and by type of heating system; simulation of the choices among the various heating systems in new dwellings; choices which depend on the behavior of the various decision-makers (households, public and private developers), on the prices of the various energy products and on the costs of the various systems;
— simulation of the need for useful energy for hot water and calculation of resulting energy demand, by category of household and dwelling;
— calculation of final energy demand for cooking;
— simulation of the evolution of electricity need for appliances and lighting and calculation of resulting electricity demand;
— calculation of urban traffic by category of cities; simulation of the choices made by the various kinds of households among the various means of transport, taking into account the transport purpose, the fixed and proportional costs of the various means and the behaviour of the households; calculation of the resulting modal distribution in urban transport and calculation of motor fuel demand for each mode.
— simulation of the evolution of educational building area and calculation of final energy demand for space heating, hot water, electrical appliances and school bus services; same for offices, retail and wholesale commerce, and the other services.

In the production sub-model, eight different energy intensive industries have been distinguished: steel, aluminum, cement, pulp and paper, glass, ammonia, ethylene, chlorine; the other sectors are grouped into four classes: food and textile, mechanical and equipment goods, other chemicals, others. Details of this sub-model are as follows:
— calculation of values for the macro-economic variables characterizing the production system: value-added, employment and productivity of industry, building and construction, agriculture;
— simulation of the evolution of labour productivity in the non-energy intensive industries; simulation of the evolution of the technical coefficients related to the energy demand for steam, for furnaces and for mechanical uses in these industries; calculation of the structure of the value added of this group of industries;
— simulation of the evolution of labour productivity in the non energy-intensive mechanical uses and space heating in each non energy-intensive industry, depending on its value added; calculation of resulting final energy demand for all of these uses, taking into account the penetration of electricity in furnaces;
— simulation of the evolution of the consumption, production and import-export, in physical terms, of the product of each energy intensive industry;

calculation of the part of production which is recycled and calculation of the "process" structure of the rest of the production;
— simulation of the evolution of specific energy consumption for steam, furnaces, electrical appliances and mechanical uses, space heating and feedstocks, by unit of production, for each process; calculation of resulting energy demand, related to each use within each process;
— calculation of heat demand for greenhouses; simulation of motor fuels demand in agriculture, on a value-added basis.
 The transport sub-model operates as follows:
— simulation of the evolution of the infrastructures of transport: mileage of railways, roads, motorways and waterways;
— simulation of the evolution of specific energy consumption of the various means of long-distance freight transport; simulation of the "desired"[2] evolution of long-distance freight traffic by trains, trucks, and barges;
— simulation of the evolution of food products traffic, on the basis of the evolution of the value added of agriculture; simulation of the evolution of the modal distribution of this traffic and calculation of the resulting energy demand;
— simulation of the evolution of traffic of building and construction materials on the basis of the evolution of value added of the building and construction sector; simulation of the evolution of the modal distribution of this traffic: calculation of the resulting energy demand;
— calculation of other manufactured and raw materials traffic, on the basis of the consumption of intermediary goods; simulation of the modal distribution of this traffic and calculation of the resulting energy demand;
— calculation of the real modal distribution of long-distance freight traffic;
— simulation of the evolution of short-distance freight traffic and calculation of resulting motor fuel demand;
— simulation of the specific consumption evolution for the various modes of passenger transport (trains, cars, planes, buses); calculation of the car ownership ratio for the different human settlement classes;
— simulation of the evolution of short trips by car and by bus;
— simulation of the evolution of the number of private long trips by class of households; calculation of the modal distribution of these trips and simulation of the resulting traffic for each mode of transport;
— simulation of the evolution of the number of professional trips; simulation of the resulting traffic for each mode of transport;
— calculation of overall passenger traffic by train; simulation of the evolution of this traffic distribution between traditional and high-speed trains; calculation of the load factors of these trains and calculation of resulting energy demand for passenger trains; the same applies for private cars.
 MEDEE 3 equations are of four types:
— equations that allow for the calculation of the energy demand for a given year;

---

[2] "Desired" means what the decision-makers would like, taking into account the relative prices of energy and the general transport and land-use policy.

— equations allowing for the simulation of the evolution of the technical and economic determinants of energy demand, from year t to year $t + 1$;
— equations which prevent inconsistencies or errors appearing during the simulation;
— tabular functions which allow for the association of quantitative values with qualitative indicators used in the scenario description; these functions are of the form: $A = f(B, C)$, where A is a quantitative variable and B and C are qualitative indicators whose values are specified by integer numbers, 1, 2, 3, . . . (see below the description of the scenario structure).

Three types of variables are linked through these equations:
— endogenous quantitative variables, for which the value is calculated every five years;
— exogenous quantitative variables, either constant or defined for each year of calculation, but independent of the evolution of the socio-economic system under consideration;
— qualitative and quantitative scenario indicators which describe the evolution of the main technical, political, social and economic features of the socio-economic system under consideration.

2.3. Scenario Design and Exploration of Long-Term Energy Demand

As we indicated previously, MEDEE 3 is fed with "scenario" assumptions which are made in a consistent and plausible way. This means two things:
— MEDEE 3 simply translates, in energy demand terms, the evolution of the socio-economic system described through the scenario assumptions;
— the quality and the pertinence of projections of long-term energy demand depend on the consistency and the plausibility of the scenario assumptions.

Consequently it is necessary to pay as much attention to the design procedure for the scenario assumptions as to the model itself. The first step in tackling this problem correctly is to decide which kind of scenario one wants to build, which depends on the way one wants to handle the future (normative versus positive scenario for instance). The definition of "scenario" used here is that "the scenario method is a synthetic approach which, on the one hand simulates, step by step and in a plausible and consistent way, a series of events leading a system to a future situation, and on the other hand, presents an overall picture of this situation"[1]. The scenario method used in the framework of the MEDEE approach involves two steps: identification of the scenario elements and of their relationships (scenario structure), design of the scenario path.

In the MEDEE approach, the scenario structure is a direct extension of the system analysis of energy demand and of the resulting construction of the simulation model, since these previous steps
— contributed to identifying the elements which either characterize or are dependent on the evolution of the socio-economic system and for which it is impossible to formalize the evolution mechanisms,

---

[1] Translated from Reference [3].

— allowed for the elaboration, among those elements, of a hierarchical structure which can be extended to the scenario structure, since a hierarchical relation between two elements can be translated into an order relation between the assumptions related to those elements.

So, three groups of scenario elements (variables) can be organized:
— those which characterize the international environment of the system and the economic and political relationships existing between the system and this environment;
— those which characterize the main economic, social, political and technological features of the development of the system under consideration;
— those which characterize secondary aspects of the evolution of the different sub-systems, at different levels, as shown in the description of MEDEE 3.

The structure formed by the elements of this last group is completely integrated in the structure of MEDEE 3 (the assumptions related to those variables are pre-recorded in the data base and called by the tabular functions). These elements are hierarchically related to the elements of the two former groups. As far as France is concerned, we consider that there exists a hierarchical relationship between the first group of elements and the second — meaning that the evolution of the French socio-economic system is influenced by the international environment and that the contrary is not true.

Three main variables characterize the long-term evolution of the world economy as far as the national economy is concerned:
— the rate of growth of world economic activity;
— the international division of labour and the worldwide location of industrial production;
— the prices of raw materials and, particularly, the price of oil.

Although it is obvious that these variables are all dependent on each other, it is impossible to formalize their relationships, and then to draw a formalized structure of this sub-scenario. Nevertheless, it is necessary to keep these relationships in mind while designing the scenario.

Two kinds of variables are part of the socio-economic scenario:
— qualitative *descriptors* of the type of society which is supposed to develop within the time period under consideration (social and political options);
— quantitative macro-economic and social variables which describe the rate, the social content and the structure of economic growth.

Nine qualitative *descriptors* have been taken into consideration which specify different aspects of the type of society: type of economic growth, urbanization, industrial development, social policy, transport system, human settlement, housing, natural environment, and energy system. As for the world scenario base, relationships between these variables exist, and must be kept in mind, but cannot be formalized (the structure depends on the scenario).

The construction of each scenario is concretely carried out as follows.
— From the basis of a pre-selected sequence of events, one establishes a full qualitative description of the scenario which will be used as a guiding line for the quantification of assumptions.
— One concretely specifies this description, with the help of qualitative *de-*

scriptors, by selecting for each one the adequate option among those available. This presupposes a clear definition of the different possible alternative options for each of these descriptors (for example three options may be associated to the descriptor "energy saving policy": 1, absence of policy; 2, moderate policy solely concerned with housing; 3, radical policy with severe regulations, . . .).
— One translates this description into macro-economic terms (growth rate, economic structure, income structure, employment, . . .) either directly if one does not have access to a macro-economic model, or if one does, by defining the few exogenous assumptions necessary to the proper functioning of this model.
— The assumptions concerning the other scenario elements (3rd group) are automatically generated from the options chosen for the qualitative descriptors. In this case, it is necessary for tabular functions to have been established previously between these descriptors and the scenario variables (which are dependent upon them), relating to each option or group of options the value which is the most significant and relevant as possible for the scenario variable. The elaboration of these functions is, on the one hand, based upon the scenario structure (relationships among elements) and on the other hand, relies upon prospective studies of the different variables. The principle in itself is simple: it consists in organizing in a logical and coherent way the significant values of a variable in the range of possibilities in terms of the different socio-economic, political and technical developments one wishes to describe.

2.4. Use of the MEDEE Models

Three major uses of the MEDEE models can be envisioned:
— explore long-term energy demand resulting from various parts of society development and energy policy, that is to say forecast long-term energy demand;
— improve the understanding of energy demand development, for instance analyze the relationship between economic growth and energy demand growth or study the potential for energy conservation or else delimitate the range of future energy demand by means of contrasted scenario;
— assist national or regional decision makers dealing with energy problems in the process of planning.

Forecasting

One category of users of the MEDEE models is made up of those who need long-term energy demand perspectives in order to assist them in decision making, but whose decisions do not affect in a significant way the economic development pattern (energy companies or international organizations for instance). In this case the use of the models consists in:
— identifying the socio-economic scenarios which seem to be the most probable taking into account the historical trends, the present policy goals of the government, the structural changes in the society that can be observed now and can be assumed in the future;
— calculating the consequences of these scenarios in terms of useful energy needs and of energy products demand;

— analyzing the sensitivity of these results to the variations of some variables whose evolution is the least known, or variables which are crucial as to energy demand.

Initially MEDEE was conceived and developed for this type of application. It was first applied in the case of France for three national companies, Electricité de France (EDF), Commissariat à l'Energie Atomique (CEA) and Elf-Aquitaine (SNEA). Further work has since then been carried out for the International Institute for Applied System Analysis (IIASA) and the European Community (EC). For the EC two types of applications have been carried out: application of MEDEE 3 to each country of the EC, which implied the constitution of a detailed data base on social, economic and energy indicators and the elaboration of forecasts for all these countries; premilinary investigation of what could be the energy demand pattern of the EC in year 2000 with MEDEE 2.

Understanding Energy Demand Growth

Research institutes or even administrations may be interested to test specific scenarios with the idea of understanding better some aspects of energy demand. In this case, the crucial point is the selection of the scenarios which have to be relevant with respect to the issue to investigate. So far several issues related to energy demand have been treated with MEDEE; the conclusions are still preliminary and need to be further investigated.

Two studies have been carried out, one for France and another one in the case of the U.S.A.

In the case of France three scenarios have been investigated and compared; these scenarios were assumed to have the same economic growth rate and demographic evolution but different socio-economic growth pattern and energy conservation policies. The first scenario (referred to as A) assumes a prolongation in the future of the past trends in terms of industrial development (high industrial growth, decline of basic materials industries, restructuration of the industry around equipment goods industries) and an active policy of energy conservation and development of new energy sources and technologies (e.g. heat pumps, solar and district heating). The second scenario (B) considers that the economic and industrial structures will remain stable up to year 2000 and that no drastic measures will be taken to save energy. The third scenario (C) describes a contrasted evolution of the French economy characterized by a strong decentralization of economic activities and a significant development of service activities. The results are presented in details in [8]. The major findings are the following: for the same economic growth rate (4%/year) final energy demand varies in 2000 between 245 Mtoe (scenarios A and C) and 315 Mtoe (B) which represents a difference of 70 Mtoe that is to say about 60% of the present oil imports; the electricity also varies significantly: 390 Twh in C, 430 Twh in A and 540 Twh in B, which represents a range of 150 Twh (i.e. the equivalent of the annual production of 25 to 30 nuclear reactors). On the period 1975—2000, the elasticity of energy demand to G.D.P. varies between 0.55 for A and C and 0.8 for B, compared to an historical value closed to 1: this shows a clear decoupling between economic activity and energy demand, even for a scenario which extrapolates more or less the past trends (B). The results show also that, whatever the scenario, the dependance to fossil fuel remains high: decline from 83% in 1975 to 68% (A), 80% (B), 77% (C) in 2000.

For the application to the U.S.A., three alternative scenarios have been considered to characterize possible evolutions of the American society, and therefore span the range of likely future energy demand in the U.S.A., for a given economic growth rate (4.5% between 1975 and 1985, 3% after). These scenarios are mainly differentiated from the point of view of the U.S.A. administration attitude towards the energy demand growth and the public response to the energy policy that could be implemented (pricing standards) (reference [9]).

Conclusion: Prospects and Scenarios

The analysis of past energy consumption as well as the methodological reflections upon forecasting inevitably lead one to question the extrapolation over a long period of time, in both principle and practice: 1980—2000 will not be a "remake" of 1960—1980, and France, Federal Republic of Germany or Italy will probably never have the same per capita energy consumption level as that of present day America. In the energy field, as in most other fields, the importance of the past fades with time and gives way to today's and tomorrow's decisions and events. The most current mode of extrapolation — the pursuit of growth exponentials — has already been denounced by the Club of Rome [1]: to illustrate and to reinforce the latter's arguments, should we calculate the temperature at which people should heat their homes and the number of hours they should spend in their cars, which are implicit to an exponential growth? This seems obvious and would not deserve any further attention if the extrapolation and the belief in a hypothetical determinism of energy demand has not underlain many decisions, taken by energy producers and governments, which will be of the uttermost importance for society in the next few decades. Indeed, it is because of this belief in the inevitable "points of growth" of energy demand that the possibilities of new energy forms are cast aside, that large scale energy production techniques are justified, and that physical shortage of fossil fuels is considered as inevitable.

Economic growth obviously influences the evolution of energy demand. However, to claim that it acts in a uniform way in time and in space and, moreover, to claim that the evolution of energy demand is a necessary condition for economic growth, is to crudely omit the complexity of the links between energy and the economy and thus to ignore the social and technological components of enegy demand. Yet, it is not due to any lack of studies concerning one or the other, or even both these aspects and in almost all countries. In the prospective analysis developed in this study, we have tried to highlight the potential role of these two components: we could not conclude without integrating them in an overall view, which we shall illustrate with these studies.

Socio-Economic Development and Energy Demand

Similar rates of economic growth may in fact conceal very diverse social and economic realities; within these, the structure of economic activities and the land use pattern have a great influence upon energy demand.

As previously mentioned, the structure of economic activities directly determines the energy demand with respect to the production of goods and services; but it goes beyond this since it reflects the structure of the consumption of households and of the administration, as well as that of foreign trade: thus, on the one hand, it integrates the saturation phenomena of certain household appliances and of the car, and, on the other hand, the desequilibrium in foreign trade — as regards the energy content — between imported and exported products. In addition, upon this structure of activities depend the volume and the structure of goods traffic (and thus its modal distribution), both of which then determine the freight transport energy demand.

The changes in the economic structures of industrialized OECD countries will no doubt be dominated in the next twenty years by the continuation of the decline of the primary sector (agriculture, mines) and by the increasing importance of the tertiary sector (services). These developments as well as those previously mentioned for industry[1] generally result in energy demand growing gradually slower than the economy; this will be accentuated by the fact that household equipment will gradually reach saturation level as well as by the consequences of these developments upon goods traffic.

The impact of the land use pattern upon energy demand, though important, is more difficult to evaluate. It is certainly influential upon the individual's needs, especially with respect to transport, but also, and above all, it influences the development conditions of techniques. Thus, urban and industrial concentration may create conditions favourable to the development of energy conservation techniques (heat recovery and distribution by means of steam networks or district heating, public transport, economies of scale in industry, . . .); however, it significantly increases mobility needs inside and outside the city. Decentralization, while lowering mobility needs, may also create favourable conditions for the valorization of local energy sources such as solar or geothermal energy or small hydroelectric plants. Moreover, as revealed by the analysis of transport modes, the fact that dwellings are more or less concentrated within urban agglomerations will lead to a more or less significant development of multiple car ownership and will allow for a more or less extensive development of public modes of transport. Similarly, still related to the land-use pattern, the development and the use of transport infrastructures are liable to alter, one way or the other, the evolution of the modal distribution of passengers and goods traffic, with obvious consequences on energy demand. It is difficult to say at present what will be the trends in the land use pattern of industrial countries: are the trends towards concentration as experienced in these last few decades going to continue or will the development of economic structures and changes in social values bring about opposite trends. There are many opinions on this issue, but for the time being it would be premature to draw any definite conclusion, except to highlight the very strong inertia and the long time constants in this field.

---

[1] See Chapter 4.

Technology and Energy

Most studies concerning the long-term prospects of energy demand emphasize the role of technology in the evolution of demand. Many of these studies particularly attempt to analyze the consequences of the development of techniques aiming at slowing down the growth of energy demand. Without claiming to have given an exhaustive list of these techniques (this was not our intention) we have however highlighted those which we consider liable to play a significant role in the energy demand evolution. As previously seen, it is necessary to distinguish between the techniques concerning existing processes and installations, the effects of which may appear in the relatively short term, and those related to new installations and processes which are spreading more slowly — but prove more long lasting — through the renewal of obsolete installations or the expansion of the equipment stock. It is essential that this distinction be made explicit in long term prospects for two main reasons:

— the development conditions for these two kinds of techniques are very different, since, in the second case, they are linked to the rate of capital accumulation and renewal, itself linked to the economic growth rate (a two-way link); whereas in the first case it is essentially the combined effect of the relative prices of energy and capital and of the incentive policies which will prove to be the determining factor;

the influence of the relative prices of energy forms and of energy and capital may differently affect technical choices, in the first and second case; the pay-back time required for the investments aiming at reducing production costs or household expenditure is much shorter than that taken into account, explicitly or implicitly, in the choice of new equipment: because of this, the expectation of changes in energy prices will have a different influence in the two cases, inducing a great disparity in the development of the two types of techniques (a close look at what was happened since 1973 well illustrates this phenomenon).

On this basis, one better perceives the grounds and the objectives of energy conservation policies (also called policies for the rational use of energy), namely to induce technical changes which are economically desirable, but which cannot result from the sole influence of market forces. In fact, this goes well beyond the problem we have mentioned: even in so far as the choice of equipment or of new processes is concerned, the price mechanism can greatly be hindered by market imperfections due, for instance, to monopoly situations or to conflicting interests between the economic agents concerned by a same technical choice (a good example is the conflict of interests between a real estate developer and the family that is going to occupy the dwelling). Thus, the prospective analysis of trends in technology cannot be reduced to an analysis in terms of relative prices and must consider energy conservation policies. These encompass several aspects, some of which we shall mention only briefly: further elaboration would lead us into a new and vast field, that of planning, which is beyond the scope of this book. Firstly, the definition of the goals of an energy conservation policy results from a necessary trade-off between the means devoted to increase the energy production and those aiming at a reduction of the consumption. This trade off and consequently the vigour of the resulting conservation policy, is mainly linked to the expected evolution in energy prices, whether imported or not. Three kinds of measures may be implemented to achieve these goals: financial incentives, in the form of direct subsidies, tax reductions or tax impositions on certain energy products; non-financial incentives aiming at inducing more rational behaviour; regulations and standards concerning the energy characteristics of buildings and equipment. In order to correctly appreciate the impact of such conservation policies upon energy demand, it is necessary to examine the effectiveness of these measures, in view of their importance (dependent upon the financial means mobilized) and of the economic sector they deal with. The difficulties encountered in the implementation of these policies are in general due to the number of decision-makers involved and to the heterogeneity of the actual situations. Regulations are easy to introduce, but their effectiveness implies a great effort to control their implementation; in addition, unable to cope with the heterogeneity of the existing situations, these regulations may prove too costly for the collectivity. The financial incentives, because they are compatible with market mechanisms, may prove efficient on the economic level, but suffer from certain, or even all the afore-mentioned restrictions.

Scenarios

Numerous energy scenarios have emerged in the last few years, which more or less emphasize the social and technological components of energy demand. Their diversity, as well as their divergent conclusions, in relation to each other and to the classical perspectives, illustrate the degree of uncertainty concerning long-term trends in energy demand and the freedom of action of nations. As the time horizon lengthens, so the range of possibilities widens, and the influence of the past fades, becoming secondary in view of the innovation possibilities, both social and technological. In the very long-term (more than 30 years), extreme scenarios may be envisaged, but neither their coherence nor their probability can be seriously appreciated; in particular, the scenarios reproducing in the far distant future, through lack of imagination, the present economic social and technical framework may not be taken seriously.

In the time horizon of this study (20 to 25 years) two kinds of scenarios may be considered according to whether the social component of energy demand is affected or not, in other words whether or not there is a change in the socio-economic development pattern. In one case, the energy demand originates in the framework of a new growth model, and we shall speak of "growth scenarios"; in the other case, there is merely an adaptation of the technological infrastructure to the new energy situation, an adaptation which is more or less important according to the expected price rises and the policies implemented by the governments; we shall then refer to "technical fix scenarios".

Although we have excluded the very long-term from our prospective analysis we shall nevertheless also refer to the "Soft Energy Path" argument, since it often appears in the debate on future energy demand.

Technical Fix Scenarios

Following 1973, there was a general agreement among energy producers and governments that the only solution to the energy crisis was to rapidly develop concentrated energy sources (coal or nuclear energy). Such an opinion rested upon the belief in a necessarily rapid growth of energy demand. Quite soon, however, this notion of the inevitable growth of demand began to be questioned; a new argument emerged, based on the conviction that the growth of energy demand would not only be affected by the increase of energy prices, but also that it could be slowed down with appropriate technical measures, and that this could be the core of an energy policy. At first the argument of experts or of independent organizations, this opinion has since spread within official energy circles[2]. Several studies in the U.S.A. (Ford Foundation [3], CONAES [7]), in the U.K., (IIED [5], SPRU [4])[3] or even in France (Ministery of Industry [6])), to mention only the most well-known, have shown that the economic and social development could continue in the next twenty or thirty years with a much slower growth rate of energy demand than in the past, and even in certain cases a certain decrease (CONAES).

The scenarios considered in these studies are all defined within the frame-work of the existing economic growth pattern, without questioning the nature of this growth or life styles, the slowing down of the evolution of demand resulting mainly from technical changes compatible with the economic growth. By doing so, the authors intended to dissociate the social from the technical changes, so that the conclusions of their studies be better accepted. Due to the inevitable and complex interactions between the technical choices and the socio-economic development, such an attitude may a priori, seem to call for criticism. Although in the very long-term it would seem difficult to ignore the feedbacks of the technical choices upon society, these effects may never-theless be considered secondary within a sufficiently short time horizon. The delays necessary for the implementation of technological innovations and the inertia of social systems are such that a horizon of 20 to 25 years seems a good compromise between the need for a long-term scope, previously mentioned, and the conditions of validity.

The methods used for the evaluation of energy needs in this kind of studies mostly resemble the phenomenological (technico-economic) methods described above. The classification of energy uses is often similar to that presented in

---

[2] D. Finon has provided an excellent analysis of the logic of the various prospective approaches which one encounters at present in the energy field [14].

[3] CONAES: Committee on Nuclear and Alternative Energy Systems; IIED: International Institute for Environment and Development; SPRU: Science and Policy Research Unit (University of Sussex).

this book. The scenario of economic growth leads to an evaluation of the levels of economic activity and social needs underlying the different uses. The energy intensities per end use (steam-energy per unit of value added or heating-energy per dwelling, . . .) are calculated from the spread of new techniques and the adaptation of existing ones. The importance and rythm of the technical development are generally evaluated from technico-economic studies, including investment costs and energy prices, and from an appraisal of the social and institutional constraints. One must nevertheless admit that these two factors are rarely made explicit in these studies; in the first case because they are often based on external information (specialized studies on energy savings, for instance), and in the second case because they remain implicit or subjective in the author's appreciation. This explains that, beyond a certain homogeneity in the main conclusions of these studies, differences — which may be significant — remain in the evaluation of the possibilities of altering the energy demand pattern at the overall level or per end-use.

We shall mainly consider four of these major conclusions:

— The energy demand of households, per dwelling or per inhabitant, could experience within the next twenty years a significant reduction, and this in spite of the equipment ownership having reached saturation level: estimated at 15% of the 1975 level for France (a 30% reduction in heating and a 25% increase for other domestic uses) in the BPET [6] scenario[4], this reduction could reach 50% in the U.K. according to the IIED study [5] and 50% also in the U.S.A. in scenario A of the CONAES [7] (60% for heating and 35% for the other uses)[5].

— The energy demand of the transport sector should only increase slightly, at least in European countries (between 0% and 20% for the U.K. [5] and France [6]), despite a substantial increase of the car stock and of the traffic. In the U.S.A., the CONAES study even reveals the possibility of a substantial reduction.

— There exist greater discrepancies in the evolution of the industrial energy demand and its relationship to industrial growth: rather low in the IIED study [5], the expected increase is of approximately 40% for France between 1975 and 2000 [6] and 80% in the scenario A of CONAES for the U.S.A. from 1972 to 2010.

— Because of these discrepancies, there exists a certain difference in the elasticities, measured ex post, of the overall consumption to the GDP; these elasticities are nevertheless always lower than 0.5 (compared to 1 or even more for some countries, over the period 1950—1973).

---

[4]   Scenario BPET ("Bas Profil Energetique Technique") of the Ministery of Industry looks at the possibility of energy savings in France by means of technical adaptations only.

[5]   Scenario A of the CONAES study relies upon the highest increase of oil price, thus leading to the most significant energy savings.

Growth Scenarios

Growth scenarios encompass all the scenarios including a socio-economic growth pattern different from that which could be extrapolated from past trends. Generally, these scenarios are designed independently of energy considerations, although they may explicitly include the energy dimension (energy saving policies, macro-economic or sectorial impacts due to the energy crisis, . . .). These scenarios may on the one hand reflect either an adaptation of the system to external constraints or changes (for example in the international division of labour) or sectorial changes, without fundamentally questioning the social pattern; on the other hand, they may also reflect a real change in the social and economic organization (in other words a global project for social change). In the first category one may find the famous "Zero Energy Growth" scenario of the Ford Foundation, or different growth scenarios studied at the IEJE, by means of the MEDEE approach[6]. In the second category, one may find for example the "new growth" regional scenario envisaged for France by the DATAR[7] in which the growth is "directed towards as great an autonomy as allowed by the resources of the country or of the regions"[8]; or even the scenario designed by the authors for France [8] (S2) which deals with a less materialistic and more qualitative growth within the framework of new relations with less developed countries; the scenarios proposed by Interfutures also belong to this category[9]. Whether they are in one or the other category, these scenarios all take into account a certain number of changes, likely to have a significant impact upon the evolution of energy demand:
— reduction of the importance of energy intensive industries, within the framework of changes in the international division of labour;
— increasing role of tertiary activities;
— decentralization of decision making centres, inducing, in particular, a greater development of renewable energy sources and an increase in the recovery of waste products, or even further energy savings;
— the questioning of private modes of transport, offset by a substantial development of public transport;
— changes in land use planning, coinciding with changes in the transport system, or even in the institutional system (decentralization).

The phenomenological approaches, because of their level of disaggregation by type of needs and of homogeneous activities, are particularly well suited to the quantification of the impacts of all these changes upon energy demand. Since the importance of these impacts depends upon the magnitude of the changes envisaged, it would be meaningless to comment upon the conclusions to which the various studies have led.

---

[6] See Chapter 5.

[7] Délégation Générale à l'Aménagement du Territoire.

[8] Reference [2], p. XIII.

[9] See Chapter 4.

The "Soft Energy Paths"

The "Soft Energy Paths" immediately set out the energy problem in terms of a social finality; energy thus becomes the justification of a break with the present society model and of the development of a society with a very low energy profile. Initially sparked off in the U.S.A. with A. Lovins [9], this movement has aroused much interest in other industrialized countries [15] (for instance the DEMO project in Denmark [11] or the ALTER project in France [10]); a scientific magazine "Soft Energy Notes" has even been published in order to establish a link between all its advocates. The philosophy which underlies Soft Energy Paths is that non renewable fossil fuels must no longer be "wasted" so as to reduce the impact upon the national environment and to avoid depriving Third World countries and future generations of these resources, and must be replaced gradually by renewable energies, considered to be "soft". Such a position implies the rejection of nuclear energy (and particularly fast breeders) and of fusion as possible long-term solutions.

In order to achieve this transition to soft energy sources, the advocates of Soft Energy Paths claim that energy demand must stop increasing and return to a moderate level, compatible with the availability of renewable energy sources that is to say with their annual flows. Energy conservation then becomes a condition for this transition. This change in the energy demand pattern involves the implementation of energy efficient techniques (which one also encounters in technical fix scenarios) but more especially a thorough change of the social values and life styles.

These scenarios rarely consider the transitional phase to the new model of society and especially deal with the equilibrium stage; in particular they do not analyze the kind of economic, social or institutional measures which should be implemented. As this stage belongs to the far distant future (50 years), constraints of all kinds may however be ignored. During the transitional phase, the energy demand continues at first to increase, because of the inertia of the economic system, then gradually decreases to a level at which it remains stable (equilibrium phase). The energy demand is evaluated from the energy needs of individuals and their mode of satisfaction, defined in a purely normative way: so many square metres and so much hot water per person, normative distribution of trips per transport mode, more durable goods, . . .

The society model underlying the Soft Energy Paths may be roughly characterized in the following way: level of material comfort similar to the existing standards of the upper social strata, greater decentralization, more equal income distribution, different work organization (especially more "creative" work, . . .).

The studies concerning Canada or the U.S.A. [12, 13] lead to a per capita energy demand which is 3 or 4 times lower than present levels; the conclusions of the European studies are much less radical but the levels reached are nevertheless significantly lower than present levels.

Energy Policy and Economic Development

In all these scenarios, the social and technological components of the energy demand are considered "exogeneous" to this demand: they are defined within the framework of the scenario, independently of the energy evolution they bring about (on the level of both the energy supply and demand). Now, one easily understands that the context in which this demand is expressed and the resultant supply system in turn influence economic growth and technological evolution, and even the organization of society [13]. The evolution of motor fuel supplies and its consequences upon transport modes in the 1960's in Europe or the differences in technology between the U.S.A. and Europe bear witness to these feedback effects. Without considering this new and fundamental debate, the importance of which increases with the time horizon, we shall merely illustrate the possible effects of energy policies upon society by means of a few brief observations.

In the medium and long-term, within a context of increasing energy prices, the economic growth rate may be affected by energy policy options in several ways:

— by the external constraint (trade balance) and the necessity of devoting an increasing share of the national income to pay for energy imports; absent from the countries which have their own energy resources or paying for their imports in their own currency, this constraint may become severe if these imports are not balanced by exports or by supplies of foreign capital (recycling of petrodollars);

— by the necessity of reserving an increasing share of the gross capital formation to invest in energy production systems gradually requiring more capital per unit of energy produced (nuclear energy, off-shore oil, . . .), thus diverting financial means which could be used for more productive (or socially more desirable) purposes;

— by excessive energy costs resulting from an adaptation of techniques insufficient in a given context of energy prices, at the level of the production of goods and services as well as that of household consumption.

In addition, any energy policy, through both its components — increase of the supply and control of the demand — necessarily affects the economic structures because of its different impacts upon the activity of the various economic sectors, which obviously depend on the type of policy and the amount of energy investments. These structural impacts in turn affect the overall growth, because of the differences in the sectorial productivities of the production factors: the improvement of the overall labour and capital productivities, a major element of the long-term economic growth (and of the future availability of these factors), partly depends on the fact that certain economic sectors with a higher productivity develop faster than others.

In addition to these effects upon the economic growth, the energy policy options may induce more thorough changes of the social content of this growth and of society in general. Thus, the energy policies are closely linked to the institutional and decision making structures on which these policies rely; certain policies require and reinforce centralized structures (for instance nuclear) whereas others would, on the contrary promote a relative decentralization of the economic decision making bodies (for example local and non renewable energy sources). Similarly, the exploitation of energy resources and the development of systems of energy production and distribution may prove more or less influential upon the land use; either directly, due to the regional aspect of certain projects (mines, nuclear plants, solar energy installations), or indirectly, through the effects upon the economic sectors (the land use organization of which is not necessarily uniform) and upon the decision making structures (the possible strenghtening of local authorities to the detriment of central government).

These effects as a whole will not be without influence upon the life styles and behaviours, stressing the possible behavioural changes directly resulting from the energy policies themselves (non-financial incentives within the framework of the energy conservation policy, for instance).

Finally the technological innovation and the development of techniques in general will be more or less affected according to the energy policies, because of the energy firms or because of the industrial sectors which are particularly stimulated by these policies, or even because of the research and development programmes.

These brief reflections, far from exhausting the subject, in fact illustrate its breadth and complexity. Without seeking to develop them further — such was not our intention — we shall, to conclude, raise one of the principal issues they bring to the foreground nowadays.

By reducing the energy consumption for a given level of economic activity, thus contributing to the partial or total loosening of certain constraints to growth, by mobilizing high productivity industrial sectors (chemical, equipment goods, electronic industries), by encouraging the decentralization trends, does not energy conservation in fact constitute the most desirable component, on the economic and social levels, of energy policies? Should it not then be the main priority since, as it is technically and economically feasible immediately, it would give the precious time necessary to prepare the replacement of hydrocarbons by other economically and socially acceptable energy sources?

Appendix 1 Data on the Residential and Tertiary Sector

Note

The data presented in these appendixes result from the compilation of data from many sources over the last five years.

Much attention has been paid to the consistency and homogeneity of all the data. Therefore some series have been kept on purpose "incomplete" in order to maintain this consistency.

Table R.1. *Demographic indicators*

		1950	1955	1960	1965	1970	1975	1978	1979	References
U.S.A.	POP (10^6)	151.9	165.1	180	193.5	203.8	213.1	218.1	221	[69, 2]
	DW (10^6)	42.8	47	53	57.3	63.4	72.5	77.8		
	CAPH	(3.5)	(3.5)	(3.4)	(3.4)	(3.2)	(3.0)	(2.8)		
Japan	POP	84.1	90.1	94.3	99.2	104.7	111.9	114.9	115.9	[116, 2]
	DW				22	26.2				
	CAPH				(4.5)	(4)				
France	POP	41.8	43.4	45.7	48.8	50.8	52.7	53.3	53.5	[12]
	DW	13.1	13.5	14.3	15.3	16.3	17.8	18.7	19	[113, 117]
	CAPH	(3.2)*	(3.2)	(3.2)	(3.2)	(3.1)	(3.0)	(2.9)	(2.8)	
F.R. Germany	POP	50.2	52.4	55.4	58.6	60.7	61.8	61.3	61.4	[12]
	DW	10.5	13.3	16.1	18.5	20.8	23.6			[6, 2]
	CAPH	(4.8)	(3.9)	(3.5)	(3.2)	(2.9)	(2.6)			
Italy	POP	46.4	48.3	50.2	52.0	53.7	55.8	56.7	56.9	[12]
	DW	10.5		13.2		15.3	16.2			[15, 2]
	CAPH	(4.4)		(3.8)		(3.5)	(3.4)			
U.K.	POP	50.1	51	52.4	54.2	55.4	55.9	55.9	55.9	[118]
	DW	13.7		15.9	17.6	18.7	19.9			[118, 119, 2]
	CAPH	(3.7)		(3.3)	(3.1)	(3)	(2.8)			
Netherlands	POP	10.1	10.9	11.5	12.4	13.1	13.7	13.9	14	[27]
	DW		2.5	2.8	3.3	3.8	4.4			[27, 119]
	CAPH		(4.4)	(4)	(3.8)	(3.4)	(3.1)			
Belgium	POP	8.7	8.9	9.2	9.5	9.7	9.8	9.8	9.8	[11, 119]
	DW			3	3.1	3.2				
	CAPH			(3.1)	(3.1)	(3.0)				

Table R.1. (*continued*)

		1950	1955	1960	1965	1970	1975	1978	1979	References
Denmark	POP	4.3	4.4	4.6	4.7	4.9	5.1	5.1	5.1	[16, 28]
	DW	1.3	1.4	1.5	1.6	1.8	2.0			
	CAPH	(3.3)	(3.1)	(3.1)	(2.9)	(2.8)	(2.6)			
Sweden	POP	7	7.3*	7.5	7.8	8.1	8.2	8.3		[80, 86, 119]
	DW	2.1	2.4	2.6	2.9	3.2	3.5			
	CAPH	(3.3)	(3.1)*	(2.9)	(2.7)*	(2.5)	(2.3)			

Comments: For some countries and years, the number of dwellings (DW) is estimated from the value of CAPH, derived from the nearest year available (census years); this is the case for France (1950, 1955, 1960 and 1965; census of 1954 and 1962); for Italy (1950, 1960 and 1970, census of 1951, 1960 and 1971), for Belgium (1960, 1965; census of 1961), for U.K. (1950; census of 1951), and Japan (1970 and 1965; census of 1963, 1968 and 1973).

POP = Population; DW = Occupied dwellings; CAPH = Ratio total population divided by number of occupied dwellings.

* Estimated.

Table R.2. *Final energy consumption of the residential and tertiary sector (PJ)*

	1950	1955	1960	1965	1970	1973	1975	1977	1978	1979	References
U.S.A.	8400	10500	11300	13700	16900	17800	16850	18300	18200	17600	[111]
Japan	200	270	470	780	1770	2750	2480	2590	2510	2590	[111]
France	570	730	850	1200	1690	2080	1920	2080	2280	2300	[112]
F.R. Germany	700	1170	1360	2070	2800	3170	2920	3170			[75, 112]
Italy	110	270	380	540	1010	1250	1260	1230	1350		[114]
U.K.	2000	2120	2140	2200	2320	2360	2290	2400	2390	2580	[73]
Netherlands	210	250	280	410	670	860	860	870	910	950	[112]
Belgium	250	280	270	380	480	550	540	540	590	630	[112]
Denmark	110	130	160	260	360	360	320	360	360	380	[111]
Sweden	150	210	270	430	560	590	560	600	530	550	[111]

1 TWh = 3.6 PJ, 1 Mtce = 29.3 PJ, 1 Mtoe = 41.8 PJ.

Table R.3. *Per capita final energy consumption of the residential and tertiary sector* (GJ/capita)

	1950	1955	1960	1965	1970	1975	1978	1979
U.S.A.	55	64	63	71	83	79	83	80
Japan	2	3	5	8	17	22	22	22
France	5	17	19	25	33	36	43	43
F.R. Germany	14	22	25	35	46	47		
Italy	2	6	8	10	19	23	24	
U.K.	40	42	41	41	42	41	43	46
Netherlands	21	23	24	33	51	63	65	68
Belgium	29	31	29	40	49	55	60	64
Denmark	26	30	35	55	73	63	71	75
Sweden	21	29	36	55	69	68	64	

Source: Tables R.1 and R.2.

Table R.4. *Per capita final energy consumption of the residential and tertiary sector with climatic corrections** (GJ/capita)

	1950	1955	1960	1965	1970	1975
U.S.A.	52	61	60	68	79	76
Japan	2	3	6	9	19	36
France	5	17	19	25	33	36
F.R. Germany	11	18	20	28	37	38
Italy	3	8	11	13	25	31
U.K.	40	42	41	41	42	41
Netherlands	18	20	21	29	44	55
Belgium	25	27	25	35	43	49
Denmark	22	25	29	46	61	53
Sweden	14	19	23	35	45	44

* Values related to a same climate of reference (France), using the following indices (France = 100; corresponding to 2400 degree-days); U.S.A. = 105, Japan = 90, F.R. Germany = 125, Italy = 75, U.K. = 100, Netherlands = 115, Belgium = 120, Sweden = 155 (see Table R.11).

Table R.5. *Per capita final energy consumption per unit of GDP** in the residential and tertiary sector* (GJ/capita/1000 $ 1970)

	1950	1955	1960	1965	1970	1975
U.S.A.	16	17	16	16	16	15
Japan	—	6	8	8	14	11
France	4	12	11	12	12	11
F.R. Germany	10	11	10	11	12	11
Italy	4	9	10	10	14	17
U.K.	28	26	23	21	19	17
Netherlands	15	14	13	15	18	20
Sweden	6	8	8	10	11	—

* Source of data on GDP: References [79] and [121].

Table R.6. *Distribution of final energy consumption in the residential and tertiary sector by energy form* (in %)

		1960	1965	1970	1974	1979
U.S.A.	C	9	5	2	1	1
	H	80	80	81	78	74
	EL	11	15	17	21	25
Japan	C	42	23	6	3	5
	H	45	62	80	80	71
	EL	13	15	14	17	24
France	C	62	43	23	12	7
	H	32	48	67	76	77
	EL	6	9	10	12	16
U.K.	C	71	58	40	27	18
	H	20	26	41	51	61
	EL	9	16	19	22	21
F.R. Germany	C	69	44	24	14	7
	H	25	48	65	70	77
	EL	6	8	11	16	16
Italy	C	43	23	9	4	2
	H	48	64	80	84	84
	EL	9	13	11	12	14
Netherlands	C	55	32	7	1	—
	H	37	59	84	89	90
	EL	8	9	9	10	10
Belgium	C	71	51	31	20	9
	H	25	44	64	71	81
	EL	4	5	5	9	10
Denmark*	C	47	20	4	2	3
	H	45	72	86	85	81
	EL	8	8	10	13	16
Sweden*	C	15	7	4	4	—
	H	72	81	83	76	73
	EL	13	12	13	20	27

C = coal, H = hydrocarbons, EL = electricity.

Source of data: OECD [111].

* The data for Denmark and Sweden should be considered carefully since district heating does not appear separately.

Table R.7. *Final energy consumption in dwellings** (PJ)

	1950	1955	1960	1965	1970	1973	1974	1975	1976	1977	References
U.S.A.	6300	7200	8800	10200	12300	12400	12300	11700			[45]
France			640**			1520	1500	1420	1470	1540	[113]
F.R. Germany					1810	1990	1820	1820	1990	1960	[6, 75]
Denmark							198		200	207	[17]
U.K.	1460	1510	1530	1530	1540	1570	1590	1550		1580	[73, 115]

Note: Only consistent data are presented here.
* Residential sector, ** 1962.

Table R.8. *Final energy consumption per dwelling* (GJ/dwelling)

	1950	1955	1960	1965	1970	1973	1974	1975	1976	1977	References
U.S.A.	147	153	166	177	192	179	174	163			[45]
Japan		14	14	19	30	30	29	32	32		[22]
France			44*			86	83	79	81	84	[113]
F.R. Germany			57	73	87	88	78	77	81	81	[6, 75]
U.K.	107	104	96	87	82	81	81	78	83	78	[73, 115]

Note: Only the reliable estimate are presented here.
* 1962.

Table R.9. *Electricity consumption per dwelling* (kWh/dwelling)

	1950	1955	1960	1965	1970	1975
U.S.A.	2840	3540	4300 (56%)	5580	8240	9420 (50%)
France	240	340	520	820	1300	1850 (59%)
F.R. Germany	300	500	800 (69%)	1300 (65%)	2100 (50%)	2900
U.K.		1400 (37%)	2100 (35%)	3250 (31%)	4130 (32%)	4470 (36%)
Italy	230		390		1270	1720 (75%)
Netherlands		710	1000	1520	2280	2830 (85%)
Belgium			500	930	1540	–
Denmark			750	1500	2720	3350

(Figures between brackets: share of specific uses).
Source: EUROSTAT [112] and IEJE.

Table R.10. *Share of energy expenditure in household budget* (energy used in dwellings) (in %)*

	1960	1965	1970	1973	1974	1975	1976	1977	1978	References
U.S.A.	2.6	2.5	2.5	2.5	2.7	3	3	3.1		[8, 69]
Japan			1.9	1.7	1.8	2	2			[22, 120]
France	3.7	3.3	3.1	3.3	3.8	3.7	3.8	3.8	4.1	[21, 79]
F.R. Germany	3.2	3.5	3.4	3.7	3.9	4	4.2	4	4.1	[21, 79]
Italy	3	3	3.1	2.9	3.3	3.1	3	3.2	3.2	[5, 21, 79, 114]
U.K.		4.8	4.8	4.2	4.4	4.6	4.9	5.1		[6, 21, 79, 115]
Netherlands			3.9	3.6	3.5	4.2	4.5	4.3	4.4	[21, 79]
Belgium	4.9	5.1	5.3	5	5.3	5.8	5.6	5.6	5.7	[21, 79]
Denmark			4.6	4.8	6.1	6.1	5.8	5.5	5.8	[21, 79]

* In current price; energy expenditure included in the rents are not taken into account.

Table R.11. *Usual values of degree days*

		Belgium	U.K.	Italy	France	U.S.A.	F.R. Germany	Netherlands	Denmark	Sweden
Number of degree days	base 18°C	2800		1800	2300 2500**	2500	3000***	2800	2900	3700
	base 16°C	2100*	2200						2700	

Source: IEJE using various sources.

* Base 15°C and outside temperature under 15°C.

** Calculated over the heating period i.e.: 212 days in one case (1/10 to 10/05 and 182 days in the other (10/10 to 10/05); figures pertaining to Paris which is represents the average French conditions.

*** Base 19°C, outside temperature under 12°C.

Note: The degree days represent the cumulated sum of the difference between the outside temperature and a reference temperature inside the dwellings (for instance 18°C means a "base 18°C"). They depend on the length of the heating period, on the outside temperature under which they are measured and on the inside temperature. Therefore according to the conventions used there may exist different values for a given country.

Appendix 2 Data on the Transportation Sector

Symbols and Definitions

pkm: passenger-kilometer (= traffic of one passenger over one kilometer)

pko: place-kilometer offered (= offer of one place-seated or stand-up over one kilometer)

sko: seat-kilometer offered (= offer of one seat over one kilometer)

vkm: vehicle-kilometer (= traffic of one vehicle over one kilometer)

tkm: ton-kilometer (= traffic of one ton of freight over one kilometer, not including the weight of the vehicle)

gtkh: gross ton-kilometer hauled (= traffic of one ton hauled by a railway engine, including both freight and the weight of the rail car, over one kilometer)

tko: ton-kilometer offered (= offer of one ton of freight capacity over one kilometer)

y: year

cap: capita

Table T.1. *Energy consumption in the transport sector 1950–1978*

	1950 Mtoe	TWh	1960 Mtoe	TWh	1970 Mtoe	TWh	1975 Mtoe	TWh	1978 Mtoe	TWh
U.S.A.	188	6	234	5	348	5	412	4	437.1	3
France	8.9	2	11.3	3	20.8	6	27.3	6	29.1	7
F.R. Germany	10.8	2	15.5	4	27.2	8	32.2	9	35.7	10
U.K.	16.8	2	20.9	2	26.6	3	29.1	3	30.8	3
Italy	3.2	2	6.5	3	16.5	4	18.8	5	21.0	5
Netherlands	1.6	–	2.8	1	6.2	1	7.3	1	8.1	1
Denmark	0.7	–	1.3	–	3.1	–	3.5	–	3.5	–
Belgium	2.1	–	2.6	1	4.3	1	5.0	1	5.4	1
Sweden	1.3	1	3.0	2	4.7	2	5.3	2	5.8	2
Japan	5.1	2	11.3	5	31.1	11	40.3	14	43.5	15
References	[14, 15, 16]		[13]		[13]		[13]		[13]	

Table T.2. *Economic growth and energy consumption trends in the transport sector, 1950–1978*

	1950–1960 GDP	EN	C	1960–1970 GDP	EN	C	1970–1978 GDP	EN	C
U.S.A.	3.2%	2.2%	0.69	3.9%	4.0%	1.03	3.3%	2.9%	0.88
France	4.6%	2.5%	0.54	5.6%	6.4%	1.14	3.9%	4.2%	1.08
F.R. Germany	8.0%	3.9%	0.49	4.7%	5.9%	1.26	2.7%	2.7%	1.0
U.K.	2.8%	2.2%	0.79	2.8%	2.5%	0.89	2.3%	1.8%	0.78
Italy	5.6%	7.2%	1.29	5.7%	9.2%	1.61	2.8%	3.0%	1.07
Netherlands	4.5%	6.5%	1.44	5.2%	7.9%	1.52	3.3%	3.3%	1.0
Denmark	3.2%*	6.4%*	2.0*	4.7%	9.1%	1.94	2.7%	1.5%	0.56
Belgium	3.1%*	2.9%*	0.94*	5.0%	4.9%	0.98	3.4%	2.8%	0.82
Sweden	3.4%	8.5%	2.5	4.6%	4.1%	0.89	1.4%	2.5%	1.79
Japan	8.1%*	8.5%*	1.05*	11.1%	10.4%	0.94	5.3%	4.3%	0.81
References	[80]			[80]			[80]		

* = 1953–1960 period.

GDP = annual growth rate of gross domestic product
EN = transport energy consumption annual growth rate
C   = elasticity EN/GDP

Table T.3. *The transport sector in the total final energy consumption, and in the oil products consumption; 1950–1977*

		1950	1960	1970	1977
U.S.A.	A	31%	30%	30%	33%
	B	58%	61%	63%	59%
	C	76%	99%	99%	99%
France	A	19%	19%	20%	22%
	B	53%	43%	31%	32%
	C	43%	76%	96%	98%
F.R. Germany	A	16%	16%	17%	18%
	B	81%	41%	29%	29%
	C	20%	63%	95%	97%
U.K.	A		18%	20%	21%
	B		48%	41%	43%
	C		67%	98%	99%
Italy	A	18%	20%	21%	20%
	B	38%	34%	29%	30%
	C	39%	83%	97%	96%
Netherlands	A	15%	19%	19%	17%
	B	46%	37%	36%	37%
	C	55%	96%	99%	99%
Denmark	A		19%	21%	23%
	B		28%	24%	27%
	C		91%	99%	99%
Belgium	A	14%	15%	14%	16%
	B	47%	34%	26%	29%
	C	39%	76%	98%	99%
Sweden	A		16%	16%	17%
	B		25%	21%	25%
	C		92%	96%	97%
Japan	A	11%	20%	17%	17%
	B	100%	36%	25%	24%
	C		62%	93%	97%

A = Share of the transport sector in the total energy consumption
B = Share of the transport sector in the consumption of oil products
C = Share of the oil products in the energy consumption of the transport sector
References: 1950 [15], 1960, 1970, 1977 [13].

Table T.4. *Car population and car ownership ratios 1950–1978*

	1950 10^6PC	COR	1960 10^6PC	COR	1970 10^6PC	COR	1975 10^6PC	COR	1978 10^6PC	COR
U.S.A.	40.2	3.75	61.7	2.90	88.8	2.29	106.7	2.00	113.7*	1.90*
France	1.5	27.9	5.6	8.23	12.9	3.94	15.3	3.44	17.4	3.06
F.R. Germany	0.60	83.3	4.5	12.76	13.9	4.49	17.9	3.45	21.2	2.89
U.K.	2.3	21.8	5.5	9.49	11.8	4.76	14.0	4.01	14.4	3.88
Italy	0.34	136.5	2.0	25.23	10.2	5.28	15.1	3.70	16.4*	3.46*
Netherlands	0.14	72.1	0.52	22.12	2.3	5.75	3.6	4.03	4.3	3.24
Denmark	0.12	35.8	0.41	11.2	1.1	4.54	1.3	3.85	1.5	3.40
Belgium	0.27	31.9	0.75	12.1	2.1	4.66	2.6	3.75	3.0	3.27
Sweden	0.25	28.0	1.2	6.25	2.3	3.49	2.8	2.97	2.9	2.86
Japan	0.03	2773.	0.46	205	8.8	11.8	17.2	6.49	21.3	5.39
References	[4]		[1, 58]	[7]	[2, 6, 7, 29, 43]					

10^6PC = Stock of private cars (in millions)
COR = Car ownership ratio (persons per private car)
* 1977.

Table T.5. *Structure of the private uses of cars, 1960–1976*

		1963		1970		1975–76		References
France	H.W.	22%*	(2100)	28%**	(3100)			[30]
	Holidays	20%	(1900)	17%	(1900)			[22]
	Other	58%	(5400)	55%	(6090)			
Netherlands	H.W.	26%		26%	(2700)	30%	(3000)	
	Holidays	19%		14%	(1400)	12%	(1200)	[22]
	Other	55%		60%	(6200)	58%	(5700)	
(week-end)						(21%	(2100))	
F.R. Germany	H.W.	23%		29%	(3240)			[20]
	Holidays	14%		12%	(1310)			
	Week-end	20%		22%	(2570)			
	Other	43%		37%	(4160)			
U.S.A.	H.W.			37%	(5340)			[5]
	Holidays			3%	(470)			
	Other			60%	(8640)			
U.K.	H.W.					33%***	(3810)	[21]
	Holidays and week-ends					21%	(2400)	
	Other					46%	(5960)	

* 1966/67, ** 1973/74, *** "Car or van as driver".
H.W. = Home-work trips
N.B.: The figures in brackets are km/year/car.

Table T.6. *Modal distribution of home-work trips*

		A	B	C	References
U.S.A.	Together	13%	78%	19%	
(1975)	Cities	11%	77%	12%	[38]
France	Paris area	25%	30%	45%	[25]
	Cities > 500 000 h	45–53%	29–33%	19–27%	
	Grenoble (1966)	62%	32%	6%	
	Rouen (1966)	49%	39%	12%	
F.R. Germany	1960		37%	63%	[3, 7]
	1970		64%	36%	N.B.: Two-wheels
	1975*	24%	51%	25%	are included in B.
	1980		72%	28%	
Denmark	1974	41%	42%	17%	[33]
Sweden (1970/71)		50%	37.5%	12.5%	[75]
(Gothenburg)					
U.K.	1965	26%	33%	43%	
	1972	16%	51%	33%	[47]

A = Share of pedestrian or 2-wheels journeys in home-work trips
B = Share of private cars journeys in home-work trips
C = Share of mass-transit journeys in home-work trips

* The figures for 1975 are not directly comparable with those of the other years (which exclude walking trips) and come from an EUROSTAT survey [3].

Table T.7. *Urban trips distances, depending on the size of the city, on the trip purpose and on the mode: France as an example, 1968/69*

Cities	Size (1000)	All urban trips (km)				Home-work trips (km)			
		P.C.	P.T.	2W	Σ	P.C.	P.T.	2W	Σ
Paris	8003	6.8	7.1	3.6	6.4	7	8	4.1	7.2
Marseille	915	3.2	3.5	3.1	3.3	3.5	3.5	3.3	3.5
Lyon	836	2.8	3.1	2.3	2.8	3.1	3.2	2.4	3.0
Rouen	348	3.1	3.7	2.7	2.4	3.4	3.9	2.8	3.3
Grenoble	281	2.5	3.0	1.9	2.3	2.8	3.4	2.1	2.5
Nancy	224	2	2.4	2	2.1	2.4	2.6	2.1	2.3
Aix (Provence)	73	1.3	1.7	1.4	1.3	1.5	1.8	1.3	1.5
Chambery	64	1.8	2.4	1.6	1.8	2.0	2.7	1.9	2.0
Dieppe	38	1.1	1.4	1.1	1.1	1.2	1.6	1.2	1.2

Source: Reference [25]

P.C. = Private car
P.T. = Public transport
2W = Two-wheels
Σ = Average

Table T.8. *Motorized urban trips other than home/work in large French cities (2 wheels included)* (number of trips/capita/year)

	1966	1976	City size in 1975
Paris	349		8 550 000
Lyon	234 (1965)	482	1 171 000
Marseille	303	493	1 071 000
Lille		398	936 000
Nice	427	478 (1973)	438 000
Grenoble	354	438 (1973)	389 000
Rouen	259 (1968)	489 (1973)	389 000
Nancy	416 (1965)	405	281 000
Orleans	383 (1968)	584	209 000

Bicycle, motorcycle, public transport and cars
Source: Reference [76]

Table T.9. *Modal distribution of motorized urban trips, depending on the size of the city and the trip purpose: France as an example 1968/69*

Cities	Size	All urban trips			Home-work trips		
	(1000)	P.C.	P.T.	2W	P.C.	P.T.	2W
Paris	8003	42%	49%	9%	50%	55%	10%
Marseille	915	56%	31%	10%	51%	33%	16%
Lyon	836	45%	37%	4%	40%	37%	23%
Rouen	348	57%	16%	13%	50%	15%	35%
Grenoble	281	53%	11%	19%	45%	9%	47%
Nancy	224	54%	24%	12%	44%	21%	35%
Aix (Provence)	73	65%	13%	14%	64%	12%	24%
Chambery	64	50%	4%	28%	46%	3%	58%
Dieppe	38	59%	8%	18%	50%	3%	47%

P.C. = Private car
P.T. = Public transportation
2W = Two-wheels
Reference: [25]; some total may not add to 100%, by lack of explanation and of sufficient information in the original reference it was not possible to correct the figures.

Table T.10. *Use of private cars: professional and private trips; interurban traffic*

Country	(Year)	Private uses	Professional uses	Interurban traffic	References
U.S.A.	(1972)	92% (14 450)	8% (1 260)		[5]
France	(1966/67)	77% (9 400)	23% (2 700)		[30]
	(1973/74)	82% (11 080)	18% (2 430)	61% (8 240)	[24]
F.R. Germany	(1963)	56% (8 690)	44% (6 700)		[20]
	(1970)	76% (11 280)	24% (3 520)		
U.K.*	(1976)	82% (11 570)	18% (2 530)		[21]
Netherlands	(1963)	42% (7 800)	58% (10 600)		
	(1970)	62% (10 300)	38% (6 600)		[22]
	(1976)	71% (9 900)	29% (4 000)	52% (7 200)	

* "Car or van as driver".
N.B.: The figures in brackets are in kilometers per year and per car.

Table T.11. *Household mobility and car ownership, France and the U.K. as examples, 1975 (km/year/household).* (Index 100 for non motorized households)

	Without a car	One car	Two or more cars	References
France				
Paris area	100	290	440	
Cities > 500 000	100	260	350	
Cities 200–500 000	100	240	330	[25]
Cities 100–200 000	100	215	290	
Cities < 100 000	100	205	270	
U.K.	100	265	375	[21]

Table T.12. *Rate of holiday departures, according to the household income and the size of cities*

Town	Country	Population (1000)	Income per capita (US $ 70)	Number of holiday trips (per household)
Toulouse	France	400	1940	2.6
Geneva	Switzerland	300	2960	3.5
Four small size towns	France	15	2300	2.2
Turin	Italy	1200	2280	2.1
Düsseldorf	F.R. Germany	2300	3260	2.0
Lisbon	Portugal	1500	850	1.9
Linz	Austria	250	1890	1.5
The Hague	The Netherlands	800	2900	1.5
Bruges	Belgium	100	2700	0.9
Valencia	Spain	500	900	0.8

Source: [27].

Table T.13. *Departures on holidays and modal distribution in the European Community, 1972**

	% of holidays* taken inside the country	Modal split of holiday departures					Modal split of holiday journeys inside the country			
		train	bus	plane	car	other**	train	bus	car	plane
F.R. Germany	46.3%	21.6%	5.5%	10.5%	60.8%	1.6%	31.2%	6.3%	59.7%	1.3%
France	84.5%	16.6%	3.2%	3.4%	75.9%	0.9%	16.8%	3.0%	78.8%	0.8%
Italy	94.5%	20.6%	6.3%	1.2%	69.5%	2.4%	20.5%	6.3%	70.8%	0.5%
Netherlands	51.8%	8.7%	5.8%	7.7%	72.2%	5.6%	8.6%	3.9%	80.7%	–
Belgium	44.3%	13.6%	7.7%	8.2%	69.6%	0.9%	10.6%	9.5%	78.8%	–
Denmark	60.2%	13.6%	6.6%	19.9%	51.5%	8.5%	17.8%	5.7%	65.4%	1.1%

* in % of journeys, ** including boat.

Source: [43].

Table T.14. *Average yearly mileages of private and commercial cars, 1950–1976 (km/year/car)*

		1950	1960	1965*	1970	1973	1974	1975	1976	References
U.S.A.	Σ	14 600	15 200	15 000	15 700	15 700	14 700	15 000	15 200	[38]
France**	P.C.			12 100	13 040	13 500	13 500	13 900	14 200	[30, 79]
F.R. Germany	P.C.			13 800	13 900					[7]
	C.C.				22 200					
	Σ			15 400	14 800	13 500	13 100	13 700	13 500	[20]
U.K.	P.C.			13 100	13 800	14 200	13 600	13 200	14 100	[21]
	Σ			16 400	17 100	19 300	18 300	18 200		
Italy	Σ		14 500	16 100	13 600	11 800	10 200	10 200	9 200	[77, 8]
Netherlands	P.C.			13 000	13 900			13 900	11 700	[22]
	C.C.			22 500	21 300			23 300	22 800	
	Σ		18 700	18 000	17 200	17 000	15 800	15 600	14 000	
Denmark	Σ							15 200		
Japan	Σ				13 750			10 230		[60, 2]

* 1966 for U.K. and 1963 for F.R. Germany.
** 1965, 1970 and 1973 data from INSEE's surveys 1966/67 and 1973/74 (interpolation for 1970).

P.C. = Private cars.
C.C. = Commercial cars.
Σ = All cars together.

Table T.15. *Passenger traffic in private cars: total, per capita, per household, per car, 1955–1975*

		1955	1960**	1970	1975	1977	References
U.S.A.	10^9 pkm	1 110 (1950)	1 820	2 680	3 300	3 600	
	km/cap		10 130	13 160	15 500	16 600	[56]
	km/hh		34 400	42 300	45 500		[35]
	pkm/P.C.		29 500	30 200	30 900	31 700	[38]
France	10^9 pkm		76.3	273	364	420	
	km/cap		1 670	5 400	6 900	7 900	
	km/hh		5 340	16 700	20 700		
	pkm/P.C.		13 750	21 200	23 800	25 100	[54]
F.R. Germany	10^9 pkm		161.7	350.6	405.4	430.9	
	km/cap		2 920	5 780	6 560	7 000	
	km/hh		10 050	13 090	17 180		[7]
	pkm/P.C.		37 280	26 000	22 600	21 500	[54]
U.K.	10^9 pkm	87.0	143.6	305.3	356.6	371	
	km/cap	1 705	2 740	5 540	6 380	6 640	[54]
	km/hh		9 030	16 320	17 920		[21]
	pkm/P.C.		25 900	26 200	25 600	26 100	[6]
Italy	10^9 pkm	38.0	60.0	212.1	279.0	288.0	[54]
	km/cap	820	1 190	3 950	5 000	5 100	[21]
	km/hh	3 620	4 530	13 900	17 220.		
	pkm/P.C.		30 150	20 830	18 500	17 600	[8]
Netherlands	10^9 pkm		15.9	79.8	103.2		[21]
	km/cap		1 380	5 630	7 530		
	km/hh		5 670	19 410	23 450		[9]
	pkm/P.C.		30 600	32 650	30 350		
Denmark	10^9 pkm	9.7	15.3	41.6	50.0		[21]
	km/cap	2 200	3 390	8 490	9 800		[32]
	km/hh	6 930	10 200	23 100	25 000		[33]
	pkm/P.C.		37 300	38 500	38 500		
Japan	10^9 pkm		40	181	251	265	
	km/cap		403	1 730	2 240	2 330	
	km/hh		1 820	6 910			[21]
	pkm/P.C.		18 200	20 600	14 600	13 400	[54]

* Estimation on the basis of vehicle traffic, of interurban passenger traffic and of mean occupancy level [38].

** 1965 for Japan.

hh = household
P.C. = Private car
cap = Capita
pkm = Passenger-km.

Table T.16. *Car ownership 1955–1975*

	1955		1960		1970		1975		References
	1	2	1	2	1	2	1	2	
U.S.A.			74%	18%	80%	29%	82%	43%	[5, 29]
France	25%	—	29%	2%	53%	8%	64%	11%	[10, 29]
F.R. Germany			26%			5%	53%		[10, 29]
U.K.	19%	—	30%	2%	52%	8%	56%	10%	[21, 29]
Italy					45%	4%	64%		[10, 11, 29]
Netherlands			26%		49%		61%		[10, 29]
Denmark			50%*				65%		[10, 29]
Belgium			30%		51%		59%		[10, 29]
Sweden					75%				[29]
Japan			6%*		22%				[29]

* 1965.

1 = Share of households owning at least one private car.
2 = Share of households owning at least two private cars.

Table T.17. *Average yearly mileages of private cars: total, per average household, per motorized household, 1965–1975*

		1965	1970	1975	References
France	10^9 vkm		168	212.7	[30]
	10^3 vkm/hh		10.3	11.9	[56]
	10^3 vkm/mh		18.6	18.7	[79]
F.R. Germany	10^9 vkm	(143)	201	245	[21]
	10^3 vkm/hh	(7.7)	9.6	10.4	[7]
	10^3 vkm/mh			19.6	
Italy	10^9 vkm		138	154	
	10^3 vkm/hh		9.0	9.5	[8]
	10^3 vkm/mh		20.1	14.9	[77]
U.K.	10^9 vkm	(116)	200	254	[21]
	10^3 vkm/hh	(6.6)	10.7	12.8	
	10^3 vkm/mh		20.5	22.8	
Netherlands	10^9 vkm	(23)	38.9	53	[21]
	10^3 vkm/hh	(7.0)	10.2	12.0	
	10^3 vkm/mh		20.9	19.7	[22]
U.S.A.	10^9 vkm	941*	1441	1680	
	10^3 vkm/hh	17.8*	22.7	23.3	[38]
	10^3 vkm/mh	24.0*	28.4	28.6	
Japan	10^9 vkm	34	121	176	[60]
	10^3 vkm/hh	1.5	4.6		
	10^3 vkm/mh	25.8	21.0		

vkm = vehicle-km.
mh = motorized household.
hh = household.
* 1960.
N.B.: Figures in brackets are estimates found in [21].

Table T.18. *Utilization costs of private cars, 1973*

	References	Total cost (US $ 73)	Motorfuels and tyres	Maintenance	Taxes + insurance	Purchase (amorti-zation)
France	[37]	13.6	24% (3.3)	17% (2.3)	23% (3.1)	36% (4.9)
F.R. Germany	[37]	12.1	23% (2.8)	24% (2.9)	28% (3.4)	25% (3.0)
Netherlands	[37]	13.1	27% (3.5)	13% (1.7)	19% (2.5)	41% (5.4)
Italy	[37]	10.2	34% (3.5)	14% (1.4)	23% (2.3)	29% (3.0)
U.K.	[37]	9.2	25% (2.3)	15% (1.4)	23% (2.1)	37% (3.4)
U.S.A. *	[38]	11.2	21% (2.4)	21% (2.3)	31% (3.5)	27% (3.0

Figures in brackets are in US $ 1973 per 100 km.
* US $ 1976.

Table T.19. *Motor fuel prices, 1970–1978* (US $/100 l)

	1970	1973	1975	1978
France	20.5	26.0	40.9	50.1
F.R. Germany	17.0	23.9	37.0	43.7
Netherlands	16.4	25.5	38.7	45.0
Italy	22.4	27.5	45.0	57.4
U.K.	17.3	20.7	37.8	32.0
U.S.A.	9.3	10.4	15.1	17.9
Japan	14.6	20.3	39.4	50.8
Sweden	17.9	22.5	35.5	36.8

Source: [13, 38].

Table T.20. *Road public transport supply, 1960–1975*

		U.S.A.	France	F.R.Germany	U.K.	Italy	Netherlands	Japan
Equipment (1)	1960	1.51	0.50**	0.68	1.51**	0.48**	0.77**	1.12
(Vehicles/10³	1970	1.86	0.65	0.77	1.40	0.60	0.73	1.82
Persons)	1975	2.17	0.78	0.97	1.43	0.79	0.72	1.97
Offer (2)	1960	39	19**	31	69**	26**		36**
		(20)		(12)	(14)	(15)		
(veh.-km/cap)[+]	1970	39	23	34	62	28	37	51
		(22)	(17)	(18)	(18)	(19)	(28)	
	1975	38	30	39	64	33	41	49
		(22)	(23)	(21)	(21)	(22)	(31)	
Traffic per								
capita (3)	1960	450	590 ****	800	1350	600	900**	810
(pkm/cap)	1970	460	630	820	1010	690	840	980
	1975	440	690*	940	970	820	810	980
Utilization								
rate (4)	1960	11.5		25.8		25.4**		18.6**
(pkm/veh.-km)	1970	11.8	27.4	24.1	16.3	24.6	22.7	19.2
(3)/(2)	1975	11.6	24.6*	24.1	15.2	24.8	19.8	20.1
Mileage	1960	25 800		15 000	46 000**	54 000**		
(km/veh/year)	1970	21 000	35 000	44 000	47 000	47 000	51 000	28 000
(2)/(1)	1975***	17 500	38 000	41 000	44 000	42 000	57 000	(25 000
		(17 900)	(36 400)	(47 000)	(43 000)	(39 000)	(52 500)	(25 000
References		[38]	[6, 43]	[7]	[21]	[8, 56]	[53]	
		[56]	[56]	[43]	[43]	[58]	[43]	[49]
			[46]	[56]	[56]	[43]	[56]	[56]
			[21]					

* 1973, ** 1965, *** Figures in brackets come from IRF for 1975 [56], **** Estimated figures.

[+] Figures in brackets: interurban traffic only.

Table T.21. *Rail passenger transport supply, 1950–1975*

		U.S.A.	France	F.R.Germany	U.K.		Italy	Nether-lands	Sweden	Japan
Infra-structures (km/km²)	1950	38	75						37	
	1960	37	71	123					34	75
	1970	35	66	119	79		77	53	27	73
	1975	34	63	116	74		69	53	27	73
(km/cap)	1950	2.36	0.98						2.35	
	1960	1.94	0.85	0.55					2.03	0.30
	1970	1.63	0.71	0.49	0.35		0.24	0.30	1.51	0.26
	1975	1.51	0.65	0.47	0.32		0.21	0.29	1.48	0.24
Equipment (cars/10³ pers.)	1950	0.25							0.67	
	1960	0.14	0.33**	0.41	0.52**				0.55	0.33
	1970	0.06	0.30	0.32	0.42		0.18	0.15	0.38	0.40
	1975	0.03	0.29	0.32	0.39		0.20	0.14	0.32	0.40
Service Offered* (10³ gtkh cap/y)	1960						1.08			
	1965	0.50	1.30		1.69					
	1970	0.16	1.54	1.45***	1.54		1.08	1.41***	1.91***	
	1975	0.09	1.76	1.87	1.59		1.11	1.28	1.93	
(sko/cap/y)	1960	0.80								
	1965		2.50		2.20		1.40			
	1970	0.30	2.80		1.50		1.60			
	1975	0.20	3.30		1.60		1.60			
References		[38]	[51,52]	[43] [7]	[21,43]		[8] [43]	[43] [53]	[1,2] [4,48]	[49] [56]

* Based on the average European value in 1971 for U.S.A. (46 gtkh/vkm) and Sweden (260 gtkh/train-km); for U.K., the same ratio is assumed for 1960 and 1970.

** 1965.

*** 1971.

gtkh = gross ton-km hauled
sko = seat-km offered.

Table T.22. *Air passenger transport, 1960– 1978*

		U.S.A.	France	F.R.Germany	U.K.	Italy	Japan
Equipment (Planes/10^6 pers.)	1960	10.2	4.1*	3.8			
	1970	11.9	7.5	8.0			
	1975	10.6	9.4	7.8			7.3
Estimated Offer *** (seat-km/cap)	1960	615	230**	26	380	140	20
		(480)			(60)	(20)	(12)
	1970	2240	500	190	550	280	250
		(1760)	(40)		(60)	(50)	(140)
	1975	2430	750	320	880	350	490
		(1870)	(75)		(65)	(70)	(280)
	1978	2830					
		(2560)					
References		[38]	[56]	[7]	[21]	[8]	[49]

* 1962.
** 1961.
*** Figures between brackets: domestic routes only (for France, only Air Inter traffic is included); for U.K. and Italy, we assumed a ratio of 20 seat-km/ton-km performed; for Japan an average load factor of 0.6 passenger-km/seat-km was assumed.

Table T.23. *Passenger traffic by public transport modes, 1950–1977* (10^9 pkm)

Country / Mode		U.S.A.	France	F.R.Germany	U.K.	Italy	Nether-lands	Sweden	Japan
Road	1955				80	24.5 (12.0)			
	1960	30.9		48.5 (33.6)	71***	29.9*** (13.9)			78.4***
	1970	40.5	32	58.4 (39)	56	37.0 (14.9)	11.0		104.7
	1975	40.6	36** (14)	67.7 (44)	54.0 (38.4)	45.9 (18.4)	11.2		108.5
	1977	40.6*		68.1	53.0		11.9		108.9 +
Rail	1950	51	29.5 ++	31 +++	38.4	23.0 +++		7 +++	106
	1960	34	32.0	40 (17.6)	39.9	31.0	8.0	5	184
	1970	17	41.0 (6.3)	38.1	35.7	34.8	8.0	5	289
	1975	16	50.7 (7.1)	37.7	35.1	39.2	8.5	5.9	324
	1977	16.5	52.3	36.5	33.0*	41.7*	8.2	5.7*	320*
Air	1950	12.8							
	1960	49	0.52***	1.6	1.7***	0.6***	0		0.7
	1970	167	1.70	6.6	2.0	1.4	0		8.8
	1975	211	2.9	8.1	2.2	2.1	0		18.7
	1977	292 +	3.7	9.3	2.3*				19.1*
References		[38]	[2,4,52, 54,65, 78,46]	[4,7]	[21,50]	[8]	[50,53]	[1,2, 4,48]	[49,54]

* 1976, ** 1973, *** 1965, + 1978, ++ 1949, +++ 1948.
N.B.: Figures in brackets relate to urban traffic; for U.S.A. the road traffic only includes interurban traffic, underground is included in road traffic.

Table T.24. *Mobility by public transport modes: 1960–1977* (km/y/cap)

		U.S.A.	France	F.R. Germany	U.K.	Italy	Nether-lands	Japan
Traffic per	1960	920	(1300)	1630	2160	1240	1670	3440*
capita in	1970	1360	1470	1700	1700	1360	1450	3830
public	1975	1500	1850	1860	1630	1620	1440	4050
transport	1977			1850	1580		1450	
Traffic per	1960	450**	(590)	880	1360	600	970	790*
capita in	1970	460	630	970	1020	690	840	1000
public road	1975	440	820	1100	980	860	820	970
transport	1977			1110	950		860	950***
Traffic per	1960	190	700	720	760	620	700	2580*
capita in	1970	80	810	650	650	650	610	2760
rail	1975	80	960	610	620	730	620	2920
transport	1977	80	980	590	590	740	590	
Traffic per	1960	280	10	30	40	10		(70)*
capita in	1970	820	30	80	30	10	–	80
air	1975	980	70	150	30	30		160
transport	1977	1350***	80	150	40			

References see Table T.22.
* 1965 (Reference [60]), ** Urban buses load factor = 15 pkm/vkm, *** 1978,
( ) Estimated figures.

Table T.25. *Distribution of passenger traffic in public transport, according to trip purposes and modes: F.R. Germany as an example, 1960–1975* (10^9 pkm)

	Rail			Road			Air		
	1960	1970	1975	1960	1970	1975	1960	1970	1975
Total	40.0	38.1	37.7	48.5	58.4	67.7	1.6	6.6	8.1
H.W.	12.8	7.1	8.1	24.0	21.3	20.6	–	–	–
L.D.	7.6	8.7	8.4	1.6	3.1	3.4	1.2	5.5	7.8
W.E.	15.0	17.2	14.6	13.3	16.4	20.0	0.4	1.1	0.3
Others	4.6	5.1	6.6	9.6	17.6	23.7	–	–	–

H.W. = Home-work.
L.D. = Long distance (professional and holidays).
W.E. = Week-end.
Source: [7].

Table T.26. *Urban trips in public modes of transport, according to the size of cities* (journeys per year and per capita)

		Conurbations	Big cities > 500 000	Cities 200–500 000	Cities 100–200 000	References
U.S.A.	(1971)	(San Francisco) 45			56	[26]
France	(1971)	(Paris) 205	(Bordeaux–Lyon) 80–140	(Douai–St. Etienne) 20–130	St. Nazaire–Besançon 10–100	[26, 57]
F.R. Germany	(1971)	(Hamburg) 178	(Duisburg–Düsseldorf) 123–166	(Bonn–Kassel) 117–179	(Osnabrück–Heidelberg) 128–305	[26]
U.K.	(1971)			(Leicester) 225		[26]
Italy	(1972)	(Rome) 257	(Naples–Milan) 170–290	45–248		[8]
Netherlands	(1971)		(The Hague) 134	(Utrecht) 113		[26]
Belgium	(1971)		(Brussels) 174	(Liège) 108		[26]
Sweden	(1971)		(Stockholm) 256	(Göteborg) 187		[26]
Switzerland	(1971)		(Zürich) 358	(Geneva) 234	(Lausanne) 252	[26]

Table T.27. *Specific energy consumption of passenger trains*

		Per gtkh 1966	1970	1975	Per Seat-km ** 1960	1970	1975
U.K.	O.P. (kJ)	–	–	300	–	–	–
	E. (Wh)	–	–	39	–	–	–
Netherlands	O.P. (kJ)	–	380	380		320	310
	E. (Wh)	–	39	39	–	33	21
Denmark	O.P. (kJ)	–	–	390***	–	–	–
	E. (Wh)	–	–	55	–	–	–
Italy	O.P. (kJ)	–	520*	520	–	340*	360
	E. (Wh)	–	34	35	–	22	24
France	O.P. (kJ)	340	300	280*	–	–	–
	E. (Wh)	23	25	22	–	–	–
F.R. Germany	O.P. (kJ)	–	–	500	–	–	–
	E. (Wh)	–	–	31	–	–	–

* 1972, ** derived from the specific consumption per gtkh, *** 1973.

O.P. = Oil products.

E. = Electricity.

gtkh = Gross ton-km hauled.

Source: [43].

Table T.28. Goods transport and industrial growth, 1955–1978

		U.S.A.	France	F.R. Germany	U.K.	Italy	Belgium	Netherlands	Sweden	Japan
Traffic per capita (10^3 tkm/cap)	1955	*10.2 (1.8)	1.7 (0.5)	1.8 (0.3)	1.3 (0.7)	0.9 (0.6)	2.0 (0.7)	1.9 (0.2)		0.4 (0)***
	1960	9.8 (2.5)	2.2 (0.7)	2.5 (0.8)	1.7 (1.2)*	1.1 (0.7)	*2.0 (0.7)	3.0 (0.7)*		0.8 (0.2)
	1970	11.8 (3.2)	3.0 (1.3)	3.3 (1.3)	2.0 (1.5)	1.5 (1.1)	2.4 (0.9)	3.6 (0.9)		1.9 (1.3)
	1974	12.9 (3.7)	3.4 (1.7)	3.5 (1.5)	2.0 (1.6)	1.5 (1.1)	2.5 (1.1)			1.7 (1.2)
	1975	11.7 (3.4)	2.9 (1.5)	3.2 (1.5)	2.1 (1.6)	1.4 (1.1)	2.3 (1.0)	3.5 (1.1)	5.5 (2.5)	1.6 (1.2)
	1978	**12.9 (4.1)	3.2 (1.7)	3.6 (1.8)	**2.2 (1.8)	1.9 (1.5)	**2.7 (1.5)	**3.6 (1.2)		1.6 (1.2)
Traffic per capita and unit of industrial production (index, 100 in 1970)	1955	***157 (103)	114 (64)	114 (49)	90 (56)	164 (148)	138 (128)	113 (52)	***333 (–)	
	1960	120 (103)	99 (82)	117 (95)	*94 (85)	128 (119)	*101 (94)	*117 (110)		122 (50)
	1970	100 (100)	100 (100)	100 (100)	100 (100)	100 (100)	100 (100)	100 (100)	100	100 (100)
	1974	94 (100)	93 (107)	99 (108)	96 (103)	88 (88)	87 (98)			77 (80)
	1975	95 (102)	88 (105)	94 (112)	106 (108)	89 (97)	90 (105)	86 (84)		82 (90)
	1978	**87 (101)	87 (105)	95 (122)	**102 (109)	113 (124)	**98 (136)	84 (106)		69 (79)
Traffic per unit of industrial value added (tkm/US $ 1970)	1974	9.6 (2.8)	3.7 (1.8)	2.6 (1.1)	2.2 (1.8)	2.3 (1.8)	2.3 (1.0)	4.4 (1.4)	5.4 (2.4)	2.1 (1.5)
References		[38]	[6, 43, 51]	[7, 51, 56]	[21, 51, 56]	[8, 51, 56]	[5, 43, 56]	[5, 43, 56]	[6, 51, 56]	[51, 60, 65, 56]

* 1965, ** 1977, *** 1950.

Figures between brackets: road transport only.

Table T.29. Goods traffic per transport modes, 1950–1978 (10^9 tkm)

		U.S.A.	France	F.R. Germany	U.K.	Italy	Netherlands	Belgium	Sweden	Japan
Road	1950	277	18.6**	15.7**	33.5**	16.2	2.6**	6.3**		3*
	1960	456	30.6	45.5		37.2				21
	1965	574	43.5	62.5	68.8	45.8	8.9	6.4	6.8	48.4
	1970	659	66.9	78.0	85.0	58.6	12.4	9.1		136.2
	1974	792	87.4	95.0	89.9	62.4	15.6	10.3	21.5	130.8
	1975	726	78.5	93.1	91.8	62.8	15.4	9.8	20.2	130.0
	1978	888*	89.1	111.7	98.0*	88.0	16.7*	14.4*	20.3	143.1*
Rail	1950	1004	46.9**	49.8**	34.9**	13.5**	3.4**	6.7**	8.2	37*
	1960	952	57.0	53.1	30.5	15.6	3.4	6.3	9.8	55
	1965	1154	64.4	58.2	25.2	15.4	3.5	6.8	13.9	57.3
	1970	1233	70.1	71.5	26.8	18.1	3.5	7.8		63.5
	1974	1363	76.5	69.5	24.2	18.1	3.4	9.1	18.5	52.5
	1975	1214	63.5	55.3	23.5	14.9	2.7	6.8	15.2	47.3
	1978	1331*	67.3	57.5	22.8*	17.4	2.7*	6.5*	14.1	41.3*
River	1950	261	19.3**	26.7**			15.3**	4.6**		
	1960	352	10.7	40.4						
	1965	419	12.5	43.6		0.5	24.1	6.1		
	1970	510	14.2	48.8		1.1	30.8	6.7		
	1974	568	13.7	51.0		1.5	29.6	5.1	8.0	
	1975	547	11.9	47.6		1.4	29.6	6.9	9.5	
	1978	589*	11.6	51.5			31.0*	5.8*		
Pipes	1950	330								
	1960	366		3.0		0.8				
	1965	490		8.9	1.3	2.3				
	1970	690	26.3	16.8	2.7	9.1		0.3		
	1974	810	33.1	16.7	4.8	10.7		1.5		
	1975	811	28.0	14.4	5.2	11.5		1.5		
	1978	874*	29.7							
References		[38]	[6, 43, 51]	[7, 51, 56]	[21, 51, 56]	[8, 51, 56]	[43, 51, 56]	[43, 51, 56]	[6, 51, 56]	[51, 56, 60, 65]

* 1977, ** 1955.

Table T.30. *Intermediate goods production*** and goods traffic, 1960–1977 (pipes and bunker excluded)*

		U.S.A.	France	F.R. Germany	U.K.	Italy	Netherlands	Belgium	Sweden	Japan
Intermediate goods production (10⁶T)	1960	179.6	34.6	53.1	42.40	26.1	4.8*	12.1*	8.3*	49.3
	1965				49.9		7.4	15.6		
	1970	248.4	58.8	91.1	52.2	55.5	10.5*	19.9		169.1
	1974	267.8	67.5	100.9	46.8	66.9	14.3	24.6	15.8	214.3
	1977	255.0	58.9	81.1	42.3	73.1	13.3	19.2		
Ratio goods traffic/intermediate goods production** (10³ tkm/t)	1960	9.8 (7.8)	2.8 (2.5)	2.6 (1.8)		2.0 (2.0)				1.6 (1.6)
	1965				1.9 (1.9)		5.0 (1.6)	1.2 (0.8)		
	1970	9.7 (7.7)	2.6 (2.3)	2.2 (1.7)	2.1 (2.1)	1.4 (1.4)	3.8 (1.3)	1.2 (0.9)		1.2 (1.2)
	1974	10.2 (8.0)	2.6 (2.4)	2.1 (1.6)	2.4 (2.4)	1.2 (1.2)	3.4 (1.3)	1.0 (0.8)	3.0	0.85 (0.85)
	1977	11.0 (8.7)	2.7 (2.5)	2.6 (2.0)	2.9 (2.9)	1.3 (1.3)	3.6 (1.4)	1.4 (1.1)	3.2	0.9 (0.9)

* Ethylene excluded, ** figures in brackets relate to road and rail traffic, *** steel, aluminum, cement, ethylene, propylene and paper.

Table T.31. *Modal distribution of goods traffic, 1955–1978* (excluding pipe lines)

		U.S.A.	France	F.R.Germany	U.K.	Italy	Netherlands	Belgium	Sweden	Japan
Road	1955	18%**	22%	17%	49%	68%	12%	36%		8%**
	1960	26%	31%	33%	73%***	70%	24%***	33%		28%
	1970	27%	44%	39%	76%	75%	26%	39%		68%
	1974	29%	49%	44%	79%	76%	32%	42%	45%	71%
	1975	29%	51%	48%	80%	79%	32%	43%	45%	73%
	1978	32%*	53%	51%	81%*	82%	33%	54%*		78%
Rail	1955	65%***	55%	54%	51%	32%	16%	38%		92%**
	1960	54%	58%	38%	27%***	30%	9%***	35%***		72%
	1970	51%	46%	36%	24%	23%	7%	33%		32%
	1974	50%	43%	32%	21%	22%	7%	37%	39%	29%
	1975	49%	41%	28%	20%	19%	6%	30%	34%	27%
	1978	47%*	40%	26%	19%**	16%	5%	24%		22%
Waterways	1955	17%**	23%	29%			72%	26%		
	1960	20%	11%	29%			67%***	32%***		
	1970	21%	10%	25%		2%	67%	28%		
	1974	21%	8%	24%		2%	61%	21%	16%	
	1975	22%	8%	24%		2%	62%	27%	21%	
	1978	21%	7%	23%		2%	62%	22%*		
Total traffic (10⁹ tkm)	1955	1540**	84.8	92.2	68.4	42.2	21.2	17.6		40**
	1960	1760	98.3	139	94***	53	37***	19.3***		76
	1970	2400	151.2	198	112	78	47	23.6		200
	1974	2720	177.6	216	114	82	49	24.5	48	183
	1975	2490	153.9	196	115	79	48	22.7	45	177
	1978	2810*	168	221	121*	107	50.4*	26.7*		186

* 1977, ** 1950, *** 1965.

Source: [66].

Table T.32. Road goods traffic, 1965–1978

		U.S.A.	Japan	France	F.R. Germany	U.K.	Italy	Netherlands	Belgium	Sweden
Total equipment (10^6 vehicles)	1965	13.1		1.23 (3%)	1.06 (10%)	2.04 (20%)	0.94 (1%)	0.24 (4%)	0.20 (6%)	
	1970	17.7		1.56 (4%)	1.23 (10%)	2.15 (17%)	1.27 (1%)	0.30 (3%)		
	1975	24.8		2.08 (5%)	1.40 (13%)	2.30 (14%)	1.57 (1%)	0.35 (6%)	0.20 (8%)	0.42 (63%)
	1978	30.5		2.50 (7%)						
Equipment per capita (veh/10^3 pers.)	1965	68		25	18	39	18	20		
	1970	87		31	20	39	24	23	21	
	1975	116		39	23	41	29	26	20	52
	1978	139		47						
Equipment utilization (10^3 tkm/veh/y)	1965	43.8		35.4	59.0	32.1	48.7	37.0	45.5	
	1970	37.2		42.9	63.4	39.5	46.1	41.3	51.5	
	1974			43.5	67.4	38.2	41.3	45.9	49.0	52.4
	1975	29.3		37.7	66.5	39.9	40.0	44.0		48.0
	1978	29.1		35.6						
Mileage per vehicle (10^3 km/veh/y)	1972	19.7	17.9	16.8	22.5	23.8	35.9		20.5	33.8
	1978	17.9*		22.5	23.0	23.6*	37.0	22.2*	19.3*	32.9**
References		[38]		[43, 56]	[43, 56]	[43, 56]	[43, 56]	[43, 56]	[43, 56]	[56]

* 1977, ** 1976.

Figures between brackets: percentages of tractors in the total stock of vehicles.

Table T.33. Rail goods traffic 1950–1978

		U.S.A.	Japan	France	F.R. Germany	U.K.	Italy	Netherlands	Belgium	Sweden
Goods traffic per capita (10^3 tkm/cap/y)	1950	6.6	0.4	1.1**	1.0**	0.6***	0.3**	0.3	0.8	
	1960	5.3	0.6	1.3	1.0	0.5****	0.4	0.3****	0.7***	
	1970	6.0	0.6	1.4	1.2	0.5	0.4	0.3	0.8	
	1974	6.5	0.5	1.7	1.1	0.4	0.4		0.9	1.9
	1975	5.7	0.4	1.5	0.9	0.5	0.3	0.2	0.7	
	1978	6.1*	0.4	1.3	0.9	0.4*	0.4	0.2*	0.6	
Equipment utilization (10^3 tkm/car/y)	1965								127	
	1970	845		233	226	114	167	200	160	
	1975	900		278	167		174	182	130	
Car mileage (10^3 km/car/y)	1960	16.7								
	1970	20.7								
	1975	20.6		19.3	18.7	7.6	16.5	19.1		
Load factor (utilization rate × loading rate)	1975	60%		38%	28%	68%	39%	33%		
Ratio tkt/gtkh	1950			0.34						
	1965			0.39				0.38		
	1970			0.40			0.37****	0.38		
	1975			0.40	0.34	0.39	0.38	0.37	0.50	
	1978			0.40						

* 1977, ** 1955, *** 1965, **** 1972.

tkt = ton-km transported.

gtkh = gross ton-km hauled.

Source: Table T.32.

Table T.34. *Vehicles for rail goods transport, 1950–1977*

		1950	1960	1965	1970	1975	1977
U.S.A.	A	11.5	9.4	7.8	7.1	6.3	5.9
	B	53	55	60	67	73	76
	C		157 (39%)	151 (39%)	147 (42%)	130 (45%)	132 (43%)
France	A			7.6	6.0	5.4	
	B					38	
	C					104 (33%)	
F.R.Germany	A			5.9	5.3	5.4	
	B					32	
	C					101 (36%)	
U.K.	A					4.4	
	B					22	
	C					33.5 (27%)	
Italy	A			2.6	2.4	2.3	
	B					27	
	C					38 (32%)	
Netherlands	A			1.8	1.5	1.1	
	B					29	
	C					21 (37%)	
Belgium	A			6.3	5.0	5.4	
	B					35	
	C						

A = Number of cars per 1000 persons.
B = Loading capacity of cars (tons).
C = Vehicles-km/cap.
N.B.: Figures in brackets relate to the share of empty running vehicles-km.
Source: Table T.32.

Table T.35. *Specific energy consumption of goods trains, 1965–1975* (per ton-km transported)

	1965		1972		1975	
	O.P. (MJ)	E. (Wh)	O.P. (MJ)	E. (Wh)	O.P. (MJ)	E. (Wh)
U.S.A.	0.46		0.46		0.42	
France	0.90	58	0.75		0.80	62
Italy			1.1	93	1.4	92
Netherlands			1.0	106	1.1	106
References	[68]	[31]	[68]	[31]	[68]	[31]

O.P. = Oil products.
E. = Electricity.

Table T.36. *Waterwap goods traffic, 1965–1975*

		France	F. R. Germany	Netherlands	Belgium
Infrastructure 10^3 km 1975		8568	6017	4803	1968
(in use)		(7080)	(4408)	(4803)	(1535)
(above 1000 t)		(1869)	(3063)	(2333)	(630)
Equipment	1965	9688	7604	20810	5901
(barges)	1970	7174	6336	19937	5928
	1974	6614	4937	19529	4611
	1975	6563	4786	19235	4182
(per km)		(0.93)	(1.09)	(4.00)	(2.72)
Capacity	1965	3.61	5.03	6.40	2.81
(10^6 t)	1970	2.99	4.52	6.68	2.61
	1974	2.93	4.31	7.14	2.44
	1975	2.94	4.22	7.11	2.32
(t per km)		(415)	(957)	(1480)	(1511)
Unitary	1965	370	660	310	480
capacity	1970	420	710	340	440
(t/barge)	1974	440	870	370	530
	1975	450	890	370	550
Equipment	1965	1.29	5.74	1.16	1.03
utilization	1970	1.98	7.66	1.54	1.13
(10^6 tkm/barge)	1974	2.07	10.33	1.52	1.11
	1975	1.81	9.94	1.54	1.65

Source: Reference [43].

Table T.37. *Specific energy consumption of barges*

	(MJ/tko)	(MJ/tkt)	References
U.S.A.	0.11–0.31	0.34 (1972)	[5, 61]
France	0.12–0.27	0.63 (1975)	[36, 59]
F.R. Germany		0.81 (1975)	[63]
Netherlands	0.19	1.84 (1972)	[73]

tkt = Ton-km transported.
tko = Ton-km offered.

Appendix 3 Data on the Industrial Sector

Table I.1. *Final energy consumption in industry* (PJ)

	1950	1955	1960	1965	1970	1974*	1975	1977	1978	1979
U.S.A.	–	–	11 390	13 830	16 700	16 700	14 900	16 000	17 800	18 600
Japan	600	910	1 530	2 260	4 510	5 150	5 100	5 800	5 870	6 090
France	790	1 000	1 220	1 580	2 090	2 070	2 000	2 130	2 210	2 530
F.R. Germany	1 180	1 760	2 030	2 370	2 830	3 220	2 930	2 920	2 990	3 190
Italy	270	450	720	1 100	1 630	1 830	1 940	1 990	1 900	2 000
U.K.	1 990	2 250	2 280	2 440	2 600	2 510	2 240	2 350	2 330	2 380
Belgium	260	340	360	430	590	680	610	650	670	680
Netherlands	140	170	240	320	500	640	760	870	1 015	1 150
Sweden	–	–	360	430	560	590	640	560	570	590

* Before 1974 non energy uses of oil are excluded for all countries except U.K. and U.S.A.; they are included after 1974.

1 Mtoe = 41.8 PJ, 1000 PJ ≃ 24 Mtoe.

Source: U.S.A., Japan, Sweden: OECD [58, 61]; France, F.R. Germany, Italy, Belgium, Netherlands 1950–1955: EUROSTAT [59], 1960–1974: OECD [58], 1975–1979: OECD [61]; U.K.: Department of Energy [60], OECD [61].

Table I.2. *Index of final energy consumption in industry* (1970 = 100)

	1950	1955	1960	1965	1970	1974		1975	1977	1978	1979
U.S.A.	–	–	68	83	100	100	100	89	96	107	111
Japan	13	20	34	50	100	114	125	113	129	130	135
France	38	48	58	76	100	99	113	96	102	106	121
F.R. Germany	42	62	72	84	100	114	124	104	103	107	113
Italy	17	28	44	68	100	113	133	121	122	117	123
U.K.	77	87	88	94	100	97	97	86	90	90	92
Belgium	44	57	61	73	100	115	127	103	110	114	115
Netherlands	28	34	48	65	100	129	177	153	175	203	230
Sweden	–	–	64	77	100	105	116	114	100	102	118

Source: Table I.1.

Table I.3. *Index of industrial production* (1970 = 100)

	1950	1955	1960	1965	1970	1974	1975	1977	1978
U.S.A.	41	57	61	82	100	120	109	128	136
Japan	6	13	28	48	100	122	110	127	134
France	–	43	59	75	100	123	114	126	128
F.R. Germany	24	41	59	77	100	111	105	116	118
Italy	20	33	50	69	100	120	108	123	126
U.K.	58	68	77	90	100	105	100	106	110
Belgium	44	54	61	81	100	120	108	118	120
Netherlands	27	40	50	67	100	125	119	127	128
Sweden	–	–	55	79	100	116	114	108	107

Source: IEJE, from U.N. indexes (Statistical Yearbook, years 1951, 1967, 1971, 1978).

Table I.4. *Share of intermediate goods industries* in the industrial value added*

	1960 ***	1965	1970**	1974
U.S.A.		$33 \begin{smallmatrix}(11)\\(9)\end{smallmatrix}$	$32 \begin{smallmatrix}(13)\\(7)\end{smallmatrix}$	$33 \begin{smallmatrix}(13)\\(8)\end{smallmatrix}$
Japan		$31 \begin{smallmatrix}(14)\\(9)\end{smallmatrix}$	$30 \begin{smallmatrix}(14)\\(10)\end{smallmatrix}$	$30 \begin{smallmatrix}(12)\\(11)\end{smallmatrix}$
France	33	34	$34 \begin{smallmatrix}(17)\\(7)\end{smallmatrix} / 37 \begin{smallmatrix}(19)\\(9)\end{smallmatrix}$	$38 \begin{smallmatrix}(19)\\(10)\end{smallmatrix}$
Italy	$33 \begin{smallmatrix}(13)\\(6)\end{smallmatrix}$	$35 \begin{smallmatrix}(14)\\(7)\end{smallmatrix}$	$34 \begin{smallmatrix}(14)\\(7)\end{smallmatrix}$	$35 \begin{smallmatrix}(15)\\(7)\end{smallmatrix}$
F.R. Germany	40	$39 \begin{smallmatrix}(12)\\(12)\end{smallmatrix}$	$40 \begin{smallmatrix}(14)\\(11)\end{smallmatrix}$	$41 \begin{smallmatrix}(15)\\(11)\end{smallmatrix}$
Netherlands	$31 \begin{smallmatrix}(15)\\(5)\end{smallmatrix}$	$32 \begin{smallmatrix}(16)\\(4)\end{smallmatrix}$	$40 \begin{smallmatrix}(24)\\(5)\end{smallmatrix}$	$45 \begin{smallmatrix}(29)\\(4)\end{smallmatrix}$ (1973)
Belgium		$28 \begin{smallmatrix}(8)\\(10)\end{smallmatrix}$	$30 \begin{smallmatrix}(9)\\(10)\end{smallmatrix}$	$30 \begin{smallmatrix}(11)\\(10)\end{smallmatrix}$

* Steel, non ferrous metals, chemicals, building materials and glass, pulp and paper; figures between brackets: share of chemicals (upper figure) and steel.

** For France and Italy there is a discontinuity in the data for 1970.

*** 1962 for Italy.

Source: OECD (values added in constant prices) [61].

Table I.5. *Distribution of final energy consumption in industry by energy form* (in %)

		1960	1965	1970	1974
U.S.A.	C	27	25	16	16
	H	60	61	69	67
	EL	13	14	15	17
Japan	C	56	31	29	29
	H	27	50	53	51
	EL	17	19	18	20
France	C	64	45	29	26
	H	24	42	58	59
	EL	12	13	13	15
F.R. Germany	C	73	51	36	30
	H	15	36	49	54
	EL	12	13	15	16
Italy	C	21	17	13	13
	H	63	68	72	71
	EL	16	15	15	16
U.K.	C	67	50	36	23
	H	23	39	51	63
	EL	10	11	13	14
Belgium	C	66	51	41	37
	H	26	39	48	51
	EL	8	10	11	12
Netherlands	C	44	25	14	11
	H	46	64	73	75
	EL	10	11	13	14

C = Coal
H = Hydrocarbons
EL = Electricity
Source of data: OECD [58].

Table I.6. *Steel production* (10^6 t)

	1950	1955	1960	1965	1970	1974	1975	1977	1978
U.S.A.	90.4	108.6	91.9	122.0	122.0	132.2	105.8	113.2	123.9
Japan	4.8	9.4	22.1	41.2	93.3	117.1	102.3	102.4	102.1
France	8.7	12.6	17.3	19.6	23.8	27	21.5	22.1	22.8
F.R. Germany	14.0	24.5	34.1	36.8	45.0	53.2	40.4	39.0	41.3
Italy	3.4	4.5	8.5	12.7	17.3	23.8	21.8	23.3	24.3
U.K.	16.6	20.1	24.7	27.4	28.3	22.3	20.1	20.4	20.3
Belgium	3.8	5.9	7.2	9.2	12.6	16.2	11.6	11.3	12.6
Netherlands	0.5	1.0	2.0	3.1	5.0	5.8	4.8	4.9	5.6

Note: 1974 represents for most countries the highest level of production with the exception of U.K. (1970), the U.S.A. (140 Mt in 1973) and Japan (119.3 Mt in 1973).
Source: EUROSTAT [57], French Statistical Yearbook [62].

Table I.7. *Per capita steel consumption* (kg/capita)

	1950	1955	1960	1965	1970	1974	1975
U.S.A.	577	630	513	678	634	694	565
France	158	224	293	332	441	472	387
F.R. Germany	218	414	505	541	654	595	534
Italy	66	119	187	222	378	428	333
U.K.	299	360	395	423	435	423	375
Netherlands	155	238	280	311	405	392	340

Source: EUROSTAT [57].

Table I.8. *Fraction of steel consumption supplied from domestic production* (in %)*

	1950	1955	1960	1965	1970	1974
U.S.A.	103	104	99	92	94	104
France	132	129	129	121	106	109
F.R. Germany	129	113	121	115	112	144
Italy	78	95	91	109	84	100
U.K.	111	110	119	119	117	94

* Ratio domestic production to consumption.

Table I.9. *Final energy consumption of the steel industry* (PJ)

	1950	1955	1960	1965	1970	1974	1979
U.S.A.			2180	2615	2264	2452	2643
			(19%)	(19%)	(13%)	(15%)	
Japan	158	233	433	774	1770	2130	1730
	(26%)	(25%)	(28%)	(34%)	(39%)	(41%)	
France	227	326	427	465	573	616	497
	(29%)	(33%)	(35%)	(29%)	(27%)	(30%)	
F.R. Germany	370	604	795	731	943	1136	863
	(31%)	(34%)	(39%)	(31%)	(33%)	(35%)	
Italy	55	84	138	229	294	405	353
	(20%)	(19%)	(19%)	(21%)	(18%)	(22%)	
U.K.			678	711	682	498	458
			(34%)	(32%)	(29%)	(22%)	
Belgium	80	125	146	176	254	310	243
	(31%)	(37%)	(40%)	(41%)	(43%)	(45%)	
Netherlands	19	28	50	74	103	119	101
	(14%)	(17%)	(21%)	(23%)	(21%)	(19%)	

Note: The percentages represent the share of the steel industry in the overall industrial energy consumption (excluding feedstocks).

Source: OECD [58, 61].

Table I.10. *Steel production by processes* (in %)

		1950	1960	1965	1968	1970	1973	1975	1978	References
U.S.A.	OH		88	72	50			19	16	[33, 38, 56]
	EL		8	11	13	15	18	20	23	
	OX		4	18	37			61	61	
Japan	OH						1	—	—	[56]
	EL					17	18	20	22	
	OX						81	80	78	
France	OH	94	91	78		60	37	23	7	[31, 56]
	EL	6	9	9		11	11	14	15	
	OX	—	—	13		29	52	63	78	
F.R. Germany	OH			72		34	22	18	11	[56, 57]
	EL			9		10	10	13	14	
	OX			19		56	68	69	75	
Belgium	OH			79		43	18	9	—	[56, 57]
	EL			5		4	4	5	4	
	OX			16		53	78	86	96	
U.K.	OH		92	67		48		23	9	[55, 56]
	EL		7	13		20		26	35	
	OX		1	20		32		50	56	
Netherlands	OH			24		15	1	1	—	[56, 57]
	EL			7		7	7	7	6	
	OX			69		78	92	92	94	
Italy	OH			40		27	17	11	6	[56, 57]
	EL			38		41	41	43	51	
	OX			22		32	42	46	43	

OH = Open hearth, Bessemer or Thomas
EL = Electric steel-works
OX = Oxygen process.

Table I.11. *Energy consumption for pig iron production* (including agglomeration)

		1960	1965	1970	1973	1975	1978
France	(a)	63	100	107	123	129	138
	(b)	30	26.9	23.8	23.5	23.4	21.9
	(c)	(−10)	(−7.7)	(−5.6)	(−4.8)	(−4.7)	(−4.4)
Italy	(a)	70	65	60	53	60	
	(b)	20	18	16	15	14	
	(c)	(−5)	(−5)	(−6)	(−4)	(−4)	
F.R. Germany	(a)	77	77	71	100	77	
	(b)	18	17	16	16	16	
	(c)	(−9)	(−6)	(−6)	(−5)	(−6)	
Netherlands	(a)	75	59	47	47	47	
	(b)	19.5	21	18.3	14.7	13	
	(c)	(−8.1)	(−4.4)	(−4.2)	(−4.4)	(−3.8)	
Belgium	(a)	47	67	85	100	110	
	(b)	16.1	15.7	15.2	15.9	15.9	
	(c)	(−9.6)	(−6.4)	(−5.7)	(−4.9)	(−5.4)	
U.K.	(a)	195	195	187	177	174	
	(b)	16.7	17.7	17.5	16.5	16.3	
	(c)	(−9)	(−6.4)	(−5.4)	(−5.0)	(−5.2)	

(a) Electricity in kWh/t of pig iron, (b) fossil fuels in GJ/t of pig iron, (c) blast furnace gas available for other uses in GJ/t.

Source: Data worked out by P. Godoy (IEJE) from IISI [55] for Italy, F.R. Germany, Netherlands, Belgium, and U.K.; France [31].

Table I.12. *Electricity consumption in electric furnaces* (kWh/t)

	1960	1965	1970	1975
Italy	640	630	620	620
F.R. Germany	600	560	510	490
U.K.	480	450	430	420

Source: Data worked out by P. Godoy (IEJE) from an IISI study [55].

Table I.13. *Energy consumption for rolling* (fossils fuels in GJ, electricity in kWh)

		1960	1965	1970	1973*	1975	1978
France	GJ/t of crude steel	5.4	5.3	4.7	4.6	4.9	5
	kWh/t	207	221	219	239	256	270
F.R. Germany	GJ/t	7.7	6.5	6.2	5.6	5.4	
	kWh/t	202	227	202	225	230	
Italy	GJ/t	4.4	4.4	3.7	3.8	3.9	
	kWh/t	175	205	205	205	205	
Belgium	GJ/t	9.8	7.6	5.9	5.5	4.9	
	kWh/t	227	186	179	183	188	
U.K.	GJ/t	9.6	9.5	8.5		7	
	kWh/t	138	168	196		209	
Netherlands	GJ/t	3.1	2.3	3.3	3.6	3.8	
	kWh/t	191	179	153	204	221	

* In 1973, the consumption was estimated to 3.8 GJ and 200 kWh in Japan and 6.3 GJ and 289 kWh/t in the U.S.A.

Note: These figures include energy consumption for rolling and other uses not accounted elsewhere; for instance, in France, the rolling alone represented 3.2 GJ/t in 1973 and 3.1 in 1979.

Source: Worked out by P. Godoy (IEJE) from IISI data [55] for all countries except France; France [31].

References

Introduction

1. W.A.E.S.: Energy global prospects 1985–2000. New York: McGraw-Hill. 1977.
2. Darmstadter, J., Dunkerley, J., Alterman, J.: How industrial societies use energy. Baltimore-London: The Johns Hopkins University Press. 1977.

Chapter I

1. Ramain, P.: Réflexion critique sur les bilans énergétiques, 176 p. Paris: Éditions du CNRS. 1977.
2. Mainguy, Y.: L'économie de l'énergie, 532 p. Paris: Dunod. 1967.
3. Girod, J.: La demande d'énergie: méthodes et techniques de modélisation, 185 p. (Collection Énergie et Société.) Paris: Éditions du CNRS. 1977.
4. NERA: The studies of the residential demand for electricity: a critique. National Economic Research Associates (NERA). 1973.
5. Landsberg, H.H.: Energy, the next twenty years, 628 p. Cambridge, Mass.: Ballinger. 1979.
6. U.S. Department of Energy: Income and price effects on petroleum consumption. An international comparison, 57 p. Washington: Department of Energy. 1980. (DOE/EIA-0183/16.)
7. Pyndyck, R.S.: The characteristics of the demand for energy. In: Energy conservation and public policy (Sawhill, J., ed.), pp. 22–45. Englewood Cliffs, N.J.: Prentice-Hall. 1979.

Chapter 2

1. Klaiss, H., Schulz, K. H.: Gebietstypischer Energieverbrauch der Haushalte. I.K.E., October 1977 (in R.S.U. Bericht Nr. 2TF.7).
2. Agence pour les Economies d'Energie (A.E.E.): Consommations énergétiques du secteur résidentiel et tertiaire, années 1973–1977. Paris: A.E.E. September 1978.
3. Nederlands Economisch Instituut (N.E.I.): Een maatschappelijke evaluate van een energie-besparingsprogramma voor woningen. Rotterdam: N.E.I.
4. VEGIN: Rapport van de commissie debiets – analyse en prognose (DAP). Nederland: VEGIN. April 1975.
5. Collections INSEE; Serie M.74–75.
6. Reents, H.: Die Entwicklung des sektoralen End- und Nutzenergiebedarfs in der Bundesrepublik Deutschland, 258 p. Jülich, F.R.G.: KFA. 1977.
7. Erdgas: Daten, Fakten, Fälle. Erdgas, F.R.G. 1978. (Information Erdgas 78/1.)
8. Romig, F., Leach, G.: Energy conservation in U.K. dwellings: domestic sector survey and insulation, 86 p. London: IIED. June 1977.

9. Chesshire, J. H., Surrey, A. J.: Estimating U.K. energy demand for year 2000, a sectoral approach, 80 p. Brighton: SPRU. February 1978.

10. Over, J. A., Sjoerdsma, A. C.: Energy conservation: ways and means, 181 p. The Hague: Future Shape of Technology Foundation. 1974.

11. Institut National de la Statistique (I.N.S.): Annuaire statistique de la Belgique, 828 p. Bruxelles: I.N.S. 1978.

12. EUROSTAT: Indicateurs sociaux pour la Communauté Européenne 1960–1975, 486 p. Luxembourg: EUROSTAT. 1977.

13. W.A.E.S.: Energy demand studies major consuming countries, 553 p. Cambridge, Mass.: M.I.T. Press. 1976.

14. Merzagora, N.: Input data of MEDEE 2/Italy. Rome: CNEN. 1978.

15. ISTAT: Annuario statistico italiano 1978. Rome: ISTAT. 1979.

16. Danmarks Statistik: Statistik arbog 1978, 596 p. Copenhague: Danmarks Statistik. 1978.

17. DEFU: Danmarks energibalance 1976, 2 p. Copenhague: DEFU. 1976.

18. Panzhauser, E., Fantl, K.: Sinnvoller Energieeinsatz im Bereich Bauen und Wohnen, 51 p. Wien: ÖMV. 1978.

19. Dole, S.: Energy use and conservation in the residential sector: a regional analysis. Santa Monica, Calif.: RAND. 19/5. (R-1641-NSF.)

20. Federal Energy Administration (F.E.A.): Residential and commercial energy use patterns 1970–1990. (Project Independence Blueprint, Vol. 1.) Washington, D.C.: F.E.A. November 1974.

21. Schipper, L., Ketoff, A., Meyers, S.: International comparison of residential energy use: indicators of residential energy use and efficiency; Part I: The data base. Berkeley, Calif.: Lawrence Berkeley Laboratory. May 1981.

22. Yoshino, H.: Change in use and conservation in the residential sector in Japan, 12 p. Tohoku University: Faculty of Engineering.

23. Collections INSEE, serie C43.

24. Schneider, A.: Der Endenergieverbrauch. VIK-Mitteilungen Nr. 4, 88–102 (1978).

25. Leach, G. et al.: A low energy strategy for the United Kingdom, 259 p. London: Science Reviews. 1979.

26. SAEF: Logement, bâtiment et travaux publics, développement urbain, Paris: SAEF. May 1978. (Dossiers d'information 1.)

27. C.B.S.: Statistical yearbook of the Netherlands, 1977, 400 p. The Hague: Staatsuitgeverij. 1978.

28. Norgard, J.: Bolig og Varme, 73 p. Lyngby (Denmark): DEMO Projektet, Technical University, Fysik Laboratorium III. 1977.

29. Danish Building Research Institute (private communication, December 1978).

30. Hammarsten, S.: A survey of Swedish buildings from the energy aspect. Energy and Buildings 2, 125–135 (1979).

31. Isolation thermique de l'habitat existant. Paris: Promalin (special issue). June 1976.

32. Electrical energy consumption in California, data collection and analysis. Appendix A (author unknown).

33. Agence pour les Economies d'Energie. Les comportements dans le secteur résidentiel et tertiaire. Paris: AEE. March 1980.

34. National Economic Development Office (NEDO): Energy conservation in the United Kingdom, 106 p. London: HMSO. 1974.

35. Chateau, B., Lapillonne, B.: Base de données du modèle MEDEE 3/France. Grenoble: IEJE. 1979.

36. Gaz de France: L'isolation thermique et le chauffage au gaz en habitat collectif neuf. Paris: G.D.F. 1978.
37. Rizzo, M.: Le bilan énergétique des immeubles collectifs. Journée d'étude du 25.04.77 sur l'utilisation rationnelle du pétrole pour le chauffage. Paris: AFTP. 1974.
38. C.C.U.E.: Les pompes à chaleur: utilisation au chauffage les locaux d'habitation. Annales des Mines, November 1977.
39. Lettre Economie et Energie (several years).
40. Stanford Research Institute (S.R.I.): Patterns of energy consumption in the United States. Springfield, Ill.: NTIS. January 1972.
41. D'Acierno, J. P., Bertolami, R. J., Clao, E. I.: Energy consumption in residential gas and electric heater. Oak Ridge, Tenn., Oak Ridge National Laboratory. 1976.
42. Anderson, K. P.: Residential energy use: an econometric analysis. Santa Monica, Calif., Rand, October 1973. (R. 1297-NSF.)
43. Debony, P.: L'amélioration des logements existants. Paris: Eyrolles. 1977.
44. INSEE: Logements, immeubles, recensement général de la population de 1975. Paris: INSEE.
45. Hirst, E., Jakson, J.: Historical pattern of residential and commercial energy uses. Energy 2, 131–140 (1977).
46. Collections de l'INSEE, série M42.
47. Base de données SIROCCO. Paris: INSEE.
48. Saros, G.: Energy demand analysis: present structures and future changes in the Swedish households, service and transportation sectors, 132 p. Stockholm: Swedish Council for Building Research. 1979. (D.12: 1979.)
49. Lapillonne, B.: Long term perspectives of the US energy demand: application of the MEDEE 2 model to the US. Energy 5, 231–257 (1980).
50. ENI (Division for planning and development): End uses of energy in Italy, 61 p. Rome: ENI. July 1978.
51. Chateau, B., Lapillonne, B.: Base de données du modèle MEDEE 3/RFA. Grenoble: IEJE. 1979.
52. Chateau, B., Lapillonne, B.: Base de données du modèle MEDEE 3/Danemark. Grenoble: IEJE. 1979.
53. Chateau, B., Lapillonne, B.: Base de données du modèle MEDEE 3/Royaume Uni. Grenoble: IEJE. 1979.
54. Chateau, B., Lapillonne, B.: Base de données du modèle MEDEE 3/Pays-Bas. Grenoble: IEJE. 1979.
55. Chateau, B., Lapillonne, B.: Base de données du modèle MEDEE 3/Italie. Grenoble: IEJE. 1979.
56. Office of Technology Assessment (O.T.A.): Residential Energy Conservation. Vol. 1, 355 p. Washington: O.T.A. July 1979.
57. Chauffage, ventilation, conditionnement, special issue (10), October 1979.
58. Notes et études documentaires. Le charbon en France. Paris: La Documentation Francaise. May 1962. (No. 2885.)
59. Building Research Establishment (BRE): Energy conservation: a study of energy consumption in buildings and possible means of saving energy in housing, 64 p. Garston: BRE. June 1975.
60. The Electricity Council: Domestic sector analysis (2 volumes). London: August 1975 and November 1978.
61. Elforbruget for husholdningsapparater (author unknown).
62. Electricité de France (E.D.F.): (Working papers.)
63. H.E.A.: Statistisches Faltblatt 1977. Frankfurt: 1978.

64. H.E.A.: Der End-Energiebedarf der Haushalte in der Bundesrepublik Deutschland 1977 nach Energieträgern und Anwendungsgebieten. (H.E.A.-Statistik.). Frankfurt: H.E.A. 1979.

65. Gaz de France (G.D.F.): Statistiques (several years). Paris: G.D.F.

66. Electricity Council: 1978 sample survey of domestic consumers (Appendix A.) London: 1979.

67. EPRI: Efficient Electricity Use. Palo Alto, Calif.: EPRI.

68. Ebersbach et al., K.F.: Technologien zur Einsparung von Energie, Teil II.2.6: Energie-anwendung Haushalt und Kleinverbrauch. München: Forschungsstelle für Energiewirt-schaft, May 1976.

69. U.S. Department of Commerce: Statistical abstract of the United States. 1976. Washington, D.C.: Bureau of the Census, Government Printing Office. 1976.

70. Collections de l'INSEE, série M71.

71. SEDES: Survey realized in June 1975 on 2000 households. Paris: SEDES.

72. O.T.A.: Residential energy consumption. Vol. II: working papers. Washington: O.T.A. April 1979.

73. Demont et al., J. A.: Domestic gas in an energy conscious future, 28 p. London: The Institution of Gas Engineers. May 1977. (114th Annual General Meeting, Bournemouth, Communication 1018.)

74. Agence pour les Economies d'Energie: Various reports. Paris: A.E.E.

75. Arbeitsgemeinschaft Energiebilanzer: Energiebilanzen der Bundesrepublik Deutschland. Düsseldorf: F.R.G. (several years).

76. H.E.A.: Überlegungen zur künftigen Entwicklung der elektrischen Wohnungsbeheizung in der Bundesrepublik Deutschland. Frankfurt: 1976.

77. Green, M. B., Rich, J.: Future trends in domestic heating by gas, 30 p. London: The Institution of Gas Engineers. November 1979. (45th meeting.)

78. Kirk, S. R.: The facts about energy. London: The Institution of Gas Engineers. April 1979. (Short residential course, Pembroke College, Oxford.)

79. EUROSTAT: Comptes Nationaux, SEC 1960–1970. Luxembourg: EUROSTAT. 1971; Comptes Nationaux, SEC 1970–1977. Luxembourg: EUROSTAT. 1979.

80. Holmsberg et al., J. G.: Conservation of energy in Swedish buildings. Conference Mondiale de l'Energie, September 1977; Vol. 2.21, pp. 1–17.

81. The National Swedish Industrial Board: Note on the conservation program in the building sector. Stockholm: 1977.

82. The National Swedish Board of Physical Planning and Building: Regulations on energy conservation in new buildings. Stockholm: 1977.

83. Saros, G.: Data on energy use and potential for energy conservation in french dwellings, 19. p. Grenoble: IEJE. 1978.

84. National Swedish Industrial Board: Private communication with H. Ljung, 1977.

85. C.S.T.B.: Evaluation du coût du renforcement de l'isolation thermique des bâtiments existants. Paris: C.S.T.B.

86. SABO: Swedish housing 1979. Stockholm: SABO. 1979.

87. Ministère de l'Environnement et du Cadre de Vie, Mission Energie et Bâtiment. Note sur le gisement des économies d'énergie dans l'habitat. Paris: 1979.

88. Conti, F., Bain, M., Maineri, M., Zanantoni, C.: Energy saving in space heating of existing houses, an assessment for the north of Italy. Ispra: CEE (System Analysis Division, JRC, Ispra). April 1978.

89. Hoglund, B. I., Johnson, B.: Energy conservation measures taken in thermal insulation and installation fields for existing buildings. Stockholm: Royal Institute of Technology. 1976.

90. Scanada Consultant Limited, Central Mortgage and Housing Corporation: Thermal efficiency in existing housing and the potential for conservation. Canada: 1976.

91. Eurima: Evolution of regulation and practice on thermal insulation of building. Eurima: 1976.

92. Raoust, M., Claux-Pesso: Quelques éléments pour évaluer le gisement d'économies d'énergie de l'architecture climatique. (Working paper.) Paris: Commissariat Général du Plan. 1979.

93. Bertelo, L.: La consommation énergétique des logements individuels chauffés à l'électricité, au gaz et au mazout, 32 p. Paris. Comité Français d'Electrothermie. 1979.

94. Ministère de l'Environnement et du Cadre de Vie: Axes de recherche, développement à promouvoir sur le thème des économies d'énergie dans le secteur résidentiel et tertiaire. (Working paper.) Paris: Commissariat Général du Plan, January 1980.

95. Nørgard, J. S.: Improved efficiency in domestic electricity use. Energy Policy 7 (1979).

96. Ward, D. S.: Executive summary, solar heating and cooling system operational results conference. Colorado Springs, Colo.: Solar heating and cooling systems operational results conference. November 17–December 1, 1978.

97. Criqui, P.: L'énergie solaire en France: approche socio-économique. Paris: CNRS. 1980.

98. Bonaïti, J. P.: Potentiel de developpement de certains types de pompes à chaleur dans l'habitat, 60 p. Grenoble: IEJE. November 1977.

99. Energy, Mines, and Resources Canada: Energy demand projections, a total energy approach. Ottawa: Ministery of Supply and Services, 1977. (Report ER 77-4.)

100. Energy, Mines and Resources Canada: Energy conservation in Canada: programs and perspectives. Ottawa: Ministery of Supply and Services, 1977. (Report ER 77-7.)

101. Shoda, T., Murakami, S., Yoshino, H.: Qualitative level of indoor environment in Japanese houses. Tokyo: University of Tokyo.

102. Clarke, W.: La Californie à l'avant garde solaire mondiale. Solaire 1, January 1980.

103. Rosenfeld et al., A.: Building energy use compilation and analysis, Part 1: Single family residence. Berkeley, Calif.: Lawrence Berkeley Laboratory, July 1979. (LBL 8912, draft.)

104. Ross, M. H., Williams, R. H.: Drilling for oil and gas in our buildings, report PU/CEES 87, July 1979.

105. Groupe de travail CFE: La surisolation thermique des bâtiments neufs d' habitation: exemple de réalisation. Paris: Comité Français d'Electrothermie (1979).

106. Schipper, L.: Raising the productivity of energy use. Berkeley, Calif.: Lawrence Berkeley Laboratory.

107. UNIPEDE: Congrès de Cannes, 1970.

108. CSTB: Cahiers du CSTB (F) no. 180, p. 103.

109. INSEE: Collections de l'INSEE. Série E, no. 42: Enquête annuelle d'entreprise dans le commerce. Paris: 1973.

110. Chateau, B.: Analyse de la demande d'énergie du secteur tertiaire. Grenoble: IEJE. 1977.

111. OCDE: Statistiques de base de l'énergie 1950–1964. Paris: OCDE. 1966.
OCDE: Bilans énergétiques des pays de l'OCDE 1973–1975. Paris: OCDE. 1977.
OCDE: Bilans énergétiques des pays de l'OCDE 1960–1974. Paris: OCDE. 1977.
OCDE: Bilans énergétiques des pays de l'OCDE 1975–1979. Paris: OCDE. 1981.

112. EUROSTAT: Bilans globaux de l'énergie 1963–1975: Luxembourg: EUROSTAT. 1977.
EUROSTAT: Energie 1950–1965. Luxembourg: EUROSTAT. 1965.
EUROSTAT: Bilans globaux de l'énergie 1970–1977. Luxembourg: EUROSTAT. 1979.

113. Agence pour les Economies d'Energie: Dossier statistique sur la consommation d'énergie dans le résidentiel, le tertiaire, les transports et l'industrie. Paris: A.E.E. 1979.
114. ENI: Energia ed Idrocarburi, 1977 and 1978. Rome: ENI.
115. Department of Energy: Digest of United Kingdom energy statistics (several years). London: HMSO.
116. Bureau of Statistics: Statistical handbook of Japan, 1978. Tokyo: Bureau of Statistics. 1978.
117. INSEE: Annuaire statistique de la France (several years). Paris: INSEE.
118. C.S.O.: Annual abstract of statistics, 1977. London: HMSO. 1977.
119. Commission Economique pour l'Europe: Etude statistique sur la situation du logement dans les pays de la CEE, vers 1970. New York: United Nations. 1978.
120. Ministery of Foreign Affairs: Statistical survey of japan economy. Tokyo: Economic and Foreign Affairs Research Association. 1978.
121. Laponche, B.: Consommation d'énergie et croissance économique, quelques comparaisons et rétrospectives. Paris: CEA. 1979. (DPg V/79-313.)

Chapter III

1. ONU: Annuaire statistique. New York: 1966.
2. ONU: Annuaire statistique. New York: 1976, 1977–1978, 1979.
3. EUROSTAT: Indicateurs sociaux pour la Communauté Européenne 1960–1975. Luxembourg: 1977.
4. ONU: Annuaire statistique. New York: 1951.
5. Shonka, D. B., Loebl, A. S., Patterson, P. D.: Transportation energy conservation data book (2nd ed.) Oak Ridge National Laboratory. 1977.
6. Ministère des Transports: Annuaire statistique des transports. Paris (several years).
7. Der Bundes-Minister für Verkehr: Verkehr in Zahlen 1978. Berlin: 1978.
8. Ministerio dei Trasporti: Libro bianco: I trasporti in Italia. Roma: 1977.
9. Centraal bureau voor de statistiek: Statistiek van het personenvervoer. The Hague: 1977.
10. INSEE: Série M55: L'équipement des ménages en biens durables au début de 1976. Paris: 1977.
11. ISTAT: Statistiche sociali, Vol. 1, ed. 1975. Rome: 1976.
12. Stichtingweg: Profiel van de mobiliteit. Stichtingweg Bulletin, December 1974.
13. OCDE: Bilans energétiques 1960–1977. Paris: 1978.
14. Statistical yearbook of the World Power Conference, no.7. London: 1954.
15. OSCE: Statistiques de l'énergie 1950–1964. Luxembourg: 1965.
16. OCDE: Statistiques de base de l'énergie, 1950–1954. Paris: 1965.
17. Laponche, B.: Consommation d'énergie et croissance économique. Quelques comparaisons et rétrospectives. Paris: CEA (DPg V79–313). 1979.
18. I.R.T.: Consommation d'énergie par la circulation routière. Paris: 1979.
19. Agence pour les Economies d'Energie: Consommation de carburant des voitures particulières. Paris: 1979.
20. Rieke, H.: Die künftige Entwicklung des Straßenverkehrs in der Bundesrepublik Deutschland. Diw (Berlin), No. 22 (1972).
21. Department of Transport: Transport statistics, Great Britain 1966–1976. London: HMSO. 1978.
22. CBS: Het bezit en gebruik van personenauto's 1976. The Hague: Staatssuitgeverij. 1978.
23. Frondaroli, A., Patrucco, P.: Transport energy consumption in two EEC countries, Part I. Italy: Fiat Centro Ricerche. 1976.

24. Collections INSEE; Série M: Enquêtes sur les conditions de vie des ménages (several years).
25. SETRA: Caractéristiques des déplacements en milieu urbain. Paris: Ministère de l'Equipement.
26. CPT/UTPUR: Les transports collectifs et la ville. Paris: Celse. 1973.
27. OCDE: The future of European passenger transport. Paris: 1977.
28. Collection INSEE, Série M: Enquête "Transports". 1966—1967.
29. OCDE: Environment implication of options in urban mobility. Paris: Environment Directorate, OCDE. 1973.
30. Collections INSEE, Série M 65/66: Le parc automobile des ménages. Enquête "Transports". 1973—1974.
31. Anfre, J., Rempp, J. M.: Les vacances des français. Economie et Statistiques, no. 101, 1978.
32. Elbek, B.: Private communication, Roskilde, Denmark.
33. Trafikforskningsgruppen (t-ATV-DSB-Vejdirektoratet TU 75, Trafikunderogelse 1975). Resume. Copenhague: Academy of Technical Sciences. May 1976.
34. Hirst, E.: Transportation energy use and conservation potential. Science and Public Affairs, November 1973.
35. Hirst, E.: Direct and indirect energy requirements for automobiles. Oak Ridge National Laboratory.
36. Chateau, B., Lapillonne, B.: Bases de données du modèle MEDEE 3/Pays Bas, France. Grenoble: IEJE. 1979.
37. RAI: De personenauto in cijfers. Amsterdam: 1975.
38. U.S. Department of Commerce: Statistical abstract of the U.S.A., 100th ed. Washington, D.C.: 1979.
39. Collections INSEE, Série C: Rapport annuel de la commission des comptes des transports de la nation (several years).
40. Pétrole Informations 10—16 October 1975.
41. Le Vert, P.: Consommation d'énergie des divers modes de transports. Sciences et Techniques, no. 36, November 1976.
42. CEE: Programme d'action communautaire pour l'emploi rationel de l'énergie. Note du Royaume Uni sur l'encouragement à l'emploi des moteurs Diesel. Bruxelles, CEE DG XVII, VII/219/76-F, 1976.
43. EUROSTAT: Annuaire statistique "Transports, Communications, Tourisme". Luxembourg (several years).
44. OCDE: Besoins de transports pour les communautés urbaines: la planification des transports de personnes. Paris: 1977.
45. FEA: Project independance. Washington, D.C.: 1974.
46. Merlin, P.: Comment économiser l'énergie dans les transports. Paris: La Documentation Française. 1977.
47. Department of the Environment: National travel survey 1972/73. London: HMSO. 1975.
48. The Nordic Council: Yearbook of nordic statistics 1977. Stockholm: 1978.
49. Bureau of Statistics: Statistical handbook of Japan 1978. Tokyo: 1978.
50. ONU/CEE: Bulletin annuel de statistiques de transports. Geneve (several years).
51. INSEE: Annuaire statistique de la France. Paris (several years).
52. SNCF: Memento statistiques 1977, 1978, 1979. Paris.
53. Netherlands Central Bureau of Statistics: Statistical yearbook of the Netherlands 1977. The Hague: Staatsuitgeverij. 1978.
54. IRF: La route. Genève: IRF. 1979.
55. Collections de l'INSEE, C56: Les transports en France 1975 et 1976. Paris.

56. IRF: Statistiques routières mondiales 1971–1975, 1974–1978. Genève: IRF.
57. Ministère de l'Environnement: Les principaux réseaux de transports collectifs urbains de province. Paris: 1977.
58. Ministero dei Trasporti: Compendio di statistiche sui trasporti, anno 1975. Rome: 1978.
59. Ministère des Transports: Les consommations unitaires d'énergie dans les transports. Paris: La Documentation Française. 1978.
60. Institute of Energy Economics: The energy conservation in Japan, facts and figures. Energy in Japan (Suppl.) December 1978.
61. Lapillonne, B.: Long-term perspectives of the U.S. energy demand: application of the MEDEE 2 model to the U.S.A. Energy 5, 231–257 (1980).
62. Leach, G. et al.: A low energy strategy for the United Kingdom, 259 p. London: Science Reviews Ltd. 1979.
63. KFA: Die Entwicklung des sektoralen End- und Nutzenergiebedarfs in der Bundesrepublik Deutschland. Jülich: 1977.
64. Chateau, B., Lapillonne, B.: Bases de données de MEDEE 3; dossier statistique annexe. Grenoble: IEJE. 1979.
65. Pillet, J. Ph.: Les économies d'énergie dans les transports. Paris: COPEDITH. 1980.
66. ONU/CEE: Accroissement des économies et de l'efficacité en matière d'énergie dans la région de la CEE. New York: ONU. 1976.
67. Department of Energy: Digest of United Kingdom energy statistics. London: HMSO (several years).
68. FEA: Project independance report. Washington, D.C.: 1974.
69. Landsberg, H. H., et al.: Energy: the next twenty years. Cambridge, Mass.: Ballinger. 1979.
70. AIE-OCDE: L'AIE et les économies d'énergie. Paris: OCDE. 1979.
71. Statistisches Bundesamt: Urlaubs- und Erholungsreisen 1976–1977. Stuttgart: Kohlhammer. 1978.
72. Villeneuve, A.: Les déplacements domicile-travail. Economie et Statistique, no. 17. November 1970.
73. Over, I. A., Sjoerdsma, A. C.: Energy conservation: ways and means. Future Shape of Technology Foundation, no. 19. The Hague. 1974.
74. IEA: Working paper. Paris: IEA. 1977.
75. OCDE: Group of experts on traffic policies for the improvement of the urban environment, Case of Göteborg, October 1976.
76. Ministère des Transports: L'automobile et la mobilité des Français. Paris: La Documentation Française. 1980.
77. ANFIA: Automobile in Cifre. Rome: 1977.
78. Commissariat Général du Plan: Prospective de la consommation d'énergie à long-terme, annexe 3: secteur des transports intérieurs. Paris: La Documentation Française. 1981.
79. Collection de l'INSEE, Série C81: Les transports en France en 1978. Paris: 1979.
80. OCDE: Comptes nationaux des pays de l'OCDE. 1961–1978.

Chapter IV

1. Commissariat Général du Plan: Une prospective de la consommation d'énergie de l'industrie 1985, 1990, 2000, Tome I, Tome II. Paris: Commissariat Général du Plan. May 1980.
2. Maillard: Rapport sur les bilans de la politique énérgetique depuis 1973. Paris: Commissariat Général du Plan. 1979.

3. IEJE: La consommation d'énergie: sa mesure et son traitement en vue d'une explication de ses déterminants et d'une amélioration des méthodes de prévision. Grenoble: IEJE. 1977.

4. Darmstadter, J., Dunkerley, J., Alterman, J.: How industrial societies use energy. Baltimore-London: The Johns Hopkins University Press. 1977.

5. Schipper, L., Lichtenberg, A. J.: Efficient energy use and well-being: the Swedish example. Berkeley: Lawrence Berkeley Laboratory. 1976.

6. Doernberg, A.: Energy use in Japan and U.S.A. Brookhaven National Laboratory. 1977.

7. Stanford Research Institute (S.R.I.): Comparison of energy consumption between West Germany and the United States. California: S.R.I. 1975.

8. W.A.E.S.: Energy demand studies: major consuming countries. Cambridge, Mass.: M.I.T. Press. 1976.

9. SOU: Energiforskning. Stockholm. SOU. 1974.

10. Energy Technology Support Unit (ETSU). Harwell, U.K.: 1978.

11. Leach, G. et al.: A low energy strategy for the United Kingdom, 259 p. London: Science Reviews. 1979.

12. ENI: The end uses of energy in Italy. Rome: ENI. 1979.

13. Reents, H.: Die Entwicklung des sektoralen End- und Nutzenergiebedarfs in der Bundesrepublik Deutschland, 258 p. Jülich: KFA. 1977.

14. Energy Research Group: A chemical heat-pump/energy device and its applications. London: Open University, September 1978.

15. Moisan: Utilisation directe de la chaleur d'origine solaire dans les processus industriels. Paris: PIRDES. 1978.

16. CEREN: Etude du marché industriel de l'énergie 1975. Paris: CEREN. 1977.

17. Department of Industry: Industrial energy thrift scheme: a preliminary analysis of the potential for energy conservation in industry. London: Department of Industry. 1977.

18. Association Technique de l'industrie du gaz en France: Combustibles gazeux et économies d'énergie dans l'industrie. Paris: Association Technique de l'industrie du Gaz. 1978.

19. U.S. Department of Energy: Energy efficiency and electric motors. Washington: U.S. Department of Energy, April 1978.

20. Brown, K.: The use of solar energy to produce process heat for industry. Golden, Colo.: Solar Energy Research Institute. 1980.

21. DATAR: Energie et régions. Paris: La Documentation Française, 1980. (Collection Travaux et Recherche de Prospective.)

22. Lettre Economie et Energie, September 1979, no. 21.

23. Murgatroyd, W., Wilkins, B. C.: The efficiency of electric motive power in industry. Energy 1, 337–345 (1976).

24. Economic Commission for Europe: Energy use in the pulp and paper industries. Geneva: CEE/ONU. August 1978.

25. Gyftopoulos, Lazaridis, Widmer: Potential fuel effectiveness in industry. Cambridge, Mass.: Ballinger. 1974.

26. EUROSTAT: Statistiques de l'énergie électrique. Luxembourg: EUROSTAT. 1978.

27. CEE: Les mutations sectorielles des économies Européennes de 1960 a la récession. Bruxelles: CEE. January 1978.

28. Commissariat Général du Plan: L'Europe, les vingt prochaines années. Paris: La Documentation Française. January 1980.

29. Interfutures: Facing the future. Paris: OECD. 1979.

30. Chateau, B., Lapillonne, B.: Essai de prévision de la demande d'énergie en France à l'an 2000. Grenoble: IEJE. 1977.

31. CSSF: L'énergie dans la sidérurgie, 49 p. Paris: CSSF. November 1979.

32. The Energy Conservation Research Center: Present state and future potentials of energy conservation in Japan. Energy in Japan, Suppl. 45.

33. Long, T. V., et al.: Economic determinants of the use of energy and materials in the US and Japanese iron and steel industries. Energy *3*, 451–460 (1978).

34. Emery, P.: Les besoins en énergie de la sidérurgie de l'an 2000. Annales des Mines, November 1978, pp. 5–18.

35. Emery, P.: L'acier et l'énergie. Paris: IRSID. November 1977, pp. 1173–1182. (In rapport IRSID RE 481.)

36. Astier, J.: L'évolution des méthodes de production de l'acier. Annales des Mines, June 1979, pp. 67–80.

37. F.E.A.: Energy conservation in the manufacturing sector 1954–1990. Washington: F.E.A. November 1974, pp. 6.2–6.68.

38. Stanford Research Institute (SRI): Patterns of energy consumption in the United States. Springfield: NTIS, January 1972, pp. 89–99.

39. Takagi, M.: Energy problems and measures to be taken against them in the Japanese steel industry. In: The steel industry and the energy crisis (Szekely, J., ed.), pp. 87–120. New York: M. Dekker. 1975.

40. Briens, F.: Besoins énergétiques de la sidérurgie. Paper presented at the Conference "Emploi du gaz naturel en sidérurgie", Paris, November 12, 1974.

41. Mutschler, P. H.: Impact of changing technology on the demand for metallurgical coal and coke produced in the United States to 1985. (Information Circular 8677.) U.S. Department of the Interior, Bureau of Mines.

42. Elliot, J. F.: Uses of energy in the production of steel. In: The steel industry and the energy crisis (Szekelcy, J., ed.), pp. 9–33. New York: M. Dekker. 1975.

43. CEE: Evolution des formes d'énergie utilisées dans l'industrie sidérurgique. ECE/STEEL *12* (1975).

44. Decker, A.: Energy accounting of steel. In: Proceedings of the 9th international TNO conference "The energy accounting of materials, products, processes and services": TNO.

45. Gordian Associates: The cement industry. Springfield: National Technical Information Service, U.S. Department of Commerce. (NATO/CCMS-46.)

46. Les problèmes énergétiques des cimenteries: Enerpresse no. 2517 (1980).

47. Federal Energy Administration: Energy conservation in the manufacturing sector 1954–1990. Washington: F.E.A. November 1974, Vol. 3 (project independence).

48. Malkin, L. S.: Energy consumption and conservation in the cement industry. London: Department of Energy, Energy Audit Series no. 7 (ENPC(79)P36).

49. Syndicat National des Fabricants de Ciments et de Chaux (SNFCC): Ciments et Chaux. Paris: SNFCC. 1979.

50. Energy in Japan (various issues).

51. ECN: Damocles energy data base. Petten: ECN. 1979.

52. Agence pour les Economies d'Energie (A.E.E.) (working paper). Paris.

53. Walker, E. A.: Statement before the joint hearings on conservation and efficient use of energy. In: Conservation and efficient use of energy, Part 4, pp. 1560–1579. Washington: Committee House of Representatives, July 12, 1973.

54. Department of Energy and Department of Industry: The aluminium industry. (Energy Audit Series no. 6.) London: Department of Industry. 1979.

55. IISI: A technological study on energy in the steel industry. Bruxelles: IISI. 1976.

56. EEC (U.N.): The study "Demand for and supply of coke to 1985". Geneva: ECE. 1980. (STEEL/R.4.)

57. EUROSTAT: Iron and steel yearbook. Luxembourg: EUROSTAT. 1977.

58. OCDE: Statistiques de base de l'énergie 1950–1964. Paris: OCDE. 1966.
    OCDE: Bilans énergétiques des pays de l'OCDE 1973–1975. Paris: OCDE. 1977.
    OCDE: Bilans énergétiques des pays de l'OCDE 1960–1974. Paris: OCDE. 1976.
59. EUROSTAT: Bilans globaux de l'énergie 1963–1975. Luxembourg: EUROSTAT. 1977.
    EUROSTAT: Energie 1950–1965. Luxembourg: EUROSTAT. 1966.
    EUROSTAT: Bilans globaux de l'énergie 1970–1977. Luxembourg: EUROSTAT. 1979.
60. Department of Energy: Digest of United Kingdom energy statistics. London: HMSO
    (several years).
61. OCDE: Bilans énergétiques des pays de l'OCDE, 1975–1979. Paris: OCDE. 1981.
62. INSEE: Annuaire statistique de la France, 1980. Paris: INSEE.

Chapter V

Selective Bibliography on Energy Demand Models

I. Deductive Models

Econometric Model

Global Models

See bibliography and analysis presented in J. Girod: La demande d'énergie: méthodes et techniques de modélisation, 185 p. Paris: Editions du CNRS.

Semi-Global or Analytical Models

Model IIES of the Energy Information Administration (U.S. Department of Energy)
Ref.: Logistics Management Institute: The International Energy Evaluation System (IIES),
    Vol. I and II. Washington: 1978.

Model PIES (Project Independence Evaluation System) of the Energy Information Administration (U.S. Department of Energy).
Ref.: Logistics Management Institute. – An Executive Summary of Volume I of the Project
    Independence Evaluation System (PIES). Washington: 1977.

Technico-Economic Models

MEDEE 2 and MEDEE 3 models of the IEJE, used by the EEC (DG12) and IIASA
Ref.: Lapillonne, B.: MEDEE 2: A model for long-term energy demand evaluation. Laxenburg:
    IIASA. 1978 (RR 78-18).
    Chateau, B., Lapillonne, B.: Long-term energy demand simulation (MEDEE 3).
    Guilford: IPC Press. 1979, pp. 120–128.

Model of the Energy Technology Support Unit (ETSU) of the U.K. Department of Energy
Ref.: Bush, R. P.: A disaggregated model of U.K. energy use for R and D planning purposes,
    ECE seminar on modelling studies and their conclusions on energy conservation and
    its impact on the economy. Washington: March 1980 (ECE/SEM 3. RII).

Model of the Economic and Statistic Division of the U.K. Department of Energy
Ref.: Department of Energy: Energy forecasting methodology. London: HMSO. 1978.
    (Energy Paper no. 29.)

Model WISE of the Wisconsin University
Ref.: Foell, W. (ed.): Management of energy environment systems: methods and case studies,
    487 p. J. Wiley. 1979.

Model IFSD (Interfuel Substitution Demand) of the Department of Energy, Mines and Resources of Canada

Ref.: Seeto, C. J., Erdman, R. W.: Assessment of potential natural gas penetration using a Canadian interfuel substitution demand model, 678 p. Dordrecht: D. Reidel. 1980, pp. 201–213.

See also the bibliography of J. Girod (op. cit.).

II. Equilibrium Models

Macro-Economic or Macro-Sectoral Models of General Equilibrium

Model ETA-Macro

Ref.: Manne, A. S.: The use and role of models: long-term energy projections for the U.S.A., 678 p. Dordrecht: D. Reidel. 1980, p. 64–79.

Model of the DEMO-Project (Denmark)

Ref.: Norgard, J. S., Meyer, N. I.: National energy systems analysis for Denmark up to year 2030. Dordrecht: D. Reidel. 1980, pp. 172–186.

Models of the "Service de la Programmation de la Politique Scientifique (SPPS)" and of the "Bureau du Plan" (Belgium)

Ref.: Osterrieth, M.: The Belgian energy models: a general introduction. Dordrecht: D. Reidel. 1980, pp. 231–236.

Bossier, F., Durvein, D., Gouzee, N.: Estimation of sectoral demand models for the Belgian economy. Dordrecht: D. Reidel. 1980, pp. 237–253.

Model EPM of the Swedish Industrial Board and of the Stockholm School of Economics (Sweden)

Ref.: Ohman, C.: Studies of optimal energy conservation programs. ECE Seminar on Modelling Studies and their Conclusions on Energy Conservation and its Impact on the Economy. Washington, D.C.: March 1980 (ECE/SEM 3.RI).

Model MSG-E developped by the Central Office of Statistics and the Economic Institute of the Oslo University

Ref.: Longva, S., Lorentsen, L., Olsen, O.: Energy in a multisectoral growth model. ECE Seminar on Modelling Studies and their Conclusions on Energy Conservation and its Impact on the Economy. Washington: March 1980 (ECE/SEM 3.R3).

Model ENOR developped by the Institut for Atomenergie (Norway) and used by the Ministry of Energy

Ref.: Ek, A., Kjlberg, J., Sira, T.: ENOR, an energy model for Norway. Dordrecht: D. Reidel. 1980, pp. 263–281.

Hudson Jorgenson Model

Ref.: Hudson, E. A., Jorgenson, D. W.: Energy policy and economic growth, in Proceedings of the Conference on Energy Modelling and Forecasting. Springfield: NTIS. 1974, pp. 41–69.

Model "Mini DMS Energie" of INSEE (France) developped by the French administration

Ref.: INSEE. Présentation du modèle Mini DMS Energie. Paris: INSEE. March 1980 (working paper).

Chains of Models

Models of the European Commission (EEC/DG12)

Ref.: Rubin, R., Romberg, E.: Energy models for the European Community. In: Energy

Models for the European Community (Strub, A., ed.), 154 p. Guilford: IPC Press, pp. 12–24.

IIASA Models

Ref.: Lukachinski, J., et al.: An integrated methodology for assessing energy economy interactions. Dordrecht: D. Reidel. 1980, pp. 303–315.

Brookhaven Models

Ref.: Lukachinski et al., J.: An integrated methodology for assessing energy economy interactions. Dordrecht: D. Reidel. 1980, pp. 303–315.

Physical Equilibrium Models

Model STER of the University of Strathclyde (Scotland)

Ref.: Hounam, I.: STER. A global energy supply model. Dordrecht: D. Reidel. 1980, pp. 447–455.

1. Chateau, B., Lapillonne, B.: La prévision à long terme de la demande d'énergie: propositions méthodologiques, 225 p. Paris: Editions du CNRS. 1977 (Collection "Energie et Société".)
2. Chateau, B., Lapillonne, B.: Long-term energy demand forecasting: a new approach. Energy Policy *6*, 140–157 (1978).
3. Julien, P. A., Lamonde, P., Latouche, P.: La méthode des scénarios. Paris: La Documentation Française. 1975. (Collection Travaux et Recherches de Prospective, no. 59.)
4. Chateau, B., Lapillonne, B.: Long-term energy demand: method of constructing scenario linked with the MEDEE 3 model. Brussels: CEE-DG XII, January 1979.
5. Chateau, B., Lapillonne, B.: Essai de prévision de la demande d'énergie en France à l'an 2000. Etude de deux scénarios contrastés, 395 p. Grenoble: IEJE. 1977.
6. Landsberg, H.: Energy the next twenty years. Cambridge, Mass.: Ballinger. 1979.
7. Chateau, B., Lapillonne, B.: Projections à l'horizon 2000 de la demande d'énergie finale de l'Europe des Neuf à l'aide du modèle MEDEE 2, 50 p. Grenoble: IEJE. 1978.
8. Chateau, B., et al.: La demande d'énergie finale de la France à l'horizon 2000, 77 p. Grenoble: IEJE. 1979.
9. Lapillonne, B.: Long-term perspectives of the US energy demand. Application of the MEDEE 2 model to the U.S. Energy *5*, 231–257 (1980).

Conclusion

1. Meadows, D., et al.: Limits to growth. New York: Universe Books. 1972.
2. DATAR: Energie et régions. Paris: La Documentation Française. 1980.
3. Energy policy project of the Ford foundation – a time to choose. Cambridge, Mass.: Ballinger. 1974.
4. Thomas, S.: Modelling U.K. energy demand to 2000. Energy Policy *1980*, pp. 17–37.
5. Leach, G., et al.: A low energy strategy for the United Kingdom. London: Science Reviews. 1979.
6. Ministère de l'Industrie: Un scénario de croissance sobre en énergie pour la France. Paris: La Documentation Française. 1980.
7. CONAES: Alternative energy demand futures to 2010. Washington: National Academy of Sciences. 1979.
8. Chateau, B., Lapillonne, B.: Long-term energy demand forecasting: a new approach. Energy Policy *6*, 140–157 (1978).
   Chateau, B., et al.: La demande d'énergie finale de la France à l'horizon 2000. Grenoble: IEJE. 1979.

9. Lovins: Soft energy paths: towards a durable peace. Cambridge, Mass.: Ballinger. 1977.
10. Groupe de Bellerive. Project ALTER. Paris: Groupe de Bellerive. 1978.
11. Norgard, J.: The gentle path of conservation. Lyngby: The Technical University, 1979 (DEMO-project).
12. Soft Energy Notes. San Francisco: International Project for Soft Energy Paths.
13. Lönnroth, M., Steen, P., Johansson, T.B.: Energy in Transition. Berkeley, Calif.: University of California Press. 1980.
14. Finon, D.: Choosing an energy forecast. Symposium of the Nobel Foundation "Managing the European Oil Transition". Stockholm: 1980 (forthcoming in the proceedings.)
15. Futuribles, no. 22, pp. 3–40, April 1979.

Subject Index

IBM-Composersatz: Springer-Verlag Wien
Umbruch und Druck: Novographic, Ing. Wolfgang Schmid, A-1230 Wien